Cordon Bleu ~ Constance Spry
ENTERTAINING

This book is dedicated to the memory

of Constance Spry and Rosemary Hume:

two remarkable women.

Cordon Bleu ~ Constance Spry

ENTERTAINING

Muriel Downes

Harold Piercy

OCTOPUS BOOKS

First published in 1985 by
Octopus Books Limited,
59 Grosvenor Street,
London W1

© Text: The Constance Spry and Cordon Bleu Group Limited

© Photography and illustration: Octopus Books Limited

ISBN 0 7064 2368 2

Produced by Mandarin Publishers Limited,
22a Westlands Road, Quarry Bay,
Hong Kong

Printed in Hong Kong

Acknowledgements

Art Director: Pedro Prá-Lopez

Stylist: Emma Hartley

Photographers:
Jan Baldwin (pages 8-13, 64-67, 96-101, 128-131)
James Jackson (pages 14-17, 30-35, 46-49, 54-59, 74-83)
Duncan McNicol (pages 18-21, 26-29, 50-53, 60-63, 102-105, 111-112, 118 bottom)
Spike Powell (pages 22-25, 36-41, 90-95, 106-113, 120-123, 132-137)
Martin Brigdale (pages 42-45, 68-73, 84-89, 114-117, 118 top left, 119, 124-127)

Illustrations: Berry Fallon Design; Russell Barnett (page 145)

Design Artwork: Technical Art Services

Food prepared for photography by Muriel Downes,
assisted by:

Eithne Swan (pages 8-13)
Janice Murfitt (pages 14-17, 46-49, 74-79, 80-83)
Clare Brennan (pages 14-17, 46-49, 64-67, 74-79, 84-89, 96-101)
Carole Handslip (pages 18-21, 26-35, 50-59)
Annie Grubb (pages 22-25, 36-45, 90-95, 106-110, 114-123, 132-137)
Helena Lappas (pages 60-63, 128-131)
Sarah Brown (pages 68-73)
Victoria Lyon (pages 102-105)
Caroline Hegarty (pages 111-112)
Pamela Howe (pages 124-127)

Flowers prepared for photography by Harold Piercy, *assisted by*
Rosemary Minter, Fred Wilkinson and Gayle Derrick.

The publishers would like to thank the following companies
for their kindness in providing materials and equipment
used in the photography for this book:

Harrods, Knightsbridge, London SW1

and
The General Trading Company, 144 Sloane Street, London SW1
Harvey Nichols, Knightsbridge, London SW1
Osborne and Little, 304 King's Road, London SW3
Divertimenti, 139 Fulham Road, London SW10
Bella Figura, 154 Fulham Road, London SW10
David Mellor, 4 Sloane Square, London SW1
The Designer's Guild, 277 King's Road, London SW3
Sanderson, 53 Berners Street, London W1
Worcester Royal Porcelain Company, Severn Street, Worcester WR1 2NE
Spode Company, Church Street, Stoke-on-Trent
Crowthers of Syon Lodge, Busch Corner, London Road, Isleworth, Middlesex
The Poster Shop, 168 Fulham Road, London SW10
The Shelfstore, 59 New King's Road, London SW6
Wilson and Gill, Rosenthal Studio Dept., 137 Regent Street, London W1
Elizabeth David, 46 Bourne Street, London SW1
Selfridges, Oxford Street, London W1
The Kite and Balloon Company, 613 Garratt Lane, London SW18
Real Flame Fireplaces, 80 New King's Road, London SW6
London Bedding Company, 26 Sloane Street, London SW1
Hirst Antiques, 59 Pembridge Road, London W11
Rassell Ltd., 80 Earl's Court Road, London W8
H. Andreas GmbH, Industriestrasse 9, 8714 Wiesentheid, West Germany
Edward Goodyear, 45 Brook Street, London W1
A. Chapman, New Covent Garden Market, London SW8
Everyday Gourmet, 229 Kensington Church Street, London W8
Stickabrick, The Green Road, Ashbourne, Derbyshire DE6 1EE
Garden Craft, 158 New King's Road, London SW6
Miranda of Sweden, 46 Pimlico Road, London SW1

The publishers would like to thank the directors and staff of Winkfield Place,
Winkfield, Berkshire for their kindness in providing such a suitable location for
a number of the menus photographed in this book.

Authors' Acknowledgements

A book of this kind could not have been attempted without a good back-up
team and in this we have been very lucky. Rosemary Minter and Fred
Wilkinson have provided invaluable support on the flower side, just as Annie
Grubb has with the food. Many thanks to Lance Sanderson at the Essex
Institute of Agriculture, and to Pat Newton and Julie Grosse for their
ever-helpful secretarial skills. All our colleagues at Winkfield Place and in
London have, as always, been most kind and encouraging. Thanks, finally, to
Andrew Jefford, our editor, for his valuable contribution.

NOTES

1. Metric and imperial measurements have been calculated separately, and are approximate rather than exact equivalents. Therefore use only one set of measurements, either metric or imperial, when preparing the recipes. Metricated equivalents of spoonfuls of dry ingredients refer to the volume occupied by the ingredient. All spoon measurements are level: specially manufactured spoon measures can be bought to give an exact result.

2. Words printed in *italics* in the recipe methods or ingredients indicate that the word in question is included in the short Directory of Cooking Terms on page 156. You will find there a full definition of the word, together with information on why, when and how to use the technique.

3. All recipes will serve the same number of people as the menu in which the recipe appears. For example, if a recipe appears in a menu for six, that recipe will serve six people.

4. Cooking times may vary according to individual ovens. Always preheat the oven to the specified temperature, and place the dishes in the centre of the oven unless otherwise indicated.

5. All eggs are standard – size 3 or 4 – unless otherwise indicated.

6. All flour is plain and all sugar is granulated unless otherwise indicated.

7. Always use the meal planners in conjunction with the recipe text: points in the meal planners refer to material covered in full in the recipes.

CONTENTS

To work with Harold Piercy and bring together the two facets of our schools has given me the greatest pleasure, and it has confirmed the idea that my career has described a full circle. At the inception of the London Cordon Bleu Cookery School, when Constance Spry and Rosemary Hume joined forces, I was lucky enough to give the demonstrations to illustrate The Constance Spry Lectures on subjects that she had made her very own. Constance was a devoted gardener, so the theme of these demonstrations covered a wide spectrum of flowers and their seeds, fruit, vegetables and herbs. Now I find myself working once again on the subject of food and its decorative floral counterpart, in a book this time, but just as before with the very greatest of pleasure.

Constance Spry loved entertaining and never waited for a special occasion to arrange a party, but invented one if necessary. I well remember such an occasion when a new table was ordered for the first teaching kitchen at Winkfield Place, large enough for 12 students to work around. The well-seasoned wood looked handsome, and it suddenly seemed to Mrs Spry the perfect setting for a party. In the space of less than a week, the guests were invited and the menu for "The Kitchen Party" was planned around a main course of smoked haddock kedgeree accompanied by small freshly-baked rolls. Sure enough, it was a great success and the first of many that were to inspire our students and – more latterly – our readers to entertain for themselves with a similar spirit of inventiveness, high style, and great fun.

Thirty years have gone by since that party, but the table is still there. So, I believe, is the spirit that I felt so strongly then, and which I hope you will find for yourselves within the covers of this book.

I was thrilled when it was suggested that I should join forces with The Cordon Bleu Cookery School to write a joint book on entertaining with food and flowers. Nothing could have pleased me more than to work with Muriel Downes on a project of this sort – and the book has indeed proved to be great fun.

I love cooking and believe strongly that flowers and food go well together. Both are concerned with the presentation of natural ingredients and materials. Careful preparation is necessary in both cases, and restraint is an important skill for arranger and cook alike to learn. ("If in doubt, leave out": it is always better to avoid an overfilled vase or plate.) Colour, shape and form have to be carefully considered, and of course food always has the extra dimension of taste to be borne in mind. The special recipes and hints worked out by Muriel always bring out the very best in Cordon Bleu food, as I know from my own experience.

In this book I have tried to choose flowers and foliage in keeping with their settings and linked in some way to the menu. It is not always easy: remember that the obvious choice is not necessarily the right one. Always remember Constance Spry's words: "Keep an open mind about the subjects you select for decoration." Consider them solely for their shape, colour or texture and disregard entirely the traditional or habitual categories in which they are usually placed. You will gain real freedom of choice for your arrangements and ensure a wide source of supply for yourself. It is immaterial whether you use garden, exotic or wild flowers, vegetables or fruit, or whether you mix them all together or use them separately. I have done each of these things in this book, trying to use as wide a range of materials as possible – and I hope it will encourage you to do the same.

Harold Piercy

SPRING LUNCH

The delicacy and sweetness of spring's first offerings are evident
throughout this special lunch, designed with an Easter slant.

JUST AS SPRING begins the year, giving everyone a first taste of the light, warmth and plenty that are to follow, so our seasonal selection of menus (which itself begins the book) commences with a light, fresh spring lunch. This opening period of the year includes Easter, of course, and so we have decided to make this into a dual-function menu, suitable either for any special entertaining you may wish to do during the spring period, or as a celebration meal for Easter Day. Hence the main course lamb, always at its best in spring and eagerly anticipated by the family at Easter; the pretty fish- and egg-based starter, and a delicious dessert that doesn't neccesarily rely on expensive imported fresh fruit.

Forward planning
Spring always seems to be a busy time of year, and Easter, too, can be hectic, particularly if you like to attend the important church services of this festival. The courses have been chosen with a restricted timetable in mind: both starter and dessert can be largely prepared in advance, and the main course is an 'all-in-one' dish that needs little monitor-

MENU

for a party of six

Eggs Connaught
with brown bread and butter

•

Leg of Lamb Printanier

•

Gâteau Diane
Melba Sauce

WINE

Red or White Rioja

ing. For further details of how to plan your preparation, see the **Meal Planner** below.

Wine suggestions
Spanish Rioja always makes a good and inexpensive accompaniment to lamb, and so we have suggested this as the wine of the meal. A red Rioja is shown in our photographs, but if you and your guests would prefer to drink a white Rioja, then that too would match the delicacy of spring lamb well. Other wines have been left to your discretion: see the **Food and Wine Matching Chart** on page 149 for general suggestions about food and wine partnerships.

A Good Friday meal
On pages 11 and 12, to extend the Easter theme of this menu, are two dishes that make an elegant, attractive lunch for Good Friday. The main course, appropriately enough, is based on fish — fillets of sole with asparagus — and the dessert is a rhubarb moscovite. White wine (perhaps a dry white Graves) would accompany this meal well.

An Easter teacake
Finally, on page 12, you'll find an Easter teacake, made with a rich, yeast-risen almond dough. Yeast cakes are traditional throughout Europe at Eastertime, and this Danish almond ring makes a refreshing change from the simnel cake often served on this occasion.

MEAL PLANNER

● **Thursday:** buy ingredients both for the Good Friday meal, and for the Easter lunch (omitting watercress) and teacake. Prepare the fish stock for the fish dish. Completely prepare the moscovite and its sauce: cover and store overnight. If you have time, make the meringue for the gâteau: store in an airtight tin.

● **Good Friday:** prepare the fish dish; remove the moscovite from the refrigerator two hours before it is to be served. Serve the Good Friday meal. Fill and finish the gâteau: store in a cool place. Make the melba sauce.

● **Easter Saturday:** buy the watercress. Begin making the almond ring. Remove the shank-bone from the lamb and make

the stock. Hard boil the eggs. Finish making the almond ring. Make the filling for the eggs: cover closely and chill overnight in the refrigerator. Finish the gâteau if you have not already done so.

● **Final preparation:** begin cooking the lamb. Finish the egg dish, and garnish it with the salmon. Finish the lamb dish immediately

before serving it as main course.

Note: This meal planner assumes you are preparing food for the complete Easter weekend. If you wish only to make the spring lunch, read the relevant parts of the meal planner, taking Thursday to mean 'three days before', Good Friday to mean 'two days before', and Easter Saturday to mean 'one day before'.

Eggs Connaught make a handsome opening for any meal, giving everyone a much-appreciated taste of smoked salmon.

Eggs Connaught

150 ml/¼ pint béchamel sauce
6 hard-boiled eggs
50 g/2 oz butter
75 g/3 oz curd cheese
5 ml/1 tsp paprika
175 g/6 oz smoked salmon pieces, finely shredded
a pinch of ground mace
a little lemon juice

To garnish:

½ bunch of watercress

Make the béchamel sauce according to the recipe on page 140 of the *Reference Section*. Split the hard-boiled eggs in two, scoop out their yolks and put the whites in a bowl of cold water. Put the yolks in a blender or food processor with the cold béchamel sauce, the butter, cheese, paprika and half the smoked salmon, and blend until smooth. Season with ground mace and a squeeze of lemon juice, and spoon into a forcing bag.

Drain and dry the egg whites and pipe the filling into them. Arrange them in a circle on a round serving dish. Scatter the remaining smoked salmon pieces over the top, and garnish with watercress.

Leg of lamb printanier

1.75-2 kg/4-4½ lb leg of lamb
50 g/2 oz butter
½ clove of garlic, crushed
15 ml/1 tbls chopped parsley
350 ml/12 fl oz white wine
450 g/1 lb small new potatoes
350 g/¾ lb small new carrots
18 small button onions
225 g/8 oz mangetout peas
175 g/6 oz button mushrooms
30 ml/2 tbls potato flour
150 ml/5 fl oz single cream
15 ml/1 tbls chopped parsley
5 ml/1 tsp chopped marjoram

OVEN TEMPERATURE: 180°C/350°F/ Gas Mark 4

The day before your lunch, remove the shankbone from the leg of lamb, and use it to make stock according to the recipe for jellied stock given on page 138 of the *Reference Section* (use only 900 ml/1½ pints water to give 600 ml/1 pint of stock). Soften the butter on a plate, work in the garlic and parsley, and spread over the lamb. Cover and chill overnight.

Let the lamb reach room temperature. Then place it in a large flameproof casserole, cover and put it over a very low heat for 30 minutes. Shake the pan from time to time. Pour the wine over the meat and leave it to bubble gently until the liquid has reduced by about one-third. Pour on the stock and season. Cover the pan, put it in the preheated oven and cook gently for 1½-1¾ hours.

Scrape the potatoes and peel the carrots. Put the onions in cold water, bring to the boil, *blanch* for 3 minutes, then drain and *refresh. Blanch* the mangetout peas for 3 minutes in boiling water, then drain and *refresh*.

When the meat has been cooking for 1¼ hours, add the potatoes and carrots, bring back to the boil and simmer for 20 minutes, either on top of the cooker or in the oven. Then add the onions and mushrooms and cook as before for a further 10 minutes. Strain the liquid from the casserole but do not remove the meat or vegetables. Cover the casserole and return to the oven, turned to its lowest setting.

Skim the fat from the cooking liquid, mix it with the potato flour and return to the liquid. Pour into a small saucepan, stir until boiling and simmer for 3 minutes, then add the cream and herbs. Reboil and check seasoning.

Place the meat on a serving dish and coat with a little sauce. Add the mangetout peas to the other vegetables in the casserole, pour over some hot sauce, and gently bring back to boiling point. Arrange some vegetables around the meat for serving: serve the remaining sauce and vegetables separately.

Leg of lamb printanier is as delicious as it is convenient: the ingredients are simmered in wine and then cream.

The crumbly texture of Gâteau Diane is the secret of its popularity; Melba sauce comes into its own as a delicious accompaniment.

Gâteau Diane

For the meringue:

5 egg whites

275 g/10 oz caster sugar

For the butter cream:

100 g/4 oz sugar

120 ml/4 fl oz water

3 egg yolks

350 g/12 oz butter

175-225 g/6-8 oz dark chocolate

For the decoration:

100 g/4 oz flaked, browned almonds

icing sugar

OVEN TEMPERATURE: 120°C/250°F/
Gas Mark ½

Prepare 3 baking sheets lined with non-stick silicone paper, marked out with 23 cm/9 in circles. Then make the meringue: whisk the egg whites until stiff, add a teaspoon of the measured sugar for each egg white, then continue whisking for about 10 seconds. Fold in the remaining sugar with a large spoon.

Divide the mixture equally be-tween the 3 baking sheets and spread it into the marked-out circles. Bake in the preheated oven for about 1 hour until lightly coloured and quite dry. Cool.

To prepare the butter cream, dissolve the sugar in the water and then boil steadily until the temperature reaches 103°C/217°F on a sugar thermometer. Pour it into the egg yolks and whisk until very thick. Cream the butter until soft with a wooden spoon or electric beater and add the egg and sugar mixture by degrees. Melt the chocolate on a plate over a pan of hot water; when it is quite smooth, work it into the butter cream.

Spread the meringue rounds with some of the butter cream and layer them one on top of the other. Coat the top and sides with more butter cream, and then cover with the almonds. Cut out strips of greaseproof paper and lay them across the cake. Dust the cake with icing sugar, then lift off the pieces of paper. Pipe rosettes of butter cream around the edge of the cake. Serve with **Melba Sauce**, made according to the recipe in the *Reference Section* on page 143.

Good Friday Lunch

The photograph showing this lunch can be found overleaf.

Fillets of sole with asparagus

3 lemon sole, each weighing 1 kg/
2 lb, to give 12 fillets

450 ml/¾ pint fish stock

a little lemon juice

seasoned flour

1 egg, beaten

white breadcrumbs

2 bundles of asparagus

1 kg/2 lb potatoes

butter to taste

15-30 ml/1-2 tbls hot milk

more beaten egg *or* melted butter

For the sauce:

250 ml/8 fl oz dry white wine

1 shallot, finely chopped

6 peppercorns

a small blade of mace

75 g/3 oz butter

2 egg yolks

40 g/1½ oz butter

40 g/1½ oz flour

seasoning

To serve:

6 large flat mushrooms, grilled

OVEN TEMPERATURE: 180°C/350°F/
Gas Mark 4

When you buy the lemon sole, ask the fishmonger to fillet and skin it for you, and to let you have the bones and fish trimmings. Use these to prepare the 450 ml/¾ pint of fish stock used for the cooking of the fish and the sauce, according to the recipe in the *Reference Section* on page 139. Fold 6 of the fillets and put them in an ovenproof dish. Sprinkle with a few drops of lemon juice and a little of the fish stock, cover with a butter wrapper or foil, and leave to one side ready for poaching. Cut the other 6 fillets into wide strips; coat them in seasoned flour, dip in the beaten egg and roll in the breadcrumbs.

Trim the asparagus, cook it in boiling water and *refresh*. Cook the potatoes, drain, dry and work to a purée in a food processor. Beat well with a nut of butter and the hot milk. Pipe the potato purée in a thick rope onto one side of a large serving dish, brush with a little beaten egg or melted butter and brown it lightly under the grill.

Fry the crumbed strips of fish in deep fat until they are golden brown (see the frying instruc-tions for the croquettes of fish on page 56), drain well and place them on a wire rack on a baking sheet to cool. When you are almost ready to serve, reheat the deep-fried strips of fish by plac-ing them on a rack in the pre-heated oven with the door ajar.

To make the white wine sauce, place the white wine and shallot, peppercorns and mace in a small saucepan, and *reduce* until there is only 10 ml/2 tsp of liquid left. Then work the 75 g/3 oz of butter until soft. Cream the egg yolks together with a nut of the butter in a bowl, then strain on the reduced wine. Place the bowl in a bain-marie (or large saucepan half-filled with warm water) and stir the mixture until thick with a whisk or wooden spatula. Add the rest of the but-ter in small pieces, stirring con-tinually. Set aside. Next make a *roux* using the second quantity of the butter and the flour. Blend in the rest of the fish stock and stir until boiling. Simmer for 1 min-ute, then draw aside and beat in the butter sauce. Check the sea-soning, cover and keep warm.

Poach the fish in the preheated oven for 8-10 minutes, then lift it onto the prepared serving dish, and coat with the sauce. Reheat the asparagus in a little butter, and use it to garnish the fish. Finally, place the pieces of fried fish in the serving dish. Serve with the flat mushrooms.

Fillets of sole with asparagus, followed by a taste of Rhubarb moscovite, makes a light but sustaining lunch for Good Friday.

Easter teacake

Danish almond ring

350 g/12 oz plain flour	
25 g/1 oz fresh yeast	
50 g/2 oz caster sugar	
225 ml/7½ fl oz warm milk	
250 g/9 oz butter, softened	
1 egg, beaten	

For the filling:

100 g/4 oz ground almonds	
100 g/4 oz caster sugar	
1 egg white	
2-3 drops almond essence	
50 g/2 oz raisins	

To finish:

225 g/8 oz apricot glaze	
glacé icing	

OVEN TEMPERATURE: 200°C/400°F/
Gas Mark 6

Sift the flour with a pinch of salt into a mixing bowl. Cream the yeast with the sugar until liquid. Add the warm milk and 50 g/2 oz of the butter and stir until dissolved, then add the beaten egg. Pour the liquid ingredients into the flour and mix to a smooth dough. Cover and leave at room temperature for about 1 hour, or until it has doubled in bulk.

Punch down the dough, turn it onto a floured board and knead lightly. Roll the dough out into an oblong and cover two-thirds of the dough with half the remaining butter, cut into pieces the size of a walnut. Fold and roll the dough as for rough puff pastry: see the recipe on page 142 of the *Reference Section*. After you have made 2 folds and turns, put on the remaining butter, fold and leave for 15 minutes. Roll and

Rhubarb moscovite

300 ml/½ pint water	
100 g/4 oz sugar	
450 g/1 lb rhubarb	
a strip of orange peel	
300 ml/½ pint milk	
3 egg yolks	
75 g/3 oz caster sugar	
20 ml/4 tsp gelatine	
150 ml/¼ pint double cream	
a little salad oil	

For the decoration:

85 ml/3 fl oz double cream, whipped (optional)	

Make a sugar syrup with the water and sugar following the method given on page 143 of the *Reference Section*. Poach the rhubarb in the sugar syrup with the orange peel.

Scald the milk by bringing it to the boil in a saucepan and then removing it from the heat. Work the egg yolks together with the caster sugar in a mixing bowl until thick and pale, then pour on the scalded milk. Stir, and return the custard to the pan. Thicken it over the heat without boiling, strain and cool. Drain the rhubarb, reserving the syrup, and rub through a nylon strainer. Divide the rhubarb purée in two, and chill half of it in the refrigerator.

Dissolve the gelatine by sprinkling it onto 65 ml/2½ fl oz of the sugar syrup and warming the syrup slightly. Mix it into the custard. Add the chilled rhubarb purée to the double cream. When the custard is on the point of setting, fold it into the cream and rhubarb mixture. Lightly oil a 1.2 litre/2 pint soufflé dish, and turn the moscovite mixture into this. Chill until set.

Add the remaining sugar syrup to the other half of the rhubarb purée to make a sauce. When the moscovite has set, turn it out onto a serving dish and pour a little sauce around it; serve the rest in a small jug. Decorate, if liked, with whipped cream.

A Danish almond ring takes centre stage at teatime on Easter Day to surprise and delight all of the family.

fold twice more, wrap in a clean tea towel and leave in the refrigerator for at least 15 minutes and preferably 30 minutes, while preparing the filling.

Mix the almonds with the sugar and work in enough beaten egg white to give a spreading consistency. Add the almond essence and raisins.

Roll out the chilled dough to a large oblong and spread with the filling. Roll up the dough, and place it in a very lightly buttered 24 cm/9½ in angel cake tin. Make a few cuts around the top, then prove it in a warm place until well risen. Bake it in the preheated oven for about 20 minutes or until it begins to colour, then turn the oven down to 180°C/350°F/ Gas Mark 4 and bake for about 1 hour, until firm to the touch.

Turn it onto a wire rack to cool. Make the apricot glaze according to the recipe in the *Reference Section* on page 143, and the glacé icing according to the recipe below. Brush over the cake with the warmed apricot glaze, and then drizzle the glacé icing over the top while the cake is still warm after baking.

Glacé icing

30 ml/2 tbls sugar syrup

100 g/4 oz icing sugar

Make a sugar syrup according to the recipe given on page 143 of the *Reference Section*. Allow it to cool completely.

When cool, add the icing sugar 15 ml/1 tbls at a time, and beat thoroughly with a wooden spatula. Enough icing sugar has been added when the icing coats the back of a spoon and looks glossy. Before drizzling the icing on the cake, warm it gently in the saucepan over a very low heat (the icing should be no hotter than hand hot).

Note: Glacé icing is useful for a number of different cakes: flavouring and colouring extracts can be added to it for special party finishes.

There is nothing nicer in spring than a bowl of hyacinths (*hyacinthus*). By using cut stems, a large number of colours can be shown in the same container; the flowers themselves are long lasting and give a wonderful perfume to the room.

These hyacinths are arranged in a glass dish which stands in an alabaster tazza. The dish rests on a cellulose wool mat to stop it from slipping and prevent any moisture from escaping. The stems are arranged in wire netting over a large pinholder.

Hyacinth flower heads are very heavy and tend to topple if left too long, so after placing your strongest and tallest stems in position, setting the outline points of the arrangement, place some shorter heads low in the group to support the taller material. Use a few leaves with each flower head to lend the arrangement diversity. If cutting from bulbs yourself, leave foliage attached to each one so that it will go on growing.

SUMMER DINNER

Elegance and simplicity are found perfectly balanced in this classic summer dinner: the ideal complement to leisurely days, lengthening evenings, and relaxing conversation.

SUMMER IS AN excellent time for entertaining: fresh ingredients are at their most plentiful, evenings at their longest, and guests, as likely as not, at their most relaxed and appreciative. In warm weather, though, appetites should be stimulated with light, pretty food, rather than cosseted and reassured with the comforting but weighty dishes of winter, so when entertaining during the summer months, try to bear this principle in mind with each of the different menus you serve.

Summer alternatives

Amongst the dishes that come into their own during the summer months are those that can be served lukewarm rather than piping hot: the first-course feuilletées of this menu are a good example. Savoury tarts and flans make excellent summer dishes, too, as do

MENU

for a party of six

Feuilletées with Prawns
and Herb Mayonnaise

•

Escalopes of Veal Niçoise

Saffron and Pepper Pilaff

•

Peaches Cordon Bleu

WINES

Mâcon Blanc or Pouilly-Fuissé

main-course salads using warm ingredients like fried bread croûtons, freshly cooked chicken or duck livers, or crisply grilled bacon.

A white burgundy such as Mâcon Villages or Pouilly-Fuissé is a good choice for the wine accompaniment, as its dry but full flavour will match, without dominating, the positive flavours of the meal. If you wish to capture that authentic Mediterranean atmosphere, though, try serving a rosé wine from Provence. These are often sold in distinctively undulating bottles with small labels.

Keeping wine cool

There are various excellent wine coolers available nowadays, ranging from the classic design shown in our photograph, to simpler versions in clear plastic or cork. Well-chilled wine can be kept cool in them for up to two hours, depending on how warm the room is.

MEAL PLANNER

● **Two days before:** make the puff pastry dough.

● **The day before:** prepare the peppers for the pilaff. Do all of the shopping.

● **The morning:** make and bake the feuilletées. Make the tomato sauce.

● **Final preparation:** fill the feuilletées. Make the peach dish and chill. Begin the pilaff. Prepare and fry veal; finish the tomato sauce and pilaff. Keep warm while you reheat the feuilletées and serve.

Feuilletées with prawns and herb mayonnaise

225 g/8 oz puff pastry dough *or*
6 ready-made bouchées

300 ml/½ pint mayonnaise

450 g/1 lb (1.2 litres/2 pints) fresh prawns

15 ml/1 tbls chopped parsley

10 ml/2 tsp fresh mixed herbs

1 lemon, cut into thin segments

For the glaze:

1 egg beaten with 5 ml/1 tsp salt

OVEN TEMPERATURE: 220°C/425°F/ Gas Mark 7

Prepare the puff pastry dough according to the recipe in the *Reference Section* on page 142. Roll out the dough very thinly (no more than 5 mm/¼ in thick), and cut with a 10 cm/4 in fluted cutter. Glaze each dough shape lightly with the egg glaze: make sure that none of the glaze runs down the sides of the dough shapes, or they will not puff properly. Lightly score a diamond grid across the top. Place on a slightly damp baking sheet and chill for 8 minutes. Bake in the preheated oven for about 10 min-

utes. Lift the baked feuilletées onto a wire rack and split each one in half.

To make the mayonnaise, see *Reference Section*, page 140. When it is ready, shell the prawns, reserving some unshelled ones for the garnish, and add the parsley and herbs to the mayonnaise. When the feuilletées are cold, fill each one with the shelled prawns and a spoonful of mayonnaise. Top with their lids.

Just before serving put them in a moderate oven (180°C/350°F/ Gas Mark 4) for 5 minutes. Serve garnished with the whole prawns and lemon segments.

Delicate, airy and finely flavoured, these Feuilletées with prawn and herb mayonnaise make a memorable starter. (Recipe on page 15.)

Escalopes of veal niçoise

6 even-sized mushrooms

6 escalopes of veal, weighing about 175 g/6 oz each

15 ml/1 tbls olive oil

25 g/1 oz butter

120 ml/4 fl oz white wine

For the tomato sauce:

450 g/1 lb ripe tomatoes

1 small onion, finely chopped

20 g/¾ oz butter

15 g/½ oz flour

120 ml/4 fl oz white wine

1 medium carrot, grated

1 large sprig of basil *or* parsley

a good pinch of salt and sugar

freshly ground black pepper

First prepare the sauce: wipe the tomatoes, cut each in half and squeeze them to remove the pips. (They do not need to be peeled as the sauce is later strained.) Strain the juices off the pips and discard the seeds. Place the onion and butter in a pan and cook slowly until the onion is golden brown. Sieve in the flour and allow it to colour. Add the tomatoes to the pan with the wine, juice from the seeds, grated carrot, basil or parsley and seasoning. Crush the tomatoes gently with a wooden spoon, cover the pan and simmer for between ¾ and 1 hour. Pass through a nylon strainer into a bowl and cover.

Wipe and trim the mushrooms, then cover and refrigerate them.

Trim the veal to remove any fat, skin or membrane. Place the escalopes between two pieces of waxed or parchment paper and gently beat out with a rolling pin to a thickness of 5 mm/¼ in. Dry them well. Heat the oil in a large frying pan, add half the butter and when foaming place three escalopes in the pan (they should be close together but not overlapping). Fry 4-5 minutes on each side, regulating the heat so as to avoid either scorching or stewing the veal. Lift the escalopes into a serving dish and keep warm. Add the rest of the butter, cook the remaining veal pieces and add them to the serving dish. Quickly fry the mushrooms and place them on top of the escalopes.

Deglaze the pan with the white wine, straining it into the tomato sauce and simmer together for 5 minutes, then check the seasoning. Spoon the sauce over the escalopes and serve, or cover with foil and keep warm until you are ready to serve with the pilaff.

Saffron and pepper pilaff

1 yellow and 1 red pepper of the same size

15 ml/1 tbls olive oil

rock salt

a good pinch of saffron threads

hot water

75 g/3 oz butter

1 large onion, finely sliced

275 g/10 oz Italian rice

seasoning

900 ml-1 litre/1½-1¾ pints stock

50 g/2 oz Parmesan *or* dry Cheddar cheese, finely grated

OVEN TEMPERATURE: 180°C/350°F/ Gas Mark 4

Prepare the peppers the day before the dinner. Slice them very finely into rings and remove the seeds. Place on a large plate, sprinkle with the oil and grind a little rock salt over them. Cover with cling film and leave them in a cool larder or refrigerator.

Begin the pilaff 1 hour before you wish to serve it. Soak the saffron in an egg-cupful of hot water. Melt 25 g/1 oz of the butter in a flameproof casserole, add the finely sliced onion, and cook slowly, uncovered, until soft and yellow. Add the rice, fry for a few minutes until the rice looks transparent then add seasoning, the saffron, and 900 ml/1½ pints of stock. Bring to the boil, cover tightly, and cook in the preheated oven until the grains are tender. Do not stir the rice at all during this period.

Remove the pan from the oven, add the prepared peppers and extra stock if necessary and carefully mix them in with a fork. Scatter half the cheese over the top and dot with another 25 g/ 1 oz butter. Cover the pan and replace in the oven turned to its lowest setting for 5-7 minutes, then lift out and keep warm at

The Mediterranean flavours of Escalopes of veal niçoise are perfectly balanced by Saffron and pepper pilaff.

the back of the stove until wanted. Stir in the final 25 g/1 oz butter and the other half of cheese with a fork just before bringing to table.

Peaches Cordon Bleu

zest and juice of 1 large orange	
50 g/2 oz caster sugar	
100 g/4 oz ratafia biscuits	
60 ml/4 tbls or more brandy	
300 ml/½ pint double cream	
10 ml/2 tsp ice-cold water	
8 large ripe peaches	

Grate the zest of the orange on the finest side of your grater and place it in a small cup with 2 teaspoonfuls of the measured sugar and 15 ml/1 tbls of the orange juice. Mix the remaining sugar and orange juice together, stir, and set aside. Put the ratafias into a soup plate and sprinkle with the brandy. (The more brandy you use the less the ratafias will hold their shape – but the better the dessert will taste!)

Pour the cream into a chilled bowl and stand in another bowl containing a little cold water and ice cubes. Whisk the cream, slowly adding the ice-cold water a little at a time, as the cream thickens. Do not over-beat. Stop when the cream leaves a trail on itself as a little is lifted out on the whisk. Stir in the orange zest mixture.

Peel and slice the peaches and pour over the sweetened orange juice. Layer the peaches with the ratafias and orange cream in a crystal bowl and serve chilled.

Classic Summer Arrangement

This arrangement is perhaps best described in stages. Remember to keep all arrangements set amongst food tall and off the table.

Begin by anchoring the stems of the back flowers across the back portion of the vase, going through your netting on to the semi-circular glass base, on which a small piece of oasis has been rested. This will stop the stems slipping. The netting has been clipped over the rim of the goblet, once again to make it more rigid.

Next, get your centre foliage in with a good curving piece coming right down over the front to stop any arrangement mechanics showing in the glass bowl. Try to find a piece of ivy (*hedera*) that has been growing in the right direction, so that it fits neatly over the vase rim.

The third step is to get width into the arrangement with stems that curve naturally. The pieces must flow and sit comfortably in the vase. Avoid a 'surprised' look with upright stems.

Grouping the flowers

Fourthly, start grouping your flowers – red hot poker (*kniphofia*), *dahlia*, rose (*rosa*) variety Peer Gynt – getting each to run right through the arrangement.

Get your large flowers and thick stems well-placed and secure in the netting, each flowing out at an angle from the vase centre. One or two of the heavier, larger flowers should go back into the centre of the vase low down.

Finally, fill in using small flowers with wiry stems – these thread in easily. Have plenty of variation of length, and flowers at all stages of development. The marigold (*calendula*), *cosmos* (variety Bright Lights) and *dimorphotheca* complete the arrangement.

AUTUMN DINNER

Autumn is traditionally a season of plenty, and this dinner generously links
the elegance of summer eating with the richer delights of winter food.

MENU

for a party of six

Leek Salad

•

Guinea Fowl en Cocotte

Fondant Potatoes

Brussels Sprouts

•

Normandy Crêpes

WINE

Hermitage

IN MANY WAYS, entertaining in the autumn and spring is more of an imaginative challenge than it is at other times of the year, as your guests will come to your table with fewer clear-cut ideas about what to expect. You can borrow recipes that come from the cookery of both summer and winter; and in autumn, particularly, you will have a wealth of fresh ingredients at your fingertips. The season of mists and mellow fruitfulness is kind to the cook.

Checking ingredients

The dishes in this menu look both forwards and backwards, and all of the ingredients should be available for a good month and a half at the beginning of autumn. Raspberry vinegar is essential for the guinea fowl: a recipe is supplied for this in the *Reference Section*, but don't forget that it should be made four or five days beforehand, so that the raspberry flavour can steep into the vinegar. If you use commercial raspberry vinegar, be sure to sweeten it first: see the recipe on page 141 for details. Look out, too, for Maris Piper potatoes: they are ideal for the fondant potato recipe, and are still available in autumn.

Choosing the wine

A rather grand wine partner to go with this menu would be Hermitage, the classic red wine of the Rhône valley: this should be at least five years old. (If it has thrown a heavy sediment, it will need decanting: see *Reference Section* page 150.) If you wish your meal to be a little less formal, or a little less expensive, any red wine from the Rhône, or any wine from the syrah grape, would accompany these autumn flavours perfectly.

MEAL PLANNER

● **Five days before:** begin the raspberry vinegar.

● **Two days before:** make the demi-glace sauce.

● **The day before:** do all the shopping. Prepare the crêpe filling. Hard boil the eggs; strain, sweeten and bottle the raspberry vinegar.

● **The morning:** prepare, cook and dress the leeks. Prepare the mayonnaise. Prepare the crêpe batter, and fry the crêpes. Stack them ready for filling.

● **Final preparation:** fill the crêpes. Brush with butter and sprinkle with sugar ready for baking. Assemble the leek salad; chill. Brown and cook the guinea fowl. Prepare and cook the potatoes. Cook the sprouts and *refresh*. Prepare the sauce for the guinea fowl, carve the birds, and allow the meat and sauce to warm together and exchange flavours as the first course is eaten. (If you wish, the carving and sauce-finishing could be done immediately after the first course.) Finish the vegetables when you are ready to eat the second course; heat the crêpes through at the same time.

Leek salad

6-8 leeks, according to size	
60 ml/4 tbls hazelnut *or* walnut oil	
1 clove garlic, peeled	
seasoning	
15 ml/1 tbls wine vinegar	
3 hard-boiled eggs, separated	
250 ml/8 fl oz mayonnaise	
paprika	

Wash the leeks thoroughly. Split in half lengthways and tie together to form two or three neat bundles. Boil the bundles in salted water until just tender (about 12 minutes). Drain and *refresh*.

Heat the nut oil in a small pan, add the whole garlic clove and fry until golden brown. Allow to cool; remove the garlic. Mix a little seasoning with the vinegar and whisk this into the oil.

Cut the leek halves into 7.5 cm/ 3 in lengths and place them in a serving dish in 6 piles. Spoon over the dressing. Cut the egg white into strips and scatter over the leeks. Make the mayonnaise according to the recipe on page 140 of the *Reference Section*. Spoon this over the salad to coat the leeks, and sieve the yolks over the top. Dust with paprika, and serve lightly chilled.

The subtly gamy taste of guinea fowl is brought out by the raspberry vinegar used in this warm and seasonal Guinea fowl en cocotte.

Guinea fowl en cocotte

450 ml/¾ pint demi-glace sauce

60 ml/4 tbls raspberry vinegar

2 plump guinea fowl

40 g/1½ oz butter, *clarified*

30 ml/2 tbls brandy

OVEN TEMPERATURE: 190°C/375°F/
Gas Mark 5

Make the demi-glace sauce and the raspberry vinegar well in advance according to the recipes given in the *Reference Section*, on page 141. Brown the two birds slowly and thoroughly in the clarified butter in a flameproof casserole. Clarified butter is necessary here if the flesh of the birds is not to stick to the bottom of the casserole. It is important for both flavour and colour that they should be browned as thoroughly as possible: hold them up with wooden spoons or wooden forks in order to get the more inaccessible parts of the birds browned. When this is completed, *flame* with the brandy. Pour over the raspberry vinegar, cover tightly and place in the preheated oven for 50-60 minutes, or until the juice from the thighs runs clear when pierced at the thickest point.

At the end of this period, remove the birds and keep them warm at the back of the stove. Turn the oven down to 120°C/250°F/Gas Mark ½. Add the demi-glace sauce to the casserole in which the birds have cooked, boil it all up well, and adjust the seasoning. *Reduce* a little if the sauce seems thin, and then pour through a very fine nylon sieve. Rinse and wipe out the casserole.

Carve the birds, replace them in the clean casserole, pour over the sauce, and serve. If you prefer, keep the meat and sauce in a very low oven for 15-20 minutes while you serve the first course, to allow the flavour of the sauce to penetrate the flesh.

Fondant potatoes

1 kg/2 lb evenly-sized new potatoes

45-50 g/1½-2 oz butter

salt

Scrape the potatoes, rinse them well in cold water and dry using paper towel or a tea towel.

Melt the butter in a sauté pan or large, heavy saucepan with a close-fitting lid, add the potatoes, cover and set over a very moderate heat. The potatoes should all be on one layer in the pan, though not packed too tightly.

Shake the pan from time to time to turn the potatoes, but do not lift the lid for the first 10-15 minutes as the steam not only helps the potatoes to cook more quickly, but also prevents sticking. Between 15 and 20 minutes after you begin cooking them, test to see if the potatoes are tender. When they are ready, season with salt and turn into a hot serving dish.

Brussels sprouts

750 g/1½ lb small firm sprouts

15 g/½ oz butter

freshly ground black pepper

During your final preparation for the meal, drop the trimmed sprouts into a pan of fast boiling salted water and cook uncovered for 3-5 minutes depending on how soft or firm you like them. Tip into a colander and *refresh* under cold running water: this will leave the sprouts with an attractive bright green colour.

When the potatoes and guinea fowl are ready, quickly toss the sprouts in hot butter. Add a twist of pepper and serve.

Normandy crêpes

For the crêpes:

pancake batter, made with 75 g/3 oz
    flour and 250 ml/8 fl oz milk

For the filling:

2 quinces

100 g/4 oz demerara *or* natural
    cane sugar

250 ml/8 fl oz water

4 large cooking apples (weighing
    1.25-1.5 kg/2½-3 lb)

juice and pared rind of ½ lemon

To finish:

25 g/1 oz butter, melted

icing sugar

Quinces used with apples in the filling for these Normandy crêpes lend an exotic though traditional touch to this popular dessert.

350 g/12 oz good apricot jam *or*
   quince jelly

grated rind and juice of ½ lemon

30 ml/2 tbls calvados *or* brandy

OVEN TEMPERATURE: 220°C/425°F/
   Gas Mark 7

Make the pancake batter according to the recipe and method in the *Reference Section*, page 143. Peel and slice the quinces thinly, then simmer until tender in a covered pan with 50 g/2 oz of the sugar and the water. Peel, core and slice the apples, then put the slices in a buttered saucepan with the lemon rind and juice; cover and cook slowly until soft and pulpy.

Remove the lemon rind, then crush the apples with a potato masher. Add the rest of the sugar to the apple purée and cook until thick. Add the quince mixture.

Test whether the pancake batter is ready for frying by dipping your small finger into the mixture. It should run off leaving just a thin film. If it is too thick, thin the batter with a little milk. When the batter is ready, fry the pancakes as thinly as possible in a 15 cm/6 in crêpe pan, or a shallow, heavy frying pan of roughly the same dimensions, and stack one on top of another until wanted.

Fill 12-16 pancakes generously with the apple mixture and place in a buttered gratin dish. Brush them with butter and dust with icing sugar. Bake in the preheated oven for 10 minutes.

Meanwhile, melt the jam or jelly with the lemon juice and rind in a small pan, and keep warm — but not over direct heat. Just before taking the crêpes to table, reheat the sauce and add the calvados or brandy to it. Spoon a little over the pancakes. Pour the remaining sauce into a small jug for serving with the pancakes.

Freezer tip: Pancakes freeze very well, and it is worth making a larger quantity when you make the base for this menu and freezing the surplus pancakes.

Mixed Autumn Colours

An antique copper bowl on short feet has been chosen to hold this all-round arrangement in orange and red. The flowers are the last of the season before the frosts begin, and the 'warm' qualities of old copper set them off perfectly. Most of the foliage and berries are from the hedgerow.

This arrangement was made by first setting 5 outline points along the base level to the vase, and then fixing the height with the stem of a daisy-type flower (*compositae*) in seed.

When doing an all-round arrangement, it's best to work in sections, one at a time, starting at the centre and working down into the vase with different lengths of stem, then out to the edge from the base of the vase: group your colours and shapes carefully, and have no two stems of the same length together. The *dahlias* used are of two distinct types known as pompon and decorative. The lily (*lilium*) is variety Firecracker. The last of the paeony (*paeonia*) foliage gives the deep red colouring. Spindle berry (*euonymus europaeus*), *berberis*, rosehip (*rosa canina* and *eglanteria*) and *viburnum* berries give different shapes and colours, and the ivy (*hedera*) helps fill the remaining gaps.

Autumn alternatives
When one thinks of autumn, orange and red colours come to mind but there are many other flowers and colours still available at that time. *Eucalyptus* makes a good light background alternative, and some silver/grey foliages (*cineraria maritima* and *helichrysum petiolatum*) are also pretty in the autumn. *Hydrangea*, rubrum lilies (*lilium auratum rubrum*) and michaelmas daisy (*aster novi-belgii*) are all attractive: their mauves, pinks and blues in amongst the grey foliage would look good in pewter or silver.

WINTER LUNCH

This simple winter lunch shows how uncomplicated seasonal entertaining can be:
a warming pie, a light creamy dessert and tasty cheese combine to provide the perfect antidote to chilly weather.

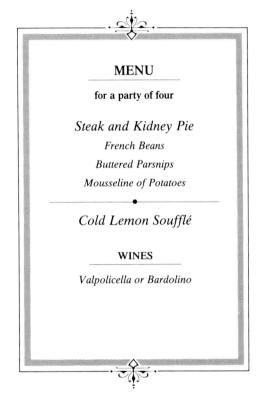

MENU

for a party of four

Steak and Kidney Pie

French Beans

Buttered Parsnips

Mousseline of Potatoes

•

Cold Lemon Soufflé

WINES

Valpolicella or Bardolino

AN EASY, TWO-COURSE lunch like this is the ideal solution to entertaining small numbers of friends memorably – particularly if you have a number of other tasks to fit into your day. Pies are a good choice as they sit quietly in the oven while you get on with other things – and you'll have no last-minute carving to worry about either. If you're really rushed (perhaps Christmas is on the way), you could always use a good quality bought puff pastry, and a microwave oven would be handy for reheating the French beans (follow manufacturer's instructions for timing and power level). The cold soufflé is simple to make, and can be fully prepared in advance if you wish.

Lunchtime entertaining

Entertaining at lunchtime, in general, makes for a less formal occasion than does entertaining in the evening, and it's nice to carry this informality over into your cooking. Certain types of food are more appropriate than others at lunchtime: pies are one example, and others include savoury flans and quiches, main-course soups, filled jacket potatoes, country stews, and – for the summer – substantial mixed salads. Eggs and egg dishes, too, are very welcome at lunchtime: omelettes, served either filled or plain, and followed by a green salad, make a light but satisfying lunch throughout the year. Avoid frying food at lunchtime, though: it can often be over-rich for those with a busy afternoon

ahead, and the cook may well be haunted by frying odours for the rest of the day!

Seeing to your guests

A good rule of thumb for a couple to bear in mind when they have guests, particularly if those guests are unfamiliar with each other, is that one person (either host or hostess) should always be in the room at any one

time. This helps to put guests at ease, and gives everyone the feeling that things are as they should be.

The finishing touches

So often it is the finishing touches that make all the difference to a meal. Simple napkins that tie in with the colour scheme you have chosen for the menu, a special silver cruet containing an appropriate mustard (English in this case): these are the things that guests will notice and remember. For a two-course meal like this it is always a good idea to have some cheese ready: this need not be a grand array. One good farmhouse cheese with a choice of biscuits or grapes to eat it with will provide the perfect end to a simple but generous lunch.

Wine for lunch

Less wine, as a rule, is needed at lunchtime than in the evening, and lighter wines are preferable to heavy, full-bodied ones high in alcohol. This doesn't mean that only white wines can be served at lunchtime, though: many dishes, like our steak and kidney pie, will be better accompanied by a red. Choose something light, such as Valpolicella or the Bardolino illustrated in the photograph, and serve it very lightly chilled (no more than half an hour in the refrigerator, or a morning in a cold pantry, will be sufficient). If you wish to drink white wine with the pie, try serving a lightly chilled, dry Soave, Frascati or Orvieto.

MEAL PLANNER

● **The day before:** do all the shopping. Make the pastry dough, and chill overnight. Completely make the soufflé if you wish: store in a cool place overnight.

● **The morning:** make and cool the soufflé, if you haven't already done so. (If it has been in the refrigerator overnight, bring it back to room temperature.) Fully prepare the pie ready for baking. Prepare the French beans and parsnips. Begin baking the pie.

● **Final preparation:** Cook the vegetables, saving the final reheating of the beans for the last minute. If you wish, the parsnips can be kept warm for up to half an hour over a very low heat on top of the stove, and the pie can also be kept warm in a low oven.

Steak and kidney pie, garnished with a selection of vegetables, makes a simple lunch into a meal which guests will remember.

French beans

450 g/1 lb French beans

15 g/½ oz butter

freshly ground black pepper

Top and tail the French beans and drop into a large saucepan of fast boiling water. Cook uncovered for no more than 2 minutes. Drain in a colander and then *refresh* under cold running water to cool quickly and 'set' their colour.

Just before serving, melt the butter in the same saucepan and toss the beans over a high heat for 1-2 minutes. Season well with the pepper. Turn into a hot dish and serve.

Note: If you feel like ringing the changes, more unusual vegetable combinations to eat with steak and kidney pie would include the cucumber with spring onions on page 99 and the celeriac and potato purée on page 39.

Buttered parsnips

1 kg/2 lb parsnips, peeled

50 g/2 oz butter

freshly ground black pepper

Cut the whole peeled parsnips into quarters, lengthwise, and trim away the centre core if it is at all tough. Cover with cold salted water, bring to the boil, and simmer until tender. Drain thoroughly and mash until smooth.

Return to the saucepan with 15 g/½ oz of the butter, and re-heat gently until the purée has lost any surplus moisture and is fully blended. Season with the pepper and stir in the rest of the butter in pieces. Serve very hot.

Note: The sweet taste of parsnips appeals to adults, particularly with savoury food, but children often like it less. Check first with any young guests, particularly those too shy to protest!

Steak and kidney pie

225 g/8 oz rough puff pastry dough

1 small onion

1 kg/2 lb lean beef shoulder steak or skirt

225 g/8 oz ox kidney, skinned and cored

30 ml/2 tbls flour, seasoned with salt and freshly ground black pepper

10 ml/2 tsp chopped parsley

approx. 175 ml/6 fl oz beef stock *or* water

For the glaze:

1 egg beaten with ½ tsp salt

OVEN TEMPERATURE: 220°C/425°F/ Gas Mark 7

Prepare the pastry dough according to the recipe in the *Reference Section* on page 142. Wrap well and chill until ready to use.

Chop the onion finely. Cut the steak and kidney into 1 cm/½ in cubes and roll in the seasoned flour. Fill an 18 cm/7 in deep pie dish with this mixture, scattering the onion and parsley between the layers of meat. Fill the dish with the stock or water.

Roll out the pastry dough into a roughly oval shape and set aside. From the trimmings make a few leaves for decoration: cut the dough into diamond shapes, score a line down the middle of the diamond, and score leaf 'veins' either side of the central line. Cut a long strip of pastry dough twice as wide as the rim of the pie dish from the outside of your large dough shape, and fix this over and under the rim of the pie dish all the way around. Dampen this dough rim with water, and place the cut oval of dough on top. Seal the edge firmly, then make a small hole in the top and decorate suitably. Brush with the beaten egg glaze and bake in the preheated oven for 35-40 minutes. Wrap a double sheet of wet greaseproof paper over and round the pie to stop the pastry burning, and continue cooking at 180°C/350°F/Gas Mark 4 for 1½-1¾ hours. Serve with the other vegetables and a mousseline of potatoes: the recipe is on page 52.

Light and fluffy, Cold lemon soufflé is finished with toasted almonds for contrast and colour. Whipped cream adds a luxurious note.

Cold lemon soufflé

4 eggs

2½ lemons

225 g/8 oz caster sugar

300 ml/½ pint double cream

10 ml/2 tsp gelatine soaked in
    a small dish containing 65 ml/
    2½ fl oz cold water

To finish:

30 ml/2 tbls ground almonds,
    browned, or ratafia crumbs

120 ml/4 fl oz double cream

Prepare a 1.2 litre/2 pint soufflé dish by folding a large sheet of greaseproof paper in half lengthwise, and then up one third again. Wrap this around your soufflé dish: the thicker portion of greaseproof paper should fit snugly beneath the narrow rim of the soufflé dish, and the rest of the paper should protrude above the rim by 4 cm/1½ in or so. Secure the greaseproof paper firmly around the dish with string.

Separate the eggs and place the yolks, grated lemon rind, strained lemon juice and sugar in a basin. Whisk all together, using an electric whisk, until it is thick and mousse-like; or hand whisk, holding the bowl over a saucepan one third full of recently boiled water. When thickened, remove and continue whisking until the bowl is cold. (No heat is necessary if an electric whisk is used.)

Half whip the 300 ml/½ pint of double cream, and fold this into the mixture. Dissolve the soaked gelatine by placing the small dish in a larger dish of hot water. Whisk the egg whites until stiff and fold into the mixture with the dissolved gelatine. Stand this soufflé mixture in a larger bowl containing ice cubes and a little water and stir very carefully until the mixture begins to thicken. Turn at once into the prepared case and set in a cool place.

When firm, remove the greaseproof paper and press the ground almonds or ratafia crumbs gently round the exposed sides. Whip the 120 ml/4 fl oz double cream, and pipe to decorate.

Dried Flower Group

Fresh flowers are both difficult to obtain and expensive during the winter months, so this arrangement uses a selection of dried flowers. The types used include dock stems (*rumex*) and foxglove shoots (*digitalis*), heads of *sedum spectabile* and *achillea*, a spray of *eryngium agavifolium* (one of the sea holly family), and *helichrysum* and statice (*limonium sinuatum*) for the yellow, white and mauve colours. Also included are a selection of dried flowers from South Africa – the sunshine bush (*leucodendron*) is prominent on the right. Hops (*humulus lupulus*) and grasses complete the arrangement.

The container used is the top of a broken alabaster vase: the stem is now missing and the oval top makes an ideal shallow vase. It also neatly echoes the oval shape of the table. Secure a block of oasis sec inside the vase with a layer of 5 cm/2 in mesh wire netting; wire this firmly to each handle. The netting helps support the brittle stems of some of the dry flowers.

Arranging dried flowers

When flower groups contain a wide mixture of varieties, as this one does, try to put colours and shapes together as far as possible. Begin this all-round arrangement by setting the end pieces at the widest points of the grouping, and from these work up into the vase centre to the highest point. Next fill in the main 'weight' in the centre: the flat head of sedum spectabile and achillea have been used here. Finally fill in the rest of the arrangement, grouping your shapes and colours as mentioned above, but remembering to check these groupings from all sides, as it is from all sides that they will be seen.

Caring for dried flowers

Always keep dried flowers dry and free from dust – though not in too hot an atmosphere or they will become brittle. After use, store them carefully in a box in a dry, dark place.

CHAMPAGNE BREAKFAST

Whether you choose to eat in bed or to gaze at each other across the kitchen table,

nothing can top a champagne breakfast for light-hearted romance.

THE SORT OF occasion that merits a champagne breakfast has to be very special – and there should accordingly be something very special about the food. At the same time, it's important that it can all be prepared the day before, and just finished on the morning of the celebration, or to some extent the 'celebration' element would be lost. This is how this menu has been devised.

Colour themes are useful aids in entertaining, and pink is a natural colour choice for all romantic meals. Here the pink 'theme' is taken from the salmon through the grapefruit to the champagne, and could be picked up in various other ways if you wish: your choice

MENU

for a celebration for two

•

Grapefruit and Grape Salad
Mushroom and Bacon Tartlets
Salmon Kedgeree
Brioches with Preserves

WINE

Rosé Champagne

of flowers might include a pretty pink variety of rose or carnation, for example.

Breakfast party alternatives
If you would like to give a less intimate champagne breakfast party for a group of people, this menu could be used as a basis for it: substitute an ordinary champagne for the rosé version; use plain grapefruit instead of pink; and use Finnan haddock to make the kedgeree. The brioches could be freshly baked on the morning of the party (getting up that little bit earlier would no longer be so inappropriate!), and quantities proportionately increased to accommodate your new guest total: double up for each couple.

BREAKFAST PLANNER

● **The afternoon before:** make and bake the pastry dough. Make and prove the brioche dough.

● **The evening before:** knock down and re-prove the brioche dough. Prepare the tart filling and hollandaise sauce. Prepare the rice and salmon, and fully prepare the grapefruit and grape salad. Bake the brioches: cool.

● **Final preparation:** put the rice into the oven on the middle shelf. Prepare the cooked egg and heat the salmon. Put the brioches into the oven on the bottom shelf. Fill the tartlet cases, top with hollandaise, and put into the top of the oven. Add the salmon, eggs and cream to the rice.

Grapefruit and grape salad

2 pink grapefruit
30 ml/2 tbls caster sugar
100 g/4 oz sweet green grapes
250 ml/8 fl oz sweet white wine (Sauternes or similar)

Cut the peel and pith from the grapefruit, divide it into segments, and dust with the sugar. Peel and pip the grapes and cover with the wine. Spoon the grapes and grapefruit into coupe glasses, cover with cling film and chill overnight.

Note: Always take the time to fully remove pith from citrus fruits, as it can be very bitter.

Mushroom and bacon tartlets

175 g/6 oz shortcrust pastry dough

For the filling:

100 g/4 oz mushrooms
4 rashers thin cut unsmoked streaky bacon
15 g/½ oz butter
1 shallot, finely chopped
120 ml/4 fl oz hollandaise sauce

OVEN TEMPERATURE: 190°C/375°F/ Gas Mark 5

Prepare the shortcrust pastry dough according to the recipe given on page 142 of the *Reference Section*: roll it out and use it to line 4 tartlet tins. *Bake blind* for 7 minutes in the preheated oven.

Wipe and trim the mushrooms and slice them thickly. Cut the bacon into 1 cm/½ in strips. Melt the butter, add the shallot, and after a few seconds frizzle the bacon gently in the butter and shallot for 2-3 minutes. Add the mushrooms, cover, and cook un-til the juice begins to run. Remove the lid, season, and increase the heat to evaporate any liquid. Cool. Prepare the hollandaise sauce according to the recipe in the *Reference Section* on page 140 (use 1 egg yolk).

Fill the pastry cases with the mushroom mixture. Top each with a spoonful of hollandaise. Five minutes before serving, heat the tartlets through on the upper shelf of the oven, as described in the **Breakfast Planner**.

Salmon kedgeree

75 g/3 oz long-grain rice, soaked for 30 minutes, drained and boiled
225 g/8 oz salmon steak, poached lightly and flaked
50 g/2 oz butter
1 egg, boiled for 8 minutes and cooled quickly in cold water
seasoning
1 raw egg
75 ml/5 tbls whipping cream

OVEN TEMPERATURE: 180°C/350°F/ Gas Mark 4

Prepare the rice and fish as indicated in the ingredients list above. Spread half the butter over the bottom and sides of a gratin dish. Turn the rice into this prepared dish and cover closely with foil. Store in a cool place.

The next morning, place the rice in the preheated oven for 15 minutes. Melt the remainder of the butter in a pan, put in the salmon and shake over heat until thoroughly hot. Add to the rice with the roughly-chopped cooked egg, season well and combine the ingredients with a fork. Add the raw beaten egg and enough cream to moisten the whole dish nicely. Return to the oven for 5 minutes to warm through finally before serving with the mushroom and bacon tartlets.

Brioches are always a treat for breakfast, particularly served warm with butter and a light fruit preserve or marmalade.

Brioches

350 g/12 oz flour
5 ml/1 tsp salt
scant 20 g/¾ oz fresh yeast
5 ml/1 tsp sugar
50 ml/2 fl oz warm milk
2 eggs
50 g/2 oz butter
25 g/1 oz caster sugar
1 egg, beaten with a pinch of salt

OVEN TEMPERATURE: 200°C/400°F/ Gas Mark 6

Sift the flour and salt into a warm basin, cream the yeast with the sugar and add to the milk and beaten eggs. Add all the liquid to the flour and beat thoroughly. Cream the butter and work into the dough with the caster sugar. Cover and allow to rise for 40 minutes in a warm place.

Push the dough down again and knead lightly on a floured board or slab. Turn the dough into lightly greased individual brioche tins (this amount will make about 12): use patty tins if you haven't any brioche tins. Cover them with a cloth and prove in a warm place until the mixture reaches the tops of the tins – allow at least 30 minutes. Glaze with the egg beaten with salt.

Bake in the preheated oven for about 12-15 minutes. Allow to cool, before storing and reheating the brioches the next day at 180°C/350°F/Gas Mark 4 for about 10 minutes.

Mushroom and bacon tartlets, served with a rich, light Salmon kedgeree, make a breakfast fit for a king – or queen.

For a simple arrangement like this the best container to use is a small, well-proportioned white vase. The roses (*rosa*) are variety Carte Blanche.

A small piece of oasis has been placed initially in the base of the vase to steady the stems and help weigh down the container and provide balance. Always set the height of the arrangement first using the smaller flower or bud at the top. This should be about one-and-a-half times the height of the vase, as a guideline. Set the second flower next: choose one with well-placed leaves. Add extra foliage at the base to fill.

These Carte Blanche roses are a fairly new variety which has wonderful lasting qualities. As the buds open, the slightly frilled petals, when seen from a distance, give one the idea that they may be camellias or gardenias. Like so many other market roses the scent is missing, but a strong point in their favour is their foliage, which is a very lovely dark green and completely free from disease. Once opened, the flower lasts well.

Alternative varieties

Other white rose varieties that would be attractive here include Jack Frost (a hybrid tea or large-flowered rose), Iceberg (a floribunda or cluster-flowered rose), and a climbing rose called Silver Moon. The Dutch variety Masterpiece would also suit.

If you wish to use pink roses, the climbing rose Swan Lake and the large-flowered Blessings and Royal Highness are all in very pretty pale pink shades, ideal for our breakfast tray.

This small, white vase is one of those known as a specimen vase, and is made of Azberg porcelain. There are many attractive alternatives – though avoid clear glass as you will not be able to use oasis.

FORMAL FISH DINNER

There is something about a fish dinner that excites the greatest enthusiasm and admiration in guests:
simplicity, both in the kitchen and on the table, is the key to success.

MENU

for a party of eight

Tomato Ice
with Fresh Prawns

•

Turbot Bretonne
with julienne of vegetables
Maître d'Hôtel Potatoes

•

Pear and Chocolate Flan
with whipped cream

•

Cheese Gougères

WINES

Manzanilla Sherry

Sancerre

THIS EXCITING AND unusual menu is perfect for those occasions when you really feel like pushing the boat out and impressing everyone, not least yourself. It is neither difficult nor particularly seasonal: while turbot is at its best in winter, it's both available and delicious throughout the year. You may well, though, have to order the turbot from your fish merchant in advance, to ensure it is in peak condition.

When entertaining with menus based around a food 'theme' (like fish, game, or vegetables) take great care to keep the meal varied and interesting. The theme should be developed both directly and indirectly – as here, where the prawn garnish is the only fish element in the first course, providing a subtle overture to the turbot *pièce de résistance*. A dessert and savoury follow.

The British savoury
Savouries are one of Britain's most under-valued contributions to the art of good eating. Enjoyed above all by the Victorians, their purpose was to refresh the palate after dessert so that the port which always followed could be enjoyed to the full. Here the idea has been combined with the French talent for producing light, rich morsels for eating on their own, in the cheese gougères. Savouries are customarily small, highly flavoured and served very hot.

Wines for the meal
Sherry, as well as being a wonderful apéritif, is a good wine to accompany Mediterranean-style starters, one of which is the tomato ice served as the first course in this menu (another one being the anchovy eggs of the **Impromptu Dinner**, page 48). Sancerre, or its counterpart on the other side of the River Loire, Pouilly-Fumé, would both make fitting accompaniments to the turbot. They are both wines made from the sauvignon blanc grape, which gives very pungent, very clean-tasting, dry white wines, perfect with a wide range of foods, but particularly good with fish. Serve well-chilled. If you would prefer something a little less dry, a German Kabinett or Spätlese wine would also match the turbot.

MEAL PLANNER

● **Three days (or more) before:** order the turbot from your fish merchant, if necessary.

● **One day before:** shop for all of the ingredients for the dinner except for the prawns and turbot. Make the tomato ice, beat and freeze it. Make the béchamel sauce, and prepare the chocolate pastry dough.

● **The morning:** collect the turbot and prawns. Prepare the vegetable julienne for the turbot dish: put into a shallow saucepan ready for cooking, and cover closely. Make the choux pastry dough, and pipe it into the ramekins. Cover and refrigerate. *Macerate* the pear slices in the sugar and brandy. Roll out the pastry dough and line the flan dish.

● **The afternoon:** bake the pear and chocolate flan. Prepare the potato dish completely except for the final baking.

● **Final preparation:** transfer the tomato ice from the freezer to the refrigerator to soften slightly about 20 minutes before serving. Cook the turbot and the vegetable julienne independently; towards the end of the turbot cooking period begin cooking the potatoes. Prepare the turbot sauce as far as the reduction of the cider. Now is the time to serve and eat the tomato ice. After the first course is eaten, finish off the turbot dish and potatoes. Bake the gougères as you eat the dessert tart.

Note: If turbot, or the similar brill, are unavailable, the main dish would be equally good made with monkfish steaks.

Tomato ice with fresh prawns

750 g/1½ lb ripe tomatoes

1 small clove garlic, blanched

2 bay leaves

3 sprigs of basil

450 ml/¾ pint thick mayonnaise, made with 4 egg yolks and lemon juice instead of vinegar

seasoning and sugar to taste

10 ml/2 tsp tomato purée

juice of 1-2 lemons

grated rind of 1 large orange

150 ml/¼ pint partially whipped double cream

For the garnish:

450 g/1 lb unpeeled prawns

Wipe the tomatoes, slice and place in a pan with the garlic and herbs. Cover, simmer to a pulp and sieve. When cool, mix in the mayonnaise (made according to the recipe in the *Reference Section*, page 140), and the rest of the ingredients in the order given. Turn into an ice churn or ice cream maker and freeze according to the manufacturer's instructions. As this is a thick, creamy mixture, it may also be turned into a 1.75 litre/3 pint plastic pudding basin and left to freeze in the ice-making compartment of your refrigerator, if large enough, or freezer. Beat twice before the ice sets hard. Remove ice from freezer and let it soften slightly in the fridge for about 20 minutes before you wish to eat it.

Peel and trim the prawns, keeping them as large as you can manage. Place a scoop of tomato ice in a prawn cocktail glass, and garnish with the prawns. Keep on crushed ice until ready to serve.

Freezer Tip: When tomatoes are plentiful in high summer, make two or three quantities of the tomato pulp for your freezer: it will be ideal for sauces and soups, as well as for special occasion recipes like this one.

The creamy summertime flavour of Tomato ice with fresh prawns subtly paves the way for the main course turbot.

Maître d'hôtel potatoes

1.5 kg/3 lb evenly-sized potatoes

100 g/4 oz butter

2 shallots, finely chopped

60 ml/4 tbls chopped parsley

seasoning

OVEN TEMPERATURE: 180°C/350°F/ Gas Mark 4

Scrub the potatoes and leave them whole, then boil or steam them gently in their skins until just tender, but not soft or floury. Drain them well, then dry, peel and slice them thickly and evenly into disc-shaped pieces.

Melt the butter in a small pan, add the finely chopped shallots, cover, and cook slowly for 2-3 minutes. Draw aside, add the parsley and plenty of salt and pepper and mix well. Place the potatoes in a hot gratin dish layered with the butter and parsley mixture and heat in the preheated moderate oven for about 15 minutes.

Note: The Cara variety of potato is excellent for this recipe.

Turbot bretonne

8 × 175 g/6 oz turbot steaks, *or*
  1 × 1.5-1.75 kg/3-4 lb chicken
  turbot, filleted, and cut into
  steaks

salt

lemon juice

600 ml/1 pint dry cider

seasoning

15 ml/1 tbls lemon juice

1 bay leaf

100 g/4 oz each of carrot, onion and
  celery

100 g/4 oz butter

2 shallots, finely chopped

40 g/1½ oz flour

15 ml/1 tbls parsley

OVEN TEMPERATURE: 180°C/350°F/
  Gas Mark 4

Soak the turbot in cold water with a little salt and lemon juice to whiten prior to cooking; rinse and dry well. Place in an oven-proof dish with the white flesh underneath, and moisten with 150 ml/¼ pint of the cider and an equal quantity of water. Add seasoning, lemon juice and bayleaf and poach in the preheated oven for 30 minutes. Baste occasionally.

Cut the vegetables into *julienne strips*, season and cook in 40 g/1½ oz of the butter in a tightly covered shallow saucepan until tender. Allow 15 minutes for this. A butter wrapper pressed down on the vegetables, and a tightly fitting lid, will help to stop the vegetables browning.

Melt 25 g/1 oz of the butter in a saucepan, add the shallots, cover and cook until soft. Pour in the remaining cider and boil rapidly until *reduced* by half, then strain on the liquor that the fish has cooked in. Keep the fish warm.

Work the remaining butter to a paste with the flour to make a *beurre manié*, whisk a small piece at a time into the liquid and stir until boiling and thickened. Add the vegetables and parsley; adjust seasoning. Remove the skin from the fish steaks, place in a dish, spoon over the sauce and julienne vegetables and serve.

Turbot bretonne is a finely-flavoured fish dish, with its sauce highlighted by the tangy taste of cider.

Pear and chocolate flan

For the pastry:

225 g/8 oz plain flour

40 g/1½ oz cocoa

120 g/4½ oz butter *or* margarine

120 g/4½ oz caster sugar

1 egg

2 egg yolks

2-3 drops vanilla essence

For the filling:

4-5 ripe dessert pears, such as Comice

15 ml/1 tbls vanilla sugar

45 ml/3 tbls brandy

To finish and serve:

1 egg white, lightly beaten, and caster sugar *or* apricot glaze *(see page 143)*

450 ml/¾ pint double cream, whipped

OVEN TEMPERATURE: 190°C/375°F/ Gas Mark 5

First prepare the dough: sift the flour together with the cocoa, then tip out onto a clean board or formica surface. Make a well in the centre and in this place the other pastry ingredients. Work to a firm paste with your finger tips and chill for 1 hour before using.

Peel, core and slice the pears. Sprinkle with the vanilla sugar and brandy. Cover and leave to soak for ½ hour. Roll out two-thirds of the dough and use it to line a 23 cm/9 in flan ring (see *Reference Section*, page 142).

Drain the pear slices and reserve the juice. Arrange the slices in the flan case. Roll out the remaining dough with any trimmings and cut into 1 cm/½ in strips. Arrange these, lattice fashion, over the pears. Bake for 30-40 minutes in the preheated oven or until firm to the touch. Do not let the pastry brown.

About 5 minutes before the flan is cooked, remove from the oven, brush lightly with egg white and dust with caster sugar. Return to the oven for a few minutes to 'frost' the top. Alternatively, glaze the lattice with apricot glaze after baking.

Serve with a bowl of the whipped cream flavoured with the reserved pear juice and brandy.

Crisp, light and served piping hot, Cheese gougères provide a memorably savoury finish to our formal fish dinner.

Chocolate pastry and a pretty lattice top make all the difference in this irresistible Pear and chocolate flan.

Cheese gougères

choux dough made with 2 eggs

350 ml/12 fl oz béchamel sauce, highly seasoned

100 g/4 oz Gruyère cheese, grated

45 ml/3 tbls double cream

OVEN TEMPERATURE: 190°C/375°F/ Gas Mark 5

Prepare the choux dough according to the recipe in the *Reference Section* on page 142, and the béchamel sauce according to the recipe on page 140. Beat 50 g/2 oz of the grated cheese into the choux mixture, and fill a forcing bag fitted with a 1 cm/½ in eclair pipe with this mixture. Pipe thinly round the bottom and sides of 8 lightly buttered ramekins to form a nest. Add the cream to the well-seasoned béchamel sauce and use half of this sauce to fill the ramekins; sprinkle the top of each with the remaining cheese and bake in the preheated oven for 15-20 minutes until well-risen and brown.

Reheat the remaining sauce and use to top up the centre of the baked choux pastries if necessary. Serve the gougères straight from the oven if possible: they are best when very hot.

Classic Rose Arrangement

For the arrangements in the centre of this table, triangular-based vases have been used, with a cherub pattern on the sides of the vase. A small block of oasis is put in each, and the arrangement uses 3-4 compound stems of polyantha roses (*rosa polyantha*), variety Dorus Rijkers. These have been cut up into lengths, and one or two open flowers have been tucked down to give weight to the centre. The effect given is that of tight posies of salmon/apricot coloured flowers, without too much green foliage interrupting the bursts of warm colour.

Arranging roses

The roses shown above are straight-stemmed florist's roses (*rosa*) – not easy to use as they have a stiff look to them. These 20 hybrid tea (large-flowered) roses, variety Pitica, have been arranged in an open shell vase. Wire netting helps the stems to flow out in a fan shape. Their foliage is large and untidy so small side-shoots of polyantha roses were added after the large Pitica leaves had been removed. Rose varieties are best displayed with their own foliage, but at times it is impossible to use it, especially late in the season when some varieties have suffered from mildew. Some of the roses have had outside petals removed because these had been damaged or had gone papery. No one will notice if done with care, but only take off what's necessary.

Vase shapes and styles are a very personal matter and to suit all occasions, a fairly wide range of shapes, sizes and textures is needed. Just as it's best to have as many different dishes to serve food in as possible, so a collection of interesting vases is well worth the effort of its acquisition. One tends to rely on a few favourites for regular use: often these are the easiest to arrange.

The use of vases

Heavy bronzes, alabaster, pewter and china in plain shapes and clean-cut designs are all particularly useful. A few different cherub figures will be useful and ornate, but coloured china can have its problems. Clear glass should be avoided when possible, and the same applies to anything with poor balance or a fragile stem.

SPORTSMAN'S DINNER

This classic game-based dinner is a treat for all your guests, sportsmen or not:
there'll be something for everybody among these four carefully contrasted courses.

THERE IS SOMETHING about game that seems to appeal to all, even the fussiest eaters. Not everyone, though, enjoys the taste of well-hung game: check how 'gamy' your pheasants are liable to be with your supplier, or if you store them yourself remember that a fortnight in a cool place is a maximum.

Two pheasants are specified in the recipe: try to ensure that at least one of these is a female bird, as they carry just that little extra bit of tender, tasty flesh. (If you buy a 'brace' of pheasants, you will get one male and one female bird.) Should pheasants be out of season, but you feel that you'd still like to try the menu, substitute guinea fowl: a domestic bird available the year round.

Serving game birds

When serving the birds, remember to warn your guests to be on their guard for lead shot in the meat. A nice and traditional touch, if your birds were splendidly feathered, is to use one or two of the finest feathers as a final decoration for the game dish – or place them

MENU

for a party of six

Pâté St. Jacques
with toast

Pheasant with Grapes
Calabrese
Celeriac and Potato Purée

Vacherin Norma

Iced Camembert

WINES

Riesling
Red Burgundy

in a silver container in the middle of the table.

Although this menu has four courses, it is by no means time-consuming to prepare, particularly if you have a freezer: the vacherin and iced Camembert could both be fully completed a number of weeks in advance, and the vacherin is in fact improved by freezing. If you have no freezer, or wish to make the whole meal freshly, follow our **Meal Planner** for preparation times.

Wines for a game menu

A fine, full-flavoured red wine, such as a red burgundy, is ideal with game. Burgundy is rarely decanted in the Burgundy region itself: this is partly because it only ever throws a light sediment, and partly because it is generally drunk fairly young (about five years old on average) at which point there will be little or no sediment anyway. A medium dry or dry white wine made from the riesling grape (good examples are produced in Germany, Alsace, Australia and California) would make an excellent accompaniment to the pâté. Serve it chilled.

MEAL PLANNER

● **Two days before:** do all the shopping. Fully prepare the vacherin if you wish: freeze it, storing it in a box or tin in the freezer, so that it is not accidentally crushed. Prepare the demi-glace sauce for the pheasant.

● **One day before:** fully prepare the iced Camembert moulds: freeze. Fully prepare the pheasant dish: cover closely and store in the refrigerator. Prepare the meringue for the vacherin if you have not already done so: store in an airtight container overnight. Prepare and chill the pâté.

● **The morning:** prepare the vegetables ready for cooking. Remove the vacherin from the freezer. If you made the vacherin meringue the day before, prepare the filling and decoration, and finish the vacherin. Prepare the vegetables ready for cooking in the evening. Set aside some grapes for the garnishing of the pheasant.

● **Final preparation:** cook the celeriac and potato purée: cover with milk and keep warm as outlined in the recipe. Transfer the Camembert moulds from freezer to refrigerator to soften slightly. Begin slowly reheating the pheasant and sauce. Make the toast and

serve the pâté. Finish the celeriac and potato purée, and cook the calabrese, immediately before serving the main course. Check the pheasant is fully reheated, then serve, garnishing with the extra black grapes.

Note: If you wished to prepare for this meal several weeks or a month or so in advance, the vacherin, camembert moulds and demi-glace sauce for the pheasant could all be frozen at that point.

Scallop roes are pounded with butter, lemon juice and brandy to form the colourful core of this seafood Pâté St. Jacques.

Pâté St. Jacques

225 g/8 oz scallops, shelled

275 g/10 oz lemon sole *or* haddock fillet

2 shallots, finely chopped

120 ml/4 fl oz white wine *or* dry vermouth

150 ml/¼ pint chicken stock

175 g/6 oz butter

25 g/1 oz flour

seasoning

5 ml/1 tsp lemon juice

5 ml/1 tsp brandy

a pinch of ground mace

lemon juice

90 ml/6 tbls double cream

To serve:

sweet paprika *or* snipped chives

thinly sliced toast

Place the scallops and fillets of sole or haddock in a large shallow frying pan with the shallots, wine and stock. Cover and poach over a very gentle heat for 5-7 minutes. Lift out the fish with a slotted spoon and let it cool. Strain the poaching liquid, return it to the pan and *reduce* it to 150 ml/¼ pint.

Prepare a thick sauce by making a *roux* with 25 g/1 oz of the butter and all of the flour. Add the reduced stock, bring to the boil and simmer for 2 minutes. Season, then tip onto a plate to cool.

Separate the roe from each scallop, carefully remove its covering membrane and when cold pound with 50 g/2 oz of the butter and the lemon juice and brandy. Place this mixture in a forcing bag fitted with a large, plain pipe.

Blend the scallops in a food processor, add the white fish, and blend again until quite smooth. (If you don't have a food processor, the scallops and fish may be put through a food mill or mincer using the finest blades you have, then rubbed through a v ire sieve.) Add the cold sauce to the fish mixture and when absorbed, add the mace and some lemon juice to taste. Cut the remaining butter into pieces and blend it into the fish mixture. Partially whip the cream, fold it into the mixture and adjust the seasoning.

Turn half the mixture into a small 600 ml/1 pint terrine. Make a slight indentation down the middle with a teaspoon and pipe in the creamed roe. Spoon the rest of the pâté mixture on top, smooth over carefully with a spatula, cover with foil and chill in the refrigerator overnight.

Serve the pâté, sprinkled with sweet paprika or snipped chives, with thin slices of toast.

Pheasant with grapes

450 ml/¾ pint demi-glace sauce

2 pheasants, plucked and drawn

50 g/2 oz butter

45 ml/3 tbls brandy

350 g/12 oz black grapes, split, pipped, but not peeled

250 ml/8 fl oz red or white wine

120 ml/4 fl oz stock

To garnish:

extra black grapes

OVEN TEMPERATURE: 180°C/350°F/ Gas Mark 4

Prepare the demi-glace sauce according to the recipe on page 141 of the *Reference Section*. Brown the pheasants slowly on all sides in the butter in a flameproof casserole, then *flame* with the brandy. Take the birds out, then add the grapes to the casserole. Cook them over a gentle heat, turning and crushing them well. Add the wine and stock (use either the jellied stock recipe given in the *Reference Section*, page 138, or a good commercial substitute like tinned consommé) and replace the pheasants. Cover closely and cook in the preheated oven for 35-45 minutes.

At the end of this period take the birds out and keep them warm in a low oven while you finish the sauce. Strain the cooking liquid and add it to the demi-glace sauce. Bring all to the boil, stirring well. Simmer the sauce to a syrupy consistency while you joint the pheasants, dividing the breast meat into four portions. Arrange the pheasant pieces in a clean casserole. Cover with some of the sauce, and pour the rest into a separate container.

Refrigerate overnight. Reheat the pheasants in a 180°C/350°F/ Gas Mark 4 oven for 30 minutes, and the remaining sauce on top of the stove in a saucepan. Serve the sauce in a sauceboat, and garnish the pheasant pieces with extra black grapes.

Serve with the celeriac and potato purée and calabrese. Calabrese should be cooked in the same way as you would cook broccoli or cauliflower: plunge evenly sized sprigs or florets into fast boiling salted water, and cook until just tender but not soft. *Refresh* with a little cold water, and then toss in a little hot butter.

Note: Full instructions have been given in the recipe above for preparing the pheasant dish in advance and reheating it on the day of the dinner. This is designed to ease the workload on a four-course menu. If, though, you wished to prepare the pheasant on the day of the dinner, or use the recipe on its own for a simpler meal, simply proceed – after jointing the pheasants – to garnishing with the grapes, and serving.

Celeriac and potato purée

| 400 g/14 oz celeriac |
| 350-450 g/¾-1 lb potatoes |
| 25 g/1 oz butter |
| seasoning |
| a little hot milk |

Peel the celeriac and cut it into eight pieces. Peel the potatoes and, if large, cut them in half. Boil the celeriac and potatoes together in salted water until both are tender; then drain and let them steam dry thoroughly before mashing them with butter and seasoning.

The purée can be kept warm by covering with hot milk as in the recipe for mousseline of potatoes on page 52, and putting into the oven or to the back of the stove. Just before you wish to serve, beat the purée with the hot milk, until it is light and fluffy. Serve immediately.

Note: Celeriac is a variety of celery cultivated for its root alone, and not for the stems that are normally eaten. It has a delicate taste and texture, brought out perfectly in this purée. It can also be eaten in salads, shredded and then either lightly cooked and dressed or dressed raw.

Other vegetables that would accompany the pheasant well include the buttered courgettes described on page 116, the spinach en branche described on page 126, and the fondant potatoes described on page 20. Potatoes in various forms are traditional with game dishes, so if you have a favourite potato recipe, particularly one that can be prepared well in advance, use it as part of this menu.

The gamebird in Pheasant with grapes is coated in a demi-glace sauce enriched with wine and crushed grapes.

Vacherin Norma brings together meringue, coffee, cream and ginger: an unforgettable combination of dessert ingredients.

Vacherin Norma

4 egg whites

25 g/1 oz caster sugar

225 g/8 oz light brown sugar

For the filling and decoration:

5 ml/1 tsp instant coffee

15 ml/1 tbls freshly boiled water

4-5 pieces glacé ginger

300 ml/½ pint double cream

5 ml/1 tsp vanilla sugar

icing sugar

OVEN TEMPERATURE: 140°C/275°F/
Gas Mark 1

Line two baking sheets with non-stick silicone paper. Beat the egg whites until they form stiff peaks, then add the caster sugar and continue to beat for about 10 seconds. Gradually fold in the brown sugar using a large metal spoon. Divide the mixture into two and spread carefully in 2 circles 20 cm/8 in in diameter, or, if you wish to use a forcing bag for a more even result, fit a 1 cm/½ in plain tube and pipe the meringue into 2 circles using a spiral motion on the prepared baking sheets.

Bake the meringue in the pre-heated oven for about 60-70 minutes or until the two rounds are dry and lightly coloured. Cool on a wire rack and when almost cold, peel off the paper.

Mix the coffee with the freshly boiled water and allow to cool; shred the ginger finely. Whip the cream, sweeten it with the vanilla sugar and place about a quarter of it in a forcing bag fitted with a large star nozzle. Keep this bag cool in the refrigerator.

Flavour the remaining cream with the coffee and water mixture, mix in the prepared ginger and use this flavoured cream to sandwich the two circles of meringue together. Dust the top of the vacherin with icing sugar and decorate with rosettes of the plain cream already reserved in the forcing bag.

The vacherin should be filled at least 1 hour before it is to be served, and it should then be cut like any cake. It will cut and taste better still after having been frozen – though if you are going to freeze it, dust it with icing sugar only after defrosting.

Iced Camembert

1 × 250 g/9 oz Camembert

1 × 60 g/2½ oz Demi-Sel cheese *or* 60 g/2½ oz full fat soft cheese

a little hot milk

30-45 ml/2-3 tbls double cream, whipped

For the garnish:

celery leaves

To serve:

small savoury biscuits and bread

Cut away the rind from the Camembert and pound it in a pestle and mortar or purée it in a food processor until smooth. Cream the Demi-Sel or full fat soft cheese with the hot milk until it has the same consistency as the Camembert. Blend the two cheeses together and add the whipped cream. The mixture should be light, creamy and even in texture, with no discernible lumps.

Fill 6 medium dariole moulds with this mixture, cover the tops with waxed or greaseproof paper, and place in the freezing compartment of the refrigerator or the freezer for at least 12 hours. (If you don't have medium dariole moulds, either half fill castle pudding moulds or fully fill large ramekin dishes, covering closely as above.)

Transfer the cheese moulds from the freezing compartment of the refrigerator or freezer to the main body of the refrigerator to soften slightly for ½ to ¾ of an hour before serving. Unmould onto small savoury biscuits of roughly the same width as the cheese moulds, garnish with celery leaves and serve with extra savoury biscuits and bread.

Note: Cheese at the end of a meal is always welcome: its creamy, savoury flavour seems to round off a meal as nothing else can. At the end of a large meal, though, a groaning cheeseboard is not really necessary; a light cheese savoury like these iced Camembert moulds will be doubly appreciated in its stead. An alternative savoury would be the cheese gougères on page 34.

Iced Camembert moulds finish a splendid meal in savoury style. Celery leaves make an excellent garnish here, as with cheese in general.

A Countryside Arrangement

The sporting theme of this menu suggested the materials chosen for this countryside arrangement: larch (*larix*) branches, with cones for shape and lichen for colour; small bulrush-like reedmace *(typha)*, leaves of royal fern (*osmunda*), *magnolia*, *grevillea robusta*, teasels *(dipsacus fullonum)*, small cardoon *(cynara scolymus)*, wheat and grasses. The two large flower heads that dominate the group are dried *protea* flowers from Africa: car-

doon (or artichoke) heads would make good substitutes if protea was not available. Gaps at the base of the arrangement have been filled in with dried heather (*erica*).

Setting the arrangement

As this is not an all-round arrangement, and the materials involved are bulky, a heavy Japanese metal trough supported by small, sturdy feet has been chosen. This makes a very stable base which will easily take the weight of the branches.

To hold these in position, a half brick of wet oasis has been used, held firmly with a layer of wire netting secured to the rim of the trough. Try to work within the confines of an imaginary triangle to give your arrangement a satisfying shape. Arrange the larch branches first, and set the height with reedmace. Next get the dried magnolia leaves flowing out over the front of the vase. The dried protea flowers have very thick woody stems and these can

be sharpened to a point at their tip to go easily into the oasis. Complete the ground work with the heather before filling out the other gaps in the arrangement with the rest of the dried stems and flower heads.

Arrangement alternatives

A vase of this type would look attractive with holly (*ilex*) and ivy (*hedera*), various berries, branches of crab apple (*malus*), and a large group of cones at the centre. Branches in blossom could take the place of larch.

VEGETARIAN DINNER

Light, colourful, and nutritious,
the best vegetarian food is a treat for eye and palate alike.

IN RECENT years the growing interest in healthy eating, as well as an increased awareness of foreign cuisines (some of them wholly vegetarian) has given vegetarianism a new image. No longer is vegetarian food seen as heavy and unimaginative fare, nor do cooks regard preparing such meals as something of a chore. It is enjoyed nowadays as a light and pleasant alternative to traditional eating, and cooking contemporary vegetable-based meals often proves both pleasant and refreshing – just as eating them does!

The word 'vegetarian', of course, can mean a number of different things: some will eat fish, and most will eat dairy produce, although very strict vegetarians (called vegans) will eat no animal products whatsoever. Our menu is ideal for the majority, as dairy products are the only non-vegetable ingredients used.

Planning vegetarian menus

These menus are not difficult to devise and plan, as long as one or two fundamental points are borne in mind. Be on your guard for 'hidden' animal ingredients, like stock or gelatine, in otherwise suitable recipes. Use vegetable stock instead of meat stocks (see the recipe in the *Reference Section* page 139) or agar-agar instead of gelatine. Health food shops generally stock these and other similar ingredients. Remember, too, that some

MENU

for a party of six

Poached Eggs Mikado

Stuffed Marrow
Vegetable Platter

Apricot and Hazelnut Streusel
with Apricot Sauce

WINES

Red and White Bulgarian Wine

vegetarians will not eat ordinary cheese, as it is curdled with rennet (an animal product): vegetarian cheeses are more and more widely available nowadays, and make good substitutes in cooking.

The importance of variety

When planning vegetarian menus, remember to put variety first. It is often thought that meatless meals are in some way 'missing' a central component, and well-intentioned compensation with substantial portions of potato and pulses can leave guests feeling fuller than they would ordinarily have been after a meat-based main course. Colour, variety and a light touch in the kitchen are, if anything, even more important for vegetarian meals than they are for conventional meat meals: try not to serve more than one starchy item per course, and to serve two light vegetables rather than one 'solid' one.

Bulgarian wines – red and white – have been chosen to partner the meal. They offer extremely good value for money, and their generous, positive flavours will accompany all the dishes perfectly: your guests can choose whichever of the two they please.

MEAL PLANNER

● **The day before:** do all the shopping. Make the vegetable stock, streusel flan and apricot sauce.

● **The morning:** fully prepare the stuffed marrow, but do not bake.

● **Final preparation:** assemble the poached eggs and rice salad. Bake the marrow and prepare the vegetable platter.

Poached eggs mikado

150 ml/¼ pint vinaigrette
300 ml/½ pint mayonnaise
6 eggs
75 g/3 oz long-grain rice, dry weight, rinsed
1 large red pepper
3-4 sticks celery
seasoning

To garnish:
1 hard-boiled egg yolk, sieved
15 ml/1 tbls finely chopped parsley
5 ml/1 tsp finely chopped chives
5 ml/1 tsp dried oregano

Make the vinaigrette and mayonnaise according to the recipes in the *Reference Section* on pages 140-1. Poach the eggs for 3 minutes each, remove carefully, and slip them into a bowl of cold water until required. (When poaching eggs, put a little vinegar into the cooking water.) Cook the rice in plenty of boiling salted water until tender. Drain well, and turn out onto a large plate to dry. Slice the red pepper, remove the seeds, *blanch* and drain.

Slice the celery and mix with the rice and pepper. Moisten all with the vinaigrette. Adjust the seasoning. Put a generous spoonful of the rice salad onto individual plates. Drain and dry the eggs and place on the top. Coat the eggs with the mayonnaise and sprinkle with the sieved egg yolk and herbs.

The bright colours and contrasting textures of Poached eggs milkado make a sparkling start to the meal. (Recipe on page 43.)

Stuffed marrow

2 small marrows
15 g/½ oz butter *or* 15 ml/1 tbls olive oil

For the filling:
750 ml/1¼ pints vegetable stock
350 g/12 oz lentils
50 g/2 oz butter
1 medium onion, chopped
1 carrot, grated
seasoning
50 g/2 oz mature Cheddar cheese, grated
4 tomatoes, peeled, seeded, and sliced into strips
900 ml/1½ pints rich tomato sauce
25 g/1 oz butter, melted *or* 30 ml/ 2 tbls olive oil

To finish:
30 ml/2 tbls sunflower seeds
30 ml/2 tbls sesame seeds
50 g/2 oz grated Parmesan cheese

OVEN TEMPERATURE: 180°C/350°F/ Gas Mark 4

Peel and cut the marrows into 3 cm/1¼ in round slices. Remove the seeds from the centre of each slice, and *blanch* them. Butter or oil a large roasting tin, and place the marrow in this.

Prepare the filling. Begin by making the vegetable stock according to the recipe on page 139 of the *Reference Section*. Remove any grit from the lentils. Melt half the butter in a flameproof casserole, and soften the onion in this. Add the lentils and the remaining butter and stir over a brisk heat for 1-2 minutes. Pour on 600 ml/1 pint of the stock, add the carrot and seasoning, and bring to the boil. Cover the pan and cook in the preheated oven for about 15 minutes. If the lentils are still firm, add a little more of the reserved stock and cook for a further 5-8 minutes. Allow the lentil mixture to cool, then stir in the cheese and tomato.

Meanwhile, make the rich tomato sauce according to the recipe on page 141 of the *Reference Section*. Spoon the lentil mixture into the circles of marrow, heaping it well, and brush with the butter or oil. Cover with foil and bake for 30-40 minutes in the same preheated oven.

After the stuffed marrow pieces have been baked, coat them in a flameproof dish or dishes with about half the sauce. Sprinkle with the sunflower and sesame seeds and Parmesan cheese and brown under the grill. Serve with the rest of the sauce.

Vegetable platter

750 g/1½ lb carrots, sliced
½ tsp salt
5 ml/1 tsp sugar
90 g/3½ oz butter
5 ml/1 tsp chopped parsley
1 large cauliflower, broken into florets
750 g/1½ lb courgettes, sliced
seasoning
450 g/1 lb French beans, sliced
350 g/12 oz button mushrooms

Peel and slice the carrots into thin rounds. Cover with cold water, add the salt, sugar and 15 g/½ oz butter and cook gently until all the water has evaporated. Keep warm in a very low oven while you prepare the other vegetables. Stir in the parsley at the last minute, before arranging the platter.

Cook the cauliflower in a little salted water until just tender but not soft, then drain and *refresh*. Heat 25 g/1 oz of the butter in a small frying pan, add the courgettes, cover with a lid and cook over a high heat for 3 minutes. Hold down the lid of the pan firmly and toss the courgettes once or twice during cooking. Season. Replace lid to keep the courgettes warm.

Cook the French beans in plenty of boiling salted water for 3 minutes. Drain, return to saucepan and dot with 15 g/½ oz butter.

Wipe and trim the mushrooms and *sauté* for 1 minute in 25 g/ 1 oz butter. Season. Leave in the warm frying pan. Heat the remaining butter to noisette brown (see page 129) and toss the cauliflower in this to reheat.

Arrange the vegetables on a warmed ovenproof platter in concentric circles, as shown in our main photograph, starting on the outside with the courgettes, and finishing in the centre with the mushrooms. Warm through for 5 minutes, covered, in a medium oven if necessary to ensure that all the vegetables are hot.

The generous flavour of Stuffed marrow, served with an assortment of vegetables from our Vegetable platter, will satisfy every appetite.

Apricot and hazelnut streusel

For the dough:

100 g/4 oz self-raising flour	
pinch of salt	
75 g/3 oz butter	
50 g/2 oz soft light brown sugar	
50 g/2 oz ground hazelnuts, toasted	
1 egg	
5 ml/1 tsp lemon juice	

For the filling:

225 g/8 oz dried apricots	
strip of lemon rind	
30 ml/2 tbls granulated sugar	
250 ml/8 fl oz water	

For the streusel:

100 g/4 oz butter	
150 g/5 oz soft light brown sugar	
5 ml/1 tsp cinnamon	
40 g/1½ oz flour	
75 g/3 oz ground hazelnuts, toasted	

OVEN TEMPERATURE: 200°C/400°F/
  Gas Mark 6

Lightly butter a 23 cm/9 in spring-form pan or a 20 cm/8 in loose bottomed cake tin. Sift the flour with a pinch of salt, rub in the butter and add the sugar and nuts; bind together with the egg beaten with the lemon juice. Knead this dough lightly. Place the dough in the prepared tin and bank it up about 2.5 cm/1 inch around the sides. Chill while preparing other ingredients.

Place the apricots in a pan with the rind, sugar and water. Cover and simmer for 40 minutes, or until most of the liquid has been absorbed. Cool. Melt the butter for the streusel mixture, then stir in the rest of the ingredients.

Spoon the apricots onto the dough and sprinkle the streusel over the top. Bake in the pre-heated oven for 35-40 minutes. After 20 minutes, turn the oven down to 190°C/375°F/Gas Mark 5. Let the flan cool for 5-10 minutes in the tin before easing it out. Serve with an apricot sauce: see the recipe in the *Reference Section* on page 143.

Easter Lilies in Clear Glass

These spectacular and highly scented Easter lilies (*lilium longiflorum*) have been chosen for our vegetarian meal, as their simple, plain beauty seems to suit the style of the dinner. Remember that all highly scented flowers should be used cautiously at table, as their scent can distract attention from the food: this is why we have used a smaller number of blooms on the main table, photographed on page 42.

Clear glass vases

A clear glass vase has been used for the lilies: these are attractive to look at, but difficult to use as 'mechanics' tend to show. Here the stems have been held in place with a small ball of wire netting: fix one or two ends over the vase rim to hold it in place.

Lilies almost seem to arrange themselves. The blooms naturally fall in certain directions: help the stems into place for a casual, fluid look. The flower heads themselves should point out in different directions.

45

IMPROMPTU DINNER

The art of having food ready for hungry guests at a moment's notice is much admired —
and less difficult to acquire than it would at first appear.

SPEED IS NATURALLY of the essence in this menu, so shopping and preparation times are of crucial importance. You will find that you already have many of the ingredients to hand in your store cupboard or refrigerator, and none of the others are difficult to find (or heavy to carry home). The only piece of preparation that could be done in advance is the making of the stock (see **Meal Planner**): if you have some ready-frozen or refrigerated this would obviously be a great help.

A menu like this is suitable for many different occasions: the unexpected arrival of old friends, an off-the-cuff celebration, a welcome break in a busy schedule. It has been designed, therefore, to meet with approval at any time of the year: summer seasonal items like new potatoes and mange-tout peas could be substituted by mousseline of potatoes (see recipe in **Fireside Supper**, page 52) and Brussels sprouts (see recipe in **Autumn Dinner**, page 20) during the chilly autumn and winter months.

The third course solution
Appetites may well vary, depending on the occasion and the season: fruits and cheese are a good choice for a third course when this

MENU

for a party of eight

Anchovy Eggs
with bread and butter

—

Fillet Steaks Cordon Bleu
with mange-tout peas
and new potatoes

—

Cheese and Fruit

WINES

Dry Sherry or Madeira
Claret (red Bordeaux)

is the case. Try to serve a variety of differently textured and flavoured cheeses: an English hard cheese, like Double Gloucester or Leicester; a blue cheese, perhaps Stilton or Roquefort; a soft cheese, for example Brie or Camembert, and perhaps a 'speciality'

cheese, like cream cheese prepared with herbs and garlic, or rolled in peppercorns. Serve with a choice of different breads and various cheese biscuits.

Aim for as wide a variety of fruits as you can manage: home-grown seasonal fruits, like apples, pears and plums, should always be included as and when available, but so too should one or two more exotic fruits, like the vitamin-rich kiwi fruit or the beautifully perfumed passionfruit.

Simple wines
The wine suggestions for this menu have deliberately been kept as simple as possible. A good dry fino sherry or sercial Madeira, both of them excellent apéritifs, would serve as first class accompaniments to the eggs: simply top up the glasses as you come to table. The steak would be best partnered by a cabernet sauvignon wine (like claret). If it is only two or three years old, let the wine 'breathe' by pouring it into a decanter about an hour before you wish to drink it: this will help bring out its flavours and aromas. Young wines will have no sediment, so you need not be excessively cautious with it as you decant. Red Bordeaux will make an excellent partner for cheeses, too.

MEAL PLANNER

● **Several days before (if possible):** prepare jellied stock and plan shopping. Both the cheese and the steak could be bought in advance, but the vegetables and fruit are best purchased as fresh as possible.

● **One and a half hours before:** prepare the eggs and their stuffing individually and cover

the fillings closely with cling film. Store the whites in cold water.

● **One hour before:** prepare the vegetables ready for cooking and make the mayonnaise. Remove cheeses from the refrigerator. Fill the eggs, and coat with the mayonnaise.

● **Final preparation:** begin cooking the new potatoes. Cook the steaks and make the

sauce in advance if you wish: keep warm together while you serve the first course. (Remember, though, that you will have to go back to the kitchen to finish the second course vegetables.) Coat the eggs with mayonnaise and serve. Cook the steaks and make the sauce now, if you have not already done so. Cook the mange-tout peas or beans immediately before serving the steaks; butter the potatoes then, too.

Anchovy eggs

8 eggs

100 g/4 oz butter, softened

10-20 ml/2-4 tsp anchovy
    essence or paste

freshly ground black pepper

400 ml/14 fl oz mayonnaise

15 ml/1 tbls boiling water

To finish:

lettuce leaves

1 tbls chopped parsley

1 tsp each chopped lemon thyme
    and snipped chives

To serve:

thin segments of lemon

brown bread and butter

Hard boil the eggs, cool quickly under cold running water, shell, and then cut carefully in two lengthways. Work the egg yolks and softened butter together with the anchovy essence or paste and season with freshly ground black pepper.

Next prepare the mayonnaise according to one of the recipes in the *Reference Section* on page 140. If you wish to use a good quality commercial mayonnaise, heighten the flavour by the addition of a little soured cream or natural yoghurt. Add the 15 ml/ 1 tbls boiling water carefully to the mayonnaise to thin it slightly and whiten its colour.

Fill the hard-boiled egg whites with the anchovy mixture, shaping each half to resemble a whole egg. Serve the eggs on crisp lettuce leaves, lightly dressed if you wish. Add the herbs to the mayonnaise and spoon it over the eggs, so that the mayonnaise covers the anchovy mixture to resemble an egg white. Serve with thin segments of lemon and brown bread and butter.

Note: Eggs and egg dishes are well-known for being difficult to match with wine. Sherry and Madeira are excellent solutions, particularly with a starter, as they may also be served as apéritifs.

The hint of anchovy in the stuffing for these Anchovy eggs points up their delicate flavour. Garnish very simply for the best results.

Fillet steak Cordon Blea receives the finest treatment: a simple sauce and light, fresh vegetables cannot be bettered as a complement to fine meat.

Fillet steaks Cordon Bleu

45 ml/3 tbls jellied stock

175 g/6 oz button mushrooms

50 g/2 oz butter

8 fillet steaks cut 1-1.5 cm/½-¾
    inch thick

seasoning

45 ml/3 tbls brandy

120 ml/8 tbls double cream

Prepare the jellied stock according to the recipe in the *Reference Section* on page 138, in advance if possible.

Wipe and trim the mushrooms. Heat a heavy frying pan, drop in a 'nut' (about 15 g/½ oz) of the butter and put in the steaks, pressing them down with a palette knife. *Dry fry* for 3 minutes on each side for a rare steak (4 minutes for medium rare, and 5 minutes on each side for well-done), then lift onto a serving dish and keep warm while you finish the sauce.

Drop the remaining butter into the pan, add the mushrooms, season and sauté briskly for 1 minute; pour on the brandy and let it bubble and *reduce* away. *Deglaze* the pan with gravy or stock, skimming if necessary, and then add the cream. Allow to simmer for a few seconds, adjust the seasoning, and then spoon sauce and mushrooms over the steak. Serve with small new potatoes and mange-tout peas or whole green beans.

The potatoes or beans should simply be boiled and buttered before serving, and the potatoes turned in a little chopped mint or parsley. Mange-tout peas are best steamed: don't give them longer than 3 minutes, in order to preserve their vivid green colour and sweet, crisp texture.

Note: If you prefer the taste of rump steak, that would be equally good here; and if you don't have time to prepare jellied stock, use the same quantity of a good tinned consommé.

Classic Mixed Group

Mixed greens and whites are always elegant in arrangements, especially with other light colours. Green *cobaea*, Iceberg roses (*rosa*) and baby *zinnia* together with small side shoots of green *nicotiana* go to make the flowers for this arrangement. The foliage is a mixture of many types and includes *adiantum* (maidenhair fern), seed heads of hornbeam (*carpinus betulus*), baby *iris*, *pelargonium* in 3 forms, and 3 small *hosta* leaves.

As this small vase is shallow, and holds little water, a piece of oasis on its own has been used to hold these short stems. There is thus little length of stem to support, and as the vase sits very firmly on its base, it should not topple over.

White roses
Iceberg, with its lovely clear white petals, is one of the most striking of all white roses. As all the individual flowers are short-stemmed, there is a tendency for them to block together. Judicial thinning is allowable if all else fails, but it's preferable to use flowers as they grow and keep them looking natural if possible. See the **Champagne Breakfast**, page 29, for some other suggestions for white roses.

Cobaea are great favourites, especially in their green form, and given a good summer, they will make wonderful climbing plants. Zinnia also need plenty of sunshine so this is ideally a group for the latter part of the summer.

This vase, though, could be used throughout the year: it looks lovely with such flowers as sweet pea (*lathyrus odoratus*), *freesia* or border carnation (*dianthus*). It may be arranged as seen here as an all-round decoration, but being raised off the table, it can also be used face-on for a small buffet table.

FIRESIDE SUPPER

Most guests will happily admit that there are times when traditional country food
provides an unmatchable sense of comfort and well being.

INFORMAL ENTERTAINING IS more than just a question of attitude on the part of you and your guests: there are very definitely certain dishes, as well as certain ways of presenting food and flowers, that are by their nature more informal than others. Stews and soups, for example, are very popular on such occasions, and they immediately establish an atmosphere of country comfort and calm. If you can eat from a wooden table – with or without a cloth – this will reinforce the atmosphere, and this is the time, too, for your oldest and best-loved serving dishes to come into play. Brown is a natural colour theme for the evening, in as many different shades as you wish.

Using dried flowers
In front of the Welsh dresser in the photograph is a log basket full of dried seed heads, grasses and flowers. These are perfect

MENU

for a party of six

*Cream of Jerusalem
Artichoke Soup*

Ragoût of Beef Flamande

Mousseline of Potatoes

Cabbage and Celery

Apples in Caramel

WINE

Red French Vin de Pays

autumn and winter decorations, and they blend in well with a wide number of colour schemes and interiors, flattering modern rooms just as they do country kitchens. Remember to keep the basket well away from any sort of open fire from which sparks might fly.

Country wines
One of the numerous and often excellent French 'Vin de Pays' wines (*Vin de Pays* means, quite literally, country wine) would be an ideal choice for this meal, and suitable for drinking throughout. Watch out for 'Vin de Pays' on the label: this is a wine category recently introduced for up-and-coming rural French wine areas, and offers many bargains at the moment. If you like Italian wine, too, this would be a good time for Chianti: do as the Italians do, if you wish, and serve the wine in small glass tumblers!

MEAL PLANNER

● **Two days before:** do all of the shopping.

● **The day before:** the beef ragoût, the apples in caramel and the soup may all be fully prepared today. Omit the cream addition.

● **The morning:** shred the cabbage and celery, and toast the hazelnuts. Prepare the other dishes if you have not yet done so.

● **Final preparation:** prepare the potatoes, and the cabbage and celery last of all.

Cream of Jerusalem artichoke soup

1 kg/2 lb Jerusalem artichokes
15 ml/1 tbls lemon juice
2 medium onions, finely sliced
50 g/2 oz butter
900 ml/1½ pints water
seasoning
a pinch of sugar
900 ml/1½ pints boiling milk
40 g/1½ oz cornflour
90 ml/6 tbls cold milk
150 ml/¼ pint whipping cream

For the garnish:

12 hazelnuts, grilled and baked to remove their skins
rock salt

Wash and peel the artichokes carefully, and keep them in a bowl of water to which 15 ml/1 tbls of lemon juice has been added. Cook the onions in half the butter for 5-6 minutes until soft. Meanwhile, rinse, dry and slice the artichokes and add to the pan with the rest of the butter. Cover and cook over a low heat for 10 minutes.

Pour in the water, add the seasoning and sugar and simmer for 15-20 minutes. Pass through a fine mouli-sieve or blend. Return the purée to the pan and whisk in the milk. Mix the cornflour with the cold milk, pour into the soup and bring to the boil, whisking all the time. Simmer for 3-4 minutes. Adjust the seasoning, remove the pan from the heat and cover closely.

Grind the toasted hazelnuts and lightly season with rock salt. Reheat the soup and pour into a warmed tureen, then swirl in the cream. (Alternatively, swirl cream into each individual soup bowl as you serve.) Finally, sprinkle on the salted ground hazelnuts.

Ragoût of beef flamande

1.5 kg/3 lb chuck steak	
40 g/1½ oz dripping	
4-6 medium onions, finely sliced	
30 ml/2 tbls flour	
1 clove garlic, crushed	
450 ml/¾ pint hot water	
600 ml/1 pint brown ale	
bouquet garni	
½ tsp salt	
½ tsp pepper	
10 ml/2 tsp wine vinegar	
a pinch of ground nutmeg	
5 ml/1 tsp sugar	

OVEN TEMPERATURE: 160°C/325°F/ Gas Mark 3

Cut the meat into large squares. Heat half the dripping in a flame-proof stew pan or casserole. Put in enough meat to cover the bottom of the pan and brown quickly. Remove from the pan. Drop in the remainder of the dripping and brown the rest of the meat as before. Remove the meat. Add the onions and allow them to brown slowly.

If necessary, pour off a little of the fat. Dust the onions with the flour, add the garlic, and replace the meat in the casserole. Add the water to the ale, pour onto the beef, add the bouquet garni and season with the salt, pepper and vinegar. Cover closely and cook gently in the preheated oven for about 1½-2 hours. When the beef is tender, adjust the seasoning, adding the nutmeg and 5 ml/1 tsp sugar.

Mousseline of potatoes

1.25 kg/2½ lb potatoes, preferably King Edward	
5 ml/1 tsp salt	
25 g/1 oz butter	
200 ml/7 fl oz hot milk	

Cover the potatoes with cold water, add 5 ml/1 tsp salt and boil gently until tender. Tip off

The brown ale used in this Ragoût of beef flamande adds a warm, homely element to the flavour: winter vegetables are the perfect accompaniment.

the water and replace the saucepan over a low heat with the lid half-on to evaporate any remaining water.

Add the butter and crush with a potato masher until smooth; then press the bulk of potatoes down into the saucepan. Pour the hot milk on top of the potatoes, put a lid on the pan and place it at the back of the stove or in a low oven, taking care not to put the handle over the flame if you have a gas oven. They will keep perfectly for up to ½ hour. Just before you serve the ragoût, take the pan from the oven or stove and beat the potatoes vigorously, either with a spoon or a hand electric beater. Only when they look as white and light as a cloud should they be turned into a serving dish.

Cabbage and celery

1.25-1.5 kg/2½-3 lb white cabbage	
3 sticks celery	
30 ml/2 tbls finely chopped parsley	
freshly ground black pepper	

Trim the cabbage, cut it into quarters and trim away most of the core; shred very finely.

Remove the strings from the celery and cut the sticks horizontally into thin slices.

Turn the cabbage and celery into a pan of fast boiling water and cook for 2-3 minutes. Drain well, return to the pan, and dry the vegetables off over a low heat. Add the finely chopped parsley and 2-3 twists of black pepper from the mill, mix well, and turn into a vegetable dish.

Apples in caramel

300 ml/½ pint water	
75 g/3 oz sugar	
6 Cox's Orange Pippin or Granny Smith apples	
4 oranges	

For the caramel:

150 g/5 oz sugar	
150 ml/¼ pint cold water	

Prepare a syrup with the water and the sugar. Peel, core and quarter the apples and poach carefully in the syrup until tender but not broken. Draw the pan aside and leave covered until cold. Pare a little rind from 1 orange and cut it into needle-like shreds. Cook them for 1 minute in boiling water, then drain and dry. Set aside for the garnish.

Peel and segment the oranges, then cut the pith and first membrane from the segments to expose the flesh. Lift the apples from the pan and put them into a glass bowl; place the oranges on top.

Strain the apple syrup if necessary and heat it in a rinsed pan. Begin making the caramel: put the sugar and cold water in a pan and dissolve over a very gentle heat. Bring to the boil and cook steadily to a rich brown caramel. Hold the pan over a bowl of lukewarm water so that the base just touches the water. Cover the hand holding the saucepan with a cloth and pour in the warm apple syrup. Tip the caramel-syrup mixture into a jug and when cool pour over the fruit. Scatter over the prepared orange zests and serve well chilled.

Note: If you have a sugar thermometer, the caramel will begin to form at 154°C/310°F. Watch very carefully once this stage is reached as the caramel can burn easily and irreversibly.

Autumn Garden Arrangement

It is always fun to ring the changes with your decorations and in this country fireside setting a few more unusual things have been chosen to go in a shallow metal trough over the fireplace. If your shelf is wide and the fire set well back, the plant material should not suffer from heat coming up from the fireplace: have a space for air to move between the cut material and chimney breast.

The decorative purple cabbage (*brassica*) tends to dominate the setting but in the autumn and winter months these plants are so spectacular that it is a shame not to use them. They are also available in green and white, and these look excellent with yellow/white or orange colours. All the members of the cabbage family tend to make water smell, so to avoid this, one should wrap the cut stem in damp cotton wool with a few drops of bleach or disinfectant added. It is then enclosed in a small plastic bag held tightly in place with a rubber band, and the whole stem is placed in the vase.

Finding the background
Sloes (*prunus spinosa*) are also most decorative and last a long time when cut: they will lose their leaves naturally after cutting and placing in a deep bucket of water, but the fruit looks so much more dramatic on the bare branches. The other berries are from privet (*ligustrum*) and buckthorn (*hippophae*). One unusual stem of interest in the centre of the group is the seed head of the ink plant (*phytolacca*). Purple grapes (*vitis*) and aubergine (*solanum melongena*) both add extra colour and shape. The trumpet-shaped flowers are *cobaea scandens*: a most useful half-hardy climbing plant. These are available in green or

purple varieties. The foliage used is pieces of *tradescantia zebrina* together with a little purple vine (*vitis*), which in late autumn is drying up quickly but still remains interesting for its shape and the felty backs of its leaves.

Building the arrangement
The arrangement was built up in stages. First, a heavy pin holder was placed in the centre of the trough, and the container was then filled with 5 cm/2 in wire netting. The main stem of sloes, firmly secured on the pin holder, set the height, and in front of this the short stem of the cabbage (slightly trimmed to size) was placed in position. From this area all the stems must radiate. Next, the vine leaves are positioned on the left hand side, and the aubergine

and grapes around the centre. Aubergines may be wired or set up on cocktail sticks.

To wire aubergines, take two pieces of 30 cm/12 in 22 gauge (71 mm) florist's stub wire, and push these through the stem end of the fruit, at about the point where the small leaves wrap around the fruit. When the wire protrudes about 10 cm/4 in to the other side of the fruit, bend it back along the aubergine's short stem. Twine the two ends of the wire together to make a longer, false stem. This wire stem can be used as an anchor to hold the aubergine into the arrangement.

To wire grapes, thread a stub wire through the bunch about 5 cm/2 in down. Bend this wire back along the main stem of the grape bunch; then twine the

wire along the bunch stem and back to make a false stem. Twist the wire stem into a hook shape to hold the bunch safely onto the netting.

Now place more of the berry stems in position to get a pleasing outline, and tuck in low down the foliage. A few pewter-coloured *hydrangea* heads can now be added and the feathery *atriplex* seed heads. Lastly, thread in the stems of cobaea.

A winter alternative
During the winter months one could make an arrangement with fresh mixed foliage on its own, or with dried foliage and flowers such as preserved beech (*fagus*), hornbeam (*carpinum*), statice (*limonium*), *helichrysum*, and seed heads of teasel (*dipsacus fullonum*) and poppies (*papaver rhoeas*).

BUFFET LUNCH

For special occasions of all sorts, a buffet lunch is as enjoyable as it is practical:

hosts and guests alike can enjoy a range of dishes at a leisurely pace.

I F YOU HAVE large numbers of guests to feed – anything upwards of eight – not only is a buffet the most manageable way of accommodating everyone, but it also means there's a chance that you'll enjoy the meal yourself, rather than spending the entire occasion rushing from kitchen to table and back.

Preparation is the key: using our **Meal Planner** you will be able to get ahead with the cooking, which in turn will leave you plenty of time for all the other little jobs that need to be done before your guests arrive.

Arranging space

Try to arrange the buffet space as simply as possible: in our photograph we have shown all the food on one sideboard for visual convenience, but spreading the food over two surfaces can often be more sensible, as you will avoid queues and bottlenecks.

Conversation groups

If possible, arrange some chairs around small side-tables: try to find enough for everyone to be able to sit down and eat in their own natural conversation groups. At the same time, it's important to keep a free flow of

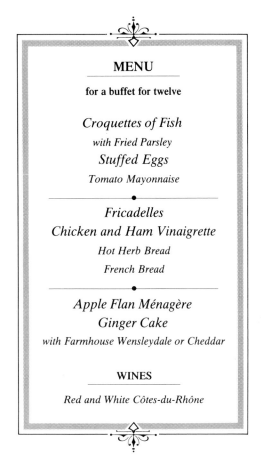

MENU

for a buffet for twelve

Croquettes of Fish
with Fried Parsley
Stuffed Eggs
Tomato Mayonnaise

•

Fricadelles
Chicken and Ham Vinaigrette
Hot Herb Bread
French Bread

•

Apple Flan Ménagère
Ginger Cake
with Farmhouse Wensleydale or Cheddar

WINES

Red and White Côtes-du-Rhône

traffic around the room, so that finished plates can be cleared away and coffee or other drinks brought in.

Children need a special thought: if there are to be more than just two or three present, they will certainly appreciate a special table of their own, and possibly somewhere to play together after the meal.

A choice of wines

Offer, if you can, a choice of red and white wine; choosing these from the same region will lend the meal coherence. A good example would be the red and white Rhône wines suggested: both are dry and full-flavoured, and will go well with a wide range of foods. Other examples would include red and white Spanish Rioja, or red wines from Australia served with whites from New Zealand.

A summer alternative

When the weather is good and you have a garden available, an open-air buffet is a marvellous idea, enjoyed by both adults and children alike. Serve the food indoors, where it can be kept cool and away from insects, and arrange your seating (no one will mind improvisation) in the garden.

MEAL PLANNER

● **Three days before:** make the ginger cake. Shop for all the non-fresh ingredients.

● **Two days before:** shop again for all fresh ingredients except fish, prawns and bread. Make the chicken stock. Make the vinaigrette. Make and finish the fricadelles: cover closely and refrigerate. Make the mayonnaise, but do not prepare the tomato mixture yet. Make the French flan pastry dough and chill in the

refrigerator. Make the glaze for the apple flan. Prepare the gammon: cover closely, and store whole.

● **The day before:** shop for the fish, prawns and bread. Hard boil the eggs and cool them under cold running water. Make the fish croquettes, and egg and crumb them: store in the refrigerator. Make the fillings for the stuffed eggs: store them, tightly covered, in the refrigerator. Cover the whites with cold water and store in a cool place. Prepare the

tomato mixture but do not add to the mayonnaise yet; keep covered overnight. Prepare the herb bread and wrap closely. Cut the gammon and cover closely.

● **Final preparation:** prepare the chicken, and make the chicken and ham vinaigrette. Prepare the apples, then roll out the dough and bake the flan; glaze. Finish the eggs and tomato mayonnaise. Reheat the fricadelles, and bake the hot herb bread. Fry the croquettes and parsley and drain well.

Croquettes of fish

450 g/1 lb fresh haddock *or* whiting fillets

15 ml/1 tbls water

1 tsp gelatine

For the sauce:

300 ml/½ pint milk

1 slice onion

½ bayleaf

a small piece of mace

50 g/2 oz butter

50 g/2 oz flour

1 egg, beaten

For coating and frying:

45 ml/3 tbls seasoned flour

1 egg

15 ml/1 tbls salad oil

dried white breadcrumbs

vegetable oil for deep frying

OVEN TEMPERATURE: 180°C/350°F/ Gas Mark 4

Place the fish in a buttered dish, scatter the 15 ml/1 tbls of water over it, and cook in the preheated oven for 8 minutes; drain, reserving the water and flake the fish. Soak the gelatine in the reserved water. Heat the milk with the flavourings (onion, bayleaf and mace), cover, remove from the heat and leave to infuse for 10 minutes, then strain. Melt the butter, add the flour away from the heat and blend in the flavoured milk. Stir over a gentle heat until boiling and then cook for 1 minute; remove the pan from the heat and stir in the soaked gelatine. Beat the fish into the sauce bit by bit and work to a smooth consistency.

Adjust the seasoning and add the beaten egg. Spread this mixture 2.5 cm/1 inch deep in a gratin dish or shallow cake tin, cover with foil or cling film and leave until quite cold or chill.

To coat the croquettes, divide the mixture into twelve equal portions and, using two knives, roll and shape them on a board floured with the 45 ml/3 tbls of flour. Beat the egg with the salad oil and pour onto a plate. Have the breadcrumbs ready on a sheet of greaseproof paper. Coat each croquette with the egg and then the crumbs; avoid using your fingers if you can.

To fry them, heat the vegetable oil for deep frying to a temperature of 190°C/375°F, taking care not to overfill your fryer: it should be no more than one-third full. (If your deep fryer is not thermostatically controlled and you have no thermometer, test the temperature by dropping a cube of bread into the fat. The correct temperature has been reached when the bread cube browns in 40 seconds.) Fry the croquettes in several batches (not more than 4 croquettes at a time) in a frying basket until golden brown, then put the whole basket onto a plate to drain initially. After 30 seconds, drain the croquettes individually on paper towels for a minute or two. Serve garnished with the fried parsley.

Fried parsley

After frying the croquettes turn the heat out under the deep fat fryer and draw the pan away from all heat sources. Place some small sprigs of parsley, tied in bunches, into the frying basket and ease them gently into the fat. Remove it as soon as the spluttering stops and while the parsley is still bright green; drain and serve with the croquettes.

Stuffed eggs

175 ml/6 fl oz béchamel sauce

100 g/4 oz large flat-topped mushrooms

65 g/2½ oz butter

1 shallot, finely chopped

100 g/4 oz prawns, shelled

6 hard-boiled eggs

100 g/4 oz curd cheese

1 tsp paprika

seasoning

Prawn- and mushroom-flavoured Stuffed eggs on the left, and Croquettes of fish on the right, are shown garnished and served with tomato mayonnaise.

For the garnish:

3 black olives

½ bunch watercress

Make the béchamel sauce according to the recipe in the *Reference Section*, page 140. Leave it to cool. Trim and wash the mushrooms, chop them finely, and then cook them briskly with 15 g/½ oz of the butter until all the moisture has evaporated. Add the shallot, and cook for a further minute; then tip onto a plate to cool. Set aside 6 prawns for a garnish and chop the remainder.

Cut the eggs in two, scoop out the yolks and rub them through a fine sieve. Cream the remaining butter with the egg yolks, curd cheese and béchamel sauce. Divide this mixture into two. Add the chopped prawns to one portion and season with paprika. Add the mushroom duxelles mixture to the second portion; check and adjust the seasoning if necessary. Using a forcing bag and small plain pipe, fill half the eggs with the prawn mixture and half with the mushroom mixture.

Place the eggs on a large round platter. Garnish the mushroom eggs with the halved olives, and the prawn and paprika eggs with the reserved prawns. Fill the centre of the plate with rich green watercress.

Tomato mayonnaise

750 ml/1¼ pints mayonnaise

6 ripe tomatoes, scalded, peeled and quartered

15 ml/1 tbls salad oil, as used in mayonnaise above

1 shallot, finely chopped

1 tsp paprika

10 ml/2 tsp tomato purée

15 ml/1 tbls boiling water

seasoning

sugar

Prepare the mayonnaise according to the recipe in the *Reference Section*, page 140: use olive oil and red wine vinegar or lemon juice for a Mediterranean flavour.

Scoop the seeds from the tomatoes into a nylon strainer and rub them well to extract their juice. Heat the tablespoonful of oil in a small pan, add the shallot and cook gently until soft, then add the paprika, tomato purée and juice from the tomato seeds. Cook together for 2-3 minutes. Strain and cool. Cut each quarter of tomato into 2 or 3 strips and set aside.

Stir 1 tablespoon of boiling water into the mayonnaise, check the seasoning, add a pinch of sugar if necessary, and add the tomato and paprika mixture. The shredded tomatoes are best added about half an hour before you begin to set up the buffet, so that the thick texture of the mayonnaise is not lost.

Fricadelles

600 ml/1 pint rich tomato sauce, heated

750 g/1½ lb beef shoulder steak, minced

225 g/½ lb minced lean pork

50 g/2 oz fresh pork fat, minced

2 medium onions, finely chopped

50 g/2 oz butter

75 g/3 oz fine dry breadcrumbs

1 tsp salt

freshly ground black pepper

250 ml/8fl oz milk *or* stock

1 beaten egg

seasoned flour

30 ml/2 tbls dripping

60 ml/4 tbls soured cream, *mixed with* 45 ml/3 tbls natural yoghurt

450 g/1 lb even-sized carrots, cut into thin rounds

1 tsp sugar

pinch of salt

a nut of butter

more soured cream and yoghurt (optional)

To serve:

French bread

OVEN TEMPERATURE: 160-180°C/ 325-350°F/Gas Mark 3-4

One or two days beforehand, prepare the rich tomato sauce

Fricadelles and Chicken and ham vinaigrette provide a perfect main course contrast. Plain French bread and hot herb bread make good accompaniments.

according to the recipe in the *Reference Section* on page 141.

Place the meats and pork fat in a mixing bowl. Cook the onions in the butter until soft and yellow, allow to cool a little and then work into the meat mixture with a wooden spoon. Add the other ingredients down to and including the beaten egg and beat well. Shape into 4 cm/1½ inch balls, roll in the seasoned flour and fry briskly in a small quantity of hot dripping until golden brown.

Lift the meatballs into a shallow ovenproof dish and spoon over the hot tomato sauce. Put into the preheated oven and bake

for 25-30 minutes. Halfway through the cooking time, turn the meatballs and spoon over the soured cream and yoghurt mixture. Return to the oven and complete the cooking.

Meanwhile cook the carrots with the seasoning, butter and just enough water to cover. Allow the water to evaporate, and the butter and sugar to form a glaze. Add the carrots to the meatballs. (The dish can be prepared ahead to this point, and refrigerated until needed.) Garnish with more soured cream and yoghurt if you wish. Serve very hot with hot French bread.

Chicken and ham vinaigrette

175 ml/6 fl oz good stock made from chicken giblets

1.5 kg/3½ lb roasting chicken, dressed weight

50 g/2 oz butter

sprig of tarragon *or* oregano

seasoning

1 kg/2 lb joint unsmoked gammon

1 onion

bouquet garni

½ *or* 1 small Galia *or* Honeydew melon, seeded

1 cucumber

225 g/½ lb large white grapes

juice of ½ lemon

For the vinaigrette:

50 ml/2 fl oz wine vinegar

200 ml/8 fl oz good olive oil

seasoning

15 ml/1 tbls chopped parsley

15 ml/1 tbls chopped tarragon *or* oregano

OVEN TEMPERATURE: 200°C/400°F/ Gas Mark 6

Make the chicken stock according to the recipe in the *Reference Section* on page 138; do this several days before you need it, if your schedule allows, or use previously made frozen stock.

Rub the chicken with the butter, putting a good 15 g/½ oz inside the bird with the herb and some seasoning, and set in a roasting tin with 150 ml/¼ pint of the stock. Cover with buttered paper and roast in the preheated oven for about 1 hour. After 15 minutes, baste the chicken and turn on its side. After 20 minutes, turn onto its other side, baste and cook for another 20 minutes, then baste again and turn breast up for the rest of the roasting period. If the stock has *reduced* completely at this point, add a spoonful more to prevent the butter burning. Baste again and return to the oven to finish the cooking. The chicken should be well-browned on all sides. Remove from the oven and cool.

Blanch the gammon, drain and

cover with fresh cold water. Add the onion and bouquet garni and bring very slowly to boiling point; simmer gently for 1 hour.

Prepare the fruit and cucumber: peel and cut the melon into cubes; peel the cucumber, cut in four lengthways and scoop out the seeds, then cut it into small sticks. Peel and pip the grapes and cover with the juice of a ½ lemon. Prepare the vinaigrette dressing, using the ingredients given, according to the method in the *Reference Section*, page 141, adding the herbs last of all.

When the chicken is tepid, remove the meat from the breast, wings, and legs. Cut the meat into bite-size pieces and moisten with a little dressing. (The chicken will not absorb the dressing so well once it has lost its warmth.) Cut an equal quantity of gammon into similar sized pieces; combine with the cucumber and fruit. Layer the chicken, ham and fruit in a large bowl, spooning vinaigrette carefully between each of the layers.

Apple flan ménagère is one of the great French desserts: rich pastry, thinly sliced apples and a pretty glaze are the secrets of its success.

Hot herb bread

100 g/4 oz butter

15 ml/1 tbls mixed dried herbs

juice of ¼ lemon

freshly ground black pepper

a little crushed garlic (optional)

1 French stick

OVEN TEMPERATURE: 220°C/425°F/ Gas Mark 7

Cream the butter together with the herbs, lemon juice, seasoning, and, if you wish, some garlic.

Cut the French stick into evenly slanting slices about 1.5 cm/ ½ in thick; spread each slice with the butter mixture and then reshape, spreading any remaining butter over the top and sides. Wrap closely in foil.

Bake for 10 minutes in the preheated oven at the temperature given. Then reduce the oven setting to 200°C/400°F/Gas Mark 6, and open the foil so that the bread browns and crisps. This will take a further 5-8 minutes. Serve immediately.

Apple flan ménagère

For the French flan pastry:

350 g/12 oz plain flour

225 g/8 oz butter *or* margarine, softened

100 g/4 oz caster sugar

1 whole egg

3 egg yolks

For the filling:

1.5 kg/3 lb Granny Smith apples

To finish:

caster sugar

450 g/1 lb apricot jam

OVEN TEMPERATURE: 190°C/375°F/ Gas Mark 5

Begin by making the pastry dough: sift the flour with a pinch of salt onto the table or marble slab, make a small well in the centre, and place all the other ingredients in this well. Using the fingertips of one hand, work the butter, sugar, whole egg and yolks together until mixed, then quickly draw in the flour and knead lightly until smooth. Wrap in a polythene bag or greaseproof paper and chill for at least 1 hour before using. Meanwhile peel, quarter and slice the apples thinly.

Roll out the dough, and use to line a 30 cm/12 in flan ring (see *Reference Section*, page 142). Crimp the edges and arrange the apples in concentric circles on the dough. Dust with caster sugar and bake in the preheated oven for about 40-45 minutes or until the apple slices begin to brown.

Leave the flan in the flan ring and on a base for about 10 minutes before removing the flan ring. Brush with the apricot glaze, made by sieving, heating and *reducing* the apricot jam until it coats a test apple slice, and slide onto a rack to cool.

Note: If you have excess glaze left over, store it in a jar, and thin it out with a little lemon juice before reuse.

Ginger cake

Note: This soft, luscious ginger cake should always be made some days in advance to allow it to mature. Serve it with a slice of Wensleydale or Cheddar cheese, as illustrated below.

100 g/4 oz butter

100 g/4 oz soft brown sugar

225 g/8 oz plain flour

1 tsp ground ginger

100 g/4 oz sultanas

275 g/10 oz black treacle

2 eggs

30-45 ml/2-3 tbls milk

½ tsp bicarbonate of soda

OVEN TEMPERATURE: 160°C/325°F/ Gas Mark 3

Line a 19-20 cm/7½-8 in round cake tin with non-stick silicone paper. Soften the butter, add the sugar and beat thoroughly until creamy. Sift all of the flour with the ground ginger, then add half of it to the sultanas, mix well, and set aside. Stir the treacle into the butter and sugar mixture, then beat in the eggs one at a time, adding each one with half the remaining flour. Mix well.

Warm the milk to no more than blood heat and dissolve the bicarbonate of soda in this. Add to the cake mixture with the combined flour and sultana mixture. Turn into the tin and bake for 1½-2 hours, reducing to 150°C/ 300°F/Gas Mark 2 after 1 hour.

A Pedestal Display

A Warwick urn is a wonderful and valuable vase to possess. This bronze one is extremely heavy and sits steadily on quite a small base. There are also silver ones available but the flower colours chosen here go particularly well in the bronze. The netting has been tied with a wire to each handle for support, because with the turned bowl-shaped lining these vases always have, the area for stems is not large, and the small amount of netting that one can get in the vase tends to slip around.

Flowers presented on a pedestal will certainly make a striking feature in your room, and one such vase is all that is really necessary to make an effective floral decoration. One good flowering or foliage pot plant could be profitably used if you feel the room is large enough for something more.

The varieties chosen

The Warwick urn contains spindle berry (*euonymus europaeus*), *hydrangea*, paeony (*paeonia*), trails of ivy (*hedera*), *cotoneaster*, gladioli (*gladiolus*), *chrysanthemum*, *gerbera* and carnation (*dianthus*), both single and spray, all the flowers being in apricot shades.

To begin the arrangement, see that your vase is perfectly clean and free from any old foliage material. Secure the wire netting after making sure that you have 4 or 5 layers of wire: the netting must touch the bottom of the vase and – for tall arrangements like this – come up above the rim to form a slightly domed shape. Use netting with holes large enough to thread the woody stems of your flowers firmly through. Clip the netting over the rim of the vase, and for extra safety twist some wire from the netting around the handles. Now place in the spindle berry stems for your background – go three-quarters of the way across the vase. Shape your branches to make a good outline, then set paeony foliage and hydrangea heads in the centre to give it weight and to hide the netting. Now add the gladioli, bringing their colouring right through the group. These are tall and should always be used on a good length of stem – don't cut their stems short. Add ivy and cotoneaster, curving them over the vase rim. The thin stems of gerbera, chrysanthemum and carnation are added last of all, threading them through the small area left in the netting. All of the stems should flow with natural lines from the centre of the vase, and colours and shapes should be grouped together harmoniously wherever this is possible.

AFTER-THEATRE SUPPER

Convenient and easy to prepare in advance yet delicious to eat,
these late night supper dishes will put the seal on a magical evening.

ANIGHT OUT AT the theatre is always a treat for everyone concerned. A meal at home at the end of the evening not only rounds off the occasion, but is also practical, as restaurant meals before – or after – a theatre trip can often be unpleasantly hurried. Giving an after-theatre supper is no more complicated than hosting an ordinary dinner party: here are one or two simple guidelines to bear in mind.

Hints for a late night supper

A useful principle to remember is that the food you choose should be simple to prepare (this is particularly important if the cook is working during the day). Make sure, too, that it can all be made ready in advance, with only reheating and garnishing to be done when you get home. Dishes or accompaniments that reheat quickly are ideal, as are dishes that cook very slowly in a low oven or slow

---

MENU

for a party of four

Tomato and Tarragon Soup

•

Smoked Haddock and Mushroom Flan

Continental Cabbage Salad

•

Blackcurrant and Raspberry Kissel

Cinnamon Biscuits

WINE

Vinho Verde

---

cooker while you are out. Alternative recipes suitable for an after-theatre meal include ragoût or beef flamande (page 52), served with hot herb bread (page 58) and red cabbage (page 130); each dish reheats well.

Light food, light wines

In general, heavy meals last thing at night are best avoided: your guests will appreciate a choice of light, varied food. Rather than serving meat, try fish or cheese dishes: flans are ideal, and always popular. A light soup is an agreeable starter, particularly in wintertime; chilled soup makes a good summer alternative. Fruit desserts draw a suitable curtain over the meal, leaving palates refreshed and appetites replete.

The wines you choose should reflect the light delicate notes of the food. Try to serve a wine – either red or white – relatively low in alcohol, like Portuguese vinho verde.

MEAL PLANNER

● **Two days before:** do all the shopping. Prepare and bake the pastry dough. Make the kissel and biscuits.

● **One day before:** prepare the soup. Prepare the cabbage salad. Prepare the hollandaise sauce, and the filling for the flan.

● **The morning:** fill the flan. Decorate the kissel with the cream. Prepare the dinner table and chill the wine.

● **Final preparation:** reheat the soup and flan: serve the meal.

Tomato and tarragon soup

1 mild red onion
1 kg/2 lb ripe tomatoes
25 g/1 oz butter
½ clove garlic, crushed
2.5 ml/½ tsp salt
15 ml/1 tbls tomato purée
300 ml/½ pint tomato juice
½ bay leaf
1.2 litres/2 pints stock, *or* good commercial consommé
seasoning
15 ml/1 tbls arrowroot
a little extra stock *or* tomato juice
10 or 12 fresh tarragon leaves

Slice the onion. Wipe the tomatoes, cut them in half and squeeze each half to remove the seeds. Rub the seeds through a strainer to extract their juice. Reserve the juice and discard the seeds.

Melt the butter in a saucepan, then add the tomatoes, onion, garlic and salt. Cover and cook very slowly for about 45 minutes. Rub all through a strainer. Rinse the pan out well, then put the tomato purée and tomato juice, together with the juice strained from the seeds and the ready-cooked tomato pulp, the bay leaf and the stock back into the rinsed pan. (Either use 2 tins of good

beef consommé plus water, or your own chicken stock: for a recipe for this, see the *Reference Section*, page 138.) Simmer for 20-30 minutes. Adjust the seasoning and remove the bay leaf. Mix the arrowroot with a little extra stock or tomato juice, and add this to the soup with the tarragon leaves. Reheat, stirring continuously, and simmer for 2 or 3 minutes more before serving.

Note: Tarragon is an excellent herb for use in the kitchen (it is particularly good with eggs, fish and chicken). It is also an easy – as well as perennial – herb to grow in the garden.

The piquancy of Tomato and tarragon soup will stimulate the palate for the dishes to come. (Recipe on page 61.)

Smoked haddock and mushroom flan

275 g/10 oz rich shortcrust pastry dough

1 kg/2 lb Finnan (smoked) haddock

cold water and milk

350 g/12 oz flat mushrooms, wiped clean

25 g/1 oz butter

hollandaise sauce made with 2 egg yolks

OVEN TEMPERATURE: 190°C/375°F/ Gas Mark 5

Begin by preparing the pastry dough according to the recipe in the *Reference Section* on page 142. Use this to line a 25 cm/ 10 in flan ring or dish, and *bake blind* in the preheated oven for 10-12 minutes, or until the pastry has set around the outside. Remove the beans and return to the oven for 4-5 more minutes, until quite dry, but not browned. Allow the pastry case to cool in the ring or dish.

Meanwhile, cover the haddock with cold water and a dash of milk in a large frying pan. Bring slowly to the boil, then cover with a large plate and turn off the heat. Leave to stand for 10 minutes before draining and flaking the fish, and removing its bones.

Sauté the whole mushrooms in the butter. Prepare the hollandaise according to the recipe in the *Reference Section* on page 140. If you have used a flan ring for your pastry case, ease the case out of the ring and slide it on to an ovenproof platter. (If you have used a flan dish leave the pastry case in the dish.) Fill the case with the fish and mushrooms, then spread the hollandaise sauce over the filling. Store the flan in a cool larder until you are ready to heat it through: allow 15 minutes in a 190°C/ 375°F/Gas Mark 5 oven for this.

Note: Scottish Finnan haddock is one of the finest of all smoked fish, and it is ideal for this dish if you can obtain it.

Smoked haddock and mushroom flan has a rich, creamy flavour, perfectly matched by fresh Continental cabbage salad and white wine.

Continental cabbage salad

450 g/1 lb white cabbage

30 ml/2 tbls sunflower oil

seasoning

15 ml/1 tbls wine vinegar

3 sticks celery, thinly sliced

1 small Cox's Orange Pippin apple, thinly sliced

Shred the cabbage very finely, then mix it with the oil, turning thoroughly until all the cabbage is coated. Season and add the vinegar, then add the celery and apple slices. Mix together well. Cover closely and chill.

Blackcurrant and raspberry kissel

225 g/8 oz blackcurrants

175 g/6 oz granulated sugar

300 ml/½ pint water

thinly pared rind, and strained juice, of 1 orange

475 ml/16 fl oz claret *or* burgundy

15 ml/1 tbls potato flour

225 g/8 oz frozen raspberries

To serve:

150 ml/5 fl oz double cream

150 ml/5 fl oz soured cream

Wash and drain the blackcurrants and place in a saucepan with the sugar, water and orange rind. Stir gently over a low heat until the currants are soft and pulpy. Crush the fruit with a potato masher or large wooden spoon. Tip into a large nylon strainer and let the juice run through of its own accord. Then press the fruit very lightly to extract more juice, but do not force the pulp through the sieve. Reserve the orange rind.

Put the blackcurrant juice, reserved rind and red wine into a pan and bring slowly to the boil. Mix the potato flour to a smooth paste with the orange juice. Remove the rind and add the potato flour paste while the kissel is simmering, stirring vigorously as you do so, then remove from the heat. Add the raspberries and pour carefully into a bowl or bowls. Dust the surface with caster sugar to prevent a skin forming. Half whip the double cream, and then add the soured cream bit by bit to this. When the kissel is cool decorate with this mixture.

Cinnamon biscuits

Note: the quantities given below will make about 25 biscuits

225 g/8 oz plain flour
large pinch of salt
large pinch of powdered cinnamon
100 g/4 oz butter, softened
grated rind of ½ lemon
100 g/4 oz caster sugar
1 egg
100 g/4 oz ground hazelnuts, toasted

OVEN TEMPERATURE: 200°C/400°F/ Gas Mark 6

Sift the flour with the salt and cinnamon. Cream the butter with the lemon rind, add the sugar and beat until fluffy. Beat in the egg, then stir in the hazelnuts and flour mixture. Let the dough rest in a cool place for 30 minutes, then roll the mixture into walnut-sized balls. Place these on a greased baking sheet, and flatten them into biscuit shapes with a wet fork. Bake in the preheated oven for 7-8 minutes.

Anemones in a Dramatic Setting

The flowers for this after-theatre meal have been chosen with the dramatic theme of the evening in mind. Brilliant red and magenta is a bold and unconventional colour combination: it works well against a dark background, and in a setting where it will not distract the eye too much.

The small metal antique vase used is ideal for a few, very bright flowers: its discreet col-ouring and delicate shape balance and counterpoint the lively blooms. *Anemones* have been used: they need a lot of water, so a vase has been chosen that has plenty of space.

Arranging anemones

Clip wire netting to the vase handles. Set the height and width first with side shoots of alder (*alnus*), then bring trails of ivy (*hedera*) across to cover the netting. (Frost-blackened ivy was used in the arrangement for its dramatic appearance, but a green ivy would work equally well). Grade the anemones: keep the larger ones for the centre of the arrangement. Bring the colour through the arrangement in patterns and groups. When the flowers are satisfactorily positioned, tuck in the thin, fine stems of privet berries (*ligustrum*) to balance and finish the arrangement.

PASTA LUNCH

The bright colours and simple combinations inspired by pasta make
a quick, easy and satisfying lunch for guests of all ages.

No ONE KNOWS more about pasta than the Italians, and it is their cuisine which provides the inspiration for this simple, tasty lunch. Pasta comes in all shapes and sizes: we've used tiny pastina in the soup, long ribbons of tagliatelle for a salad, and flat sheets of lasagne in an original main course fish dish. Pasta can be flavoured and coloured with tomato (as the red tagliatelle shown opposite and overleaf has been) or spinach (like the green lasagne shown on page 66).

Pasta is widely available nowadays both fresh and dried: fresh pasta in general needs to be cooked for less time than does dried pasta, and both varieties are ready when the pasta is *al dente* (see page 156 for a full explanation of this phrase).

A convenience food

Pasta can make a good claim to being one of the first real 'convenience foods', and this

MENU

for a party of four

Minestra with Pastina

•

Italian Salad

•

Lasagne Verdi di Pesce

•

Almond Cake

Apricot Compote

WINE

Red and White Italian
Vino da Tavola

makes it an attractive and nutritious proposition for entertaining. A complete pasta meal can, literally, be ready in hours, or in the case of a one-course meal with salad, in minutes. There are very few ingredients, either, that will not go happily with pasta, and this means that it is one of the best foods for your own kitchen experiments.

Drinking in style

Pasta has a style all of its own: simple, visually attractive, immediately appealing. Match your wine to this very Italian approach to cooking and eating with a young Italian *vino da tavola* like the excellent Sicilian example shown. Either red or white will go with the dishes chosen: serve both, and then your guests can choose the one they would prefer. The fish lasagne, in fact, is a good example of a fish dish that does go well with light red wines – contrary to most people's expectations.

MEAL PLANNER

● **Two days before:** make the almond cake.

● **The day before:** do all of the shopping for the remaining courses. Fully complete the lasagne: store in the refrigerator overnight. Make the apricot compote. Prepare the ingredients for the salad and soup.

● **The morning:** make the salad and the soup.

● **Final preparation:** reheat the lasagne.

Minestra with pastina

1 carrot
1 onion
2 sticks celery
30 ml/2 tbls olive oil
about 1.25 litres/2¼ pints water *or* light stock
½ bay leaf
1 small leek
6 French beans
seasoning
2 small potatoes, peeled
1 clove garlic
2 tomatoes, skinned, seeded and chopped
40 g/1½ oz dried pastina
10 ml/2 tsp finely chopped parsley
freshly grated Parmesan cheese

Cut the carrot, onion and celery into medium-sized *julienne strips*. Heat the oil in a saucepan, put in the vegetable strips and fry until they are beginning to colour. Stir occasionally. Pour on the water or stock, and add the bay leaf. Cut the leek and beans into shreds and add both to the pan. Season lightly and simmer for 30-40 minutes. If the soup seems over-thick at any point, add more stock or water.

Add the potatoes, cut into the same size of strip as the other vegetables, and simmer for a further 20 minutes. Crush the garlic with a little salt. Add the tomatoes to the soup with the garlic, pastina and parsley. Simmer for a further 10 minutes, adjust the seasoning and serve sprinkled with the cheese.

Note: Minestra just means 'soup' in Italian, and should not be confused with minestrone. Minestrone is more of a meal in itself, containing white beans, peas and ham among other filling ingredients.

Minestra with pastina opens the lunch. (Recipe on page 65.)

Italian salad

225 g/8 oz fresh tomato tagliatelle
30-45 ml/2-3 tbls olive oil
100 g/4 oz firm white mushrooms
½ red pepper
½ yellow pepper
6 black olives
6 green olives
vinaigrette dressing
100 g/4 oz Italian salami, sliced
100 g/4 oz mortadella, sliced

Cook the pasta in plenty of boiling salted water until *al dente* (between 3 and 5 minutes). Strain and dress with the olive oil.

Wipe and slice the mushrooms and mix them with the pasta. Slice and *blanch* the peppers, *refresh* and dry. Stone the olives. Prepare the vinaigrette dressing according to the recipe in the *Reference Section* on page 141. Cut the meats into small strips and add to the pasta with the peppers and olives. Mix through the vinaigrette dressing.

Lasagne verdi di pesce

225 g/8 oz dried green lasagne
15 ml/1 tbls vegetable oil
450 g/1 lb tomatoes
30 ml/2 tbls olive oil
1 shallot, finely chopped
1 large clove garlic, peeled

The lively colours of this Italian salad find their reflection in its excitingly flavoured ingredients.

15 ml/1 tbls tomato purée
bouquet garni
1 stick celery, roughly chopped
a strip of orange rind
salt, sugar and freshly ground
    black pepper to taste
450 g/1 lb fresh cod fillets
350 g/12 oz smoked haddock fillets
600 ml/1 pint béchamel sauce
50 g/2 oz dry Cheddar cheese,
    grated

OVEN TEMPERATURE: 190°C/375°F/
Gas Mark 5

Cook the pasta, a few sheets at a time, in plenty of boiling salted water. (Add 15 ml/1 tbls vegetable oil to the cooking water to prevent the pasta sticking together.) Allow about 10 minutes for each batch to cook.

Lift the sheets from the pan and place on a clean wet tea towel. Wipe the tomatoes, cut out the core of each and squeeze out their seeds. Slice the tomatoes roughly. Heat the oil, add the shallot, and cook until golden. Add the tomatoes, the whole clove of garlic, the tomato purée, bouquet garni, celery, orange rind and seasonings. Cover and simmer gently for 15-20 minutes. Rub through a nylon strainer.

Lightly poach the fillets of fish in gently simmering water until just cooked: drain and cool. When cool, break into large flakes and mix carefully with the sieved tomato sauce. Prepare the béchamel sauce according to the recipe in the *Reference Section* on page 140.

Butter a square flameproof dish measuring 20 × 15 cm/ 8 × 6 in, then spoon in a layer of fish and place the lasagne on top. Spoon on a layer of the béchamel sauce. Continue layering the dish in this way until the container is full; finish with a layer of béchamel. Sprinkle the cheese thickly over the top and place in the preheated oven to heat through (this will take about 30 minutes from room temperature, and 50-60 minutes to heat straight from the refrigerator).

Lasagne verdi di pesce offers new tastes and textures in a well-loved format that all will enjoy.

Almond cake

100 g/4 oz butter

150 g/5 oz caster sugar

3 eggs

90 g/3½ oz ground almonds

40 g/1½ oz potato flour

15 ml/1 tbls kirsch

25 g/1 oz almonds, blanched and split

OVEN TEMPERATURE: 180°C/350°F/ Gas Mark 4

Prepare a 20-21.5 cm/8-8½ in French sponge cake tin ('moule-a-manqué'), or a sandwich tin of the same dimensions, by wiping the sides of the tin with softened butter, then coating with caster sugar and dusting with sifted flour. Cut and fit a circle of non-stick silicone paper to the base. Work the butter until soft and light in colour, then add the sugar and beat until white. Whisk the eggs to a froth and add them gradually to the butter and sugar with the almonds; beat for 3-4 minutes. Fold the potato flour into the mixture with the kirsch; turn into the prepared tin and decorate with the almonds.

Bake the cake for 1 hour in the preheated oven. The cake is ready when it shrinks from the sides of the tin. Let it cool in the tin for 5 minutes before cooling fully on a rack. Serve with **Apricot Compote**, made according to the recipe on page 143 of the *Reference Section*.

This group of fruits, vegetables and foliage has been made up using items that one would find in a typical kitchen. It shows some of the possibilities for arrangements in a kitchen setting, and demonstrates exactly what can be done without using flowers.

Arranging a still life

The arrangement has been placed on a block of wet oasis inside a shallow dish, which has in turn been placed on a wicker tray. Use whatever fruit and vegetables you have to hand, integrating them with garden and houseplant foliage.

Place the oasis at the back of the dish, and position this in turn well back in the tray. Put the melon between the oasis and the front rim of the dish, and then position the *yucca* foliage to give the arrangement height. To the left place a frond of holly fern (*certomium falcatum*), and to the right a silver grey artichoke (*cynara scolymus*). Over the front rim of the basket on the left a sprig of variegated laurel (*aucuba japonica*) has been positioned, and on the right a leaf of Japanese aralia (*fatsia japonica*).

Adding more materials

A few more leaves and some more fruits were used to build up the arrangement around these basic outline stems. To steady any fruits or vegetables that might otherwise roll about, put a cocktail stick into their bases or stems: this will hold them firmly and make a 'leg' to go into the oasis. The green pepper, fennel and mushrooms have all been treated in this way. Once you have interesting materials positioned in the basket, add small pieces of foliage to fill in any gaps. Flowers of daphne (*daphne laureola*) and hellebore (*helleborus foetidus*), both of them green-flowered plants, add the final touch.

If you would prefer a red colour scheme to the green one we have shown, you could use red cabbage, aubergine, red-skinned onion, black grapes, red plums and radishes. Red varieties of *dracaena* and beet-root leaves (*beta vulgaris conditiva*) could replace the greener pieces of foliage.

These are, in fact, easy arrangements to do and nothing need be wasted: all the ingredients are dual-purpose, in the sense that they can be eaten once the arrangement is dismantled. You could try an all-vegetable arrangement (cauliflowers make an excellent centrepiece) or an all-fruit group, but remember that foliage helps to fill gaps and add interest.

BARBECUE PARTY

The aromatic smoke of spicy meats, cooked in the warm summer air,
lends an exotic touch to outdoor entertaining.

THERE IS SOMETHING undeniably exciting about a barbecue. This springs from the fact that not only is one eating outdoors, but also cooking outdoors. Whether you hold your party in a quiet city garden or amidst splendid country scenery, a little of this pleasure and excitement will rub off on everyone, making it truly an occasion to remember.

Safety first
A barbecue is, of course, potentially dangerous, and your first priority should be ensuring that it is a safe, happy affair. Never leave the fire unguarded, and always see that it is well-protected from its surroundings and any dry, combustible materials. Be particularly careful in hot, windy conditions when sparks might fly off on the breeze. If there are children present, make sure that they stay safely away from the fire. (Keep a fire extinguisher handy in case of accidents.) Clear a special area where you can put hot cooking implements ready. Smoke can be a problem, too: check beforehand that your neighbours will not object – or invite them along to enjoy the fun, too!

A single barbecue cannot cope with every

MENU

for a party of eight

Stuffed Tomatoes Paphos

Spiced Chicken Breasts
Barbecued Pork Chops
Savoury Rice
Gratin of Potato and Spring Onion
Spiced Plums or Apricots
Sweet and Sour Cucumber
Mixed Green Salad

Lemon Feather Cake
Mixed Berry Compote

Country Cider

dish for a large party, so it is always a good idea to have some stand-by dishes prepared beforehand. Variety is important, and in warm weather some cool, crisp salads are most welcome. Country cider is our suggestion for drinking with the barbecue: it will go with almost anything, and being low in alcohol, can be drunk in thirst-slaking draughts. If you would prefer to drink wine, see the **Wine Suggestions** below left.

MEAL PLANNER

● **Two days before:** buy all the ingredients except the chicken breasts and pork chops. Prepare the spiced plums or apricots, the mixed berry compote and savoury rice.

● **One day before:** prepare the tomatoes and stuffing, but do not fill yet. Make and fill the lemon feather cake. Buy the chicken breasts and pork chops.

● **Final preparation:** marinate the chicken breasts and chops. Stuff the tomatoes. Make the sweet and sour cucumber and salad, and make and bake the gratin.

Wine Suggestions
Carafes of Californian rosé taste suitably lighthearted and are always pretty. The larger sized bottles of popular Italian wines like Valpolicella, Chianti or Lambrusco would go down well; for a special treat some bottles of Barolo (a powerfully flavoured red wine from Piedmont) would make a perfect match for spicy meats and open-air appetites.

Stuffed tomatoes Paphos

150 ml/6 tbls lemon mayonnaise	
350 g/12 oz flat mushrooms	
25 g/1 oz butter	
seasoning	
8 large 'beefsteak' tomatoes	
3 × 200 g/7 oz tins tuna fish	
30 ml/2 tbls chives, chopped	

To garnish:

lettuce or watercress

Begin by making the mayonnaise according to the recipe on page 140 of the *Reference Section*; use lemon juice instead of vinegar to make a lemon mayonnaise. Next wash the mushrooms, squeeze out the water and chop them finely. *Sauté* them in the butter until the

purée leaves the sides of the pan. Season and leave to cool.

Skin the tomatoes, cut in half and scoop out the seeds. Drain and pound the tuna until smooth, add the mushroom purée, and bind with lemon mayonnaise.

Spoon this mixture into the tomatoes, sprinkle chives over the top of each, and arrange on a serving platter. Garnish with lettuce or watercress.

The tunafish used in Stuffed tomatoes Paphos makes them a particular favourite of fish-lovers. (Recipe on page 69.)

Spiced chicken breasts

60 ml/4 tbls oil

1 clove of garlic, crushed

a pinch of turmeric

a pinch of cayenne

8 chicken breasts, with skin

150 ml/¼ pint stock

Chinese sweet and sour sauce

oil for brushing

OVEN TEMPERATURE: 160°C/325°F/
   Gas Mark 3

Mix the oil with the garlic, turmeric and cayenne, and rub over the chicken breasts. Leave for 1 hour.

Place the breasts in a gratin dish, pour round the stock (use either the chicken giblet stock in the *Reference Section* on page 138, or a good commercial version), cover with greaseproof paper and cook in the preheated oven for 30 minutes. Lift onto a washable tray or large plate, then brush with Chinese sweet and sour sauce and salad oil.

Place the breasts skin side down on the barbecue and leave just long enough for the skin to brown. Turn them and cook for no more than 1 minute on the other side. Serve while still piping hot, and do not allow to overcook.

Barbecued pork chops

8 loin chops, trimmed

300 ml/½ pint oil

1 bottle of proprietary orange and
   sherry sauce

Brush the chops with oil and spoon over about a third of the bottle of sauce. Leave the chops to marinate in this for 1 hour, turning them from time to time.

Place the chops on the barbecue and cook for 5-7 minutes on each side, brushing the meat from time to time with oil to keep it moist. Baste with more sauce at the end of the cooking period, just before you serve them. Let your guests help themselves to whichever accompaniments they wish with both the chicken and the pork.

Savoury rice

350 g/12 oz long-grain rice, dry
   weight

up to 100 ml/3½ fl oz vinaigrette

5 ml/1 tsp paprika

100 g/4 oz prawns, peeled

75 g/3 oz almonds, split

Cook the rice until tender, then drain and dry. Make the vinaigrette according to the recipe in the *Reference Section* on page 141: flavour it with the paprika rather than black pepper.

Add the prawns and almonds to the rice, and moisten with the flavoured vinaigrette. Check the seasoning carefully: this is particularly important with rice salads. Mix all the ingredients together thoroughly before serving.

Spiced plums or apricots

450 g/1 lb plums *or* apricots

150 ml/¼ pint water

150 ml/¼ pint white wine

30 ml/2 tbls wine vinegar

5 cm/2 in stick of cinnamon

6 peppercorns

1 clove

100 g/4 oz sugar

Halve the fruit and remove the stones. Place all the other ingredients in a saucepan and dissolve the sugar slowly. Add the fruit and poach it for about 15 minutes or until tender. Remove the fruit with a slotted spoon. *Reduce* the cooking syrup until thick: strain it over the fruit and chill well.

Barbecued pork chops are shown here served with Gratin of potato and spring onion, Spiced plums and some Mixed green salad.

Sweet and sour cucumber

1 cucumber

salt

15 ml/1 tbls caster sugar

15 ml/1 tbls wine vinegar

lemon juice to taste

freshly ground black pepper to taste

Peel the cucumber and cut into slices. Sprinkle with salt, cover with a plate, and put in the refrigerator for 1 hour. Meanwhile mix the sugar and vinegar together, then add the lemon juice and pepper to taste. Rinse and dry the cucumber well with paper towels. Add the dressing to the cucumber and mix thoroughly. Arrange in a bowl and serve.

Gratin of potato and spring onion

600-900 ml/1-1½ pints stock

1.5 kg/3 lb potatoes

2 bunches of spring onions

75 g/3 oz beef dripping or butter

75 g/3 oz Cheddar cheese, grated

seasoning

OVEN TEMPERATURE: 200°C/400°F/ Gas Mark 6

A day or two in advance, make the stock. A light chicken, beef or vegetable stock would all be suitable: see recipes on pages 138 and 139 of the *Reference Section*. Slice the potatoes thinly. Trim the spring onions and cut them into evenly sized pieces with scissors.

Rub an ovenproof dish thickly with half the dripping or butter and put in the spring onions, potatoes and half the grated cheese in layers. Season well and finish with a layer of neatly arranged potatoes. Scatter with the remaining cheese, dot with dripping and pour in the stock.

Bake in the preheated oven for 1-1¼ hours until tender and brown in colour.

Note: Timing can be difficult to perfect for barbecues, and this dish has been chosen as it can be kept warm quite happily for up to 45 minutes in a very low oven. If the top is darkly brown at the end of the cooking period, cover loosely with foil.

Mixed green salad

a good mixture of green salad ingredients including Webb's lettuce, curly endive, cos lettuce, cucumber, summer celery, green pepper, avocado pear

150 ml/¼ pint vinaigrette

Wash all the ingredients apart from the avocado pear, dry them in a salad spinner and leave them wrapped in a clean tea towel in a large mixing bowl. Make the vinaigrette according to the recipe on page 141 of the *Reference Section*. Turn the salad ingredients out of the cloth and put them in a large salad bowl. Halve and peel the avocado pear: half each half, and then slice each quarter. Mix the avocado with the rest of the salad ingredients. Whisk up the dressing and pour it into the bowl: toss the salad with two large wooden spoons and serve in bowls or on plates.

Salad notes: Alternatives to this attractive mixed green salad might include a plain green salad made with lettuce, a salad of Chinese leaves, or the continental cabbage salad recipe given on page 62.

Always try to toss salad at the last possible moment to avoid any wilting of its crisp ingredients, then serve the salad immediately after tossing.

Spiced chicken breasts are certain to please, and Savoury rice and Sweet and sour cucumber can both be prepared in advance.

Lemon feather cake is as light as its name suggests: potato flour and beaten eggs are the secrets of its success.

and bake in the preheated oven for about 50-60 minutes. Cool on a wire rack.

To make the filling, whip the cream until firm and fold in the lemon curd. Split the cake in two using a sharp serrated bread knife, and fill with the lemon cream. Reassemble and dust with icing sugar.

Mixed berry compote

450 g/1 lb gooseberries	
400 ml/14 fl oz water	
350 g/12 oz sugar	
450 g/1 lb raspberries	
225 g/8 oz blackcurrants	
225 g/8 oz blackberries	
225 g/8 oz strawberries	

Top and tail the gooseberries and put them in a pan with 175 ml/ 6 fl oz water. Simmer gently to soften the skins, then add 100 g/ 4 oz of sugar. When it has dissolved, cook slowly for a further 10 minutes and leave to cool.

Put the remaining sugar in another pan with the rest of the water and dissolve this over a low heat, then boil for 5 minutes. Pour half of this hot syrup over the raspberries and the rest over the blackcurrants and blackberries. Wash the strawberries, then hull them, and cut any particularly large ones in half.

When all the fruit is cool, turn it into a large glass bowl and serve with the lemon feather cake.

Note: This delicious compote is excellent with the feather cake, but it is also very good on its own as a low calorie summer dessert.

Lemon feather cake

6 eggs	
275 g/10 oz caster sugar	
1 lemon	
150 g/5 oz potato flour	

For the filling:

300 ml/½ pint double cream	
225 g/8 oz lemon curd	

To finish:

90 ml/6 tbls icing sugar, sifted	

OVEN TEMPERATURE: 180°C/350°F/ Gas Mark 4

Butter a 25 cm/10 in moule à manqué tin (or a sandwich tin of roughly the same dimensions) and line the base with a disc of buttered greaseproof paper. Dust first with caster sugar and then with potato flour.

Separate the eggs. Work the egg yolks and sugar together with the juice and grated rind of the lemon using an electric beater, until thick and light in colour. Add the potato flour and beat thoroughly. Whisk the egg whites until stiff with a balloon whisk and fold this into the mixture. Turn into the prepared tin

Mixed berry compote gathers together summer's finest fruits to make a perfect match for the Lemon feather cake.

A Trough Of Mixed Houseplants

A fibreglass trough is the ideal container for these foliage house plants. Although expensive to buy, they are long lasting and well worth the initial outlay, for you can use the plants decoratively inside the house in winter just as you can outside in summer. Take care not to choose plants with very vigorous root systems which, after a few years, will fill the trough and burst its sides.

Try to select plants to give a variety of leaf shapes and colours. Those that trail should be planted at the front of the trough in order to soften the hard rim. Keep the taller plants to the back of the trough, and the lower ones at the sides. The plants should be planted in good compost. It is essential that they be allowed to drain freely, but at no time should they be allowed to dry out.

Ivy (*hedera*) has been used trailing around the bust and the trough: trellis is the perfect background for this. If kept very dry, ivy will colour well and not grow too fast.

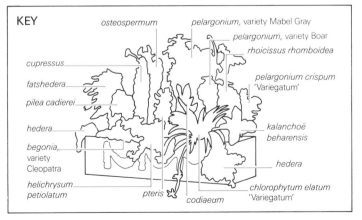

KEY

osteospermum

pelargonium, variety Mabel Gray

pelargonium, variety Boar

rhoicissus rhomboidea

cupressus

fatshedera

pilea cadierei

hedera

begonia, variety Cleopatra

helichrysum petiolatum

pteris

codiaeum

chlorophytum elatum 'Variegatum'

hedera

kalanchoë beharensis

pelargonium crispum 'Variegatum'

CHILDREN'S PICNIC

Preparing food for a family picnic can be as much of an adventure as actually eating it,
especially when you try new departures from your normal repertoire.

PICNICS, AS WE probably all remember, are extremely important events in the lives of those not yet in their teens: a lot of anticipation and excitement goes into them, and it is a shame if this is disappointed. With a little forethought – and luck with the weather – this need never be the case. Food for children's picnics should ideally be amusing and tasty, and like all picnic food it should look and taste right when served tepid: the temperature, one hopes, of a warm summer's day.

Try to get some pretty paper plates, cups and napkins: these will all add to the atmosphere. This menu includes jellies, and they will be doubly appreciated if the jelly moulds are in characterful shapes.

Packing the hamper itself is a matter of no small importance. Everything should be double-wrapped in cling film and polythene bags, to stop 'leaks', and anything that can be squashed – like the flans or the moulded jellies – should either be packed in solid

HAMPER

for a party of ten

Salad Pittas
with Chipolata Sausages
Devilled Drumsticks
Cheese Crumb Flans
Wholemeal Salad Rolls

Luncheon Plum Cake
Fresh Fruit Jelly

Home-made Lemonade

containers, or left until last and placed at the top. You may well find that it's easier to assemble the salad pittas at the picnic spot you have chosen, and the jellies are best unmoulded at the picnic spot. Choose bottles with very firm stoppers – or screw tops – for the lemonade, and make sure that there is no possibility of these being broken in transit. Don't forget a cutting knife for the cake, and pepper and salt; plenty of extra napkins in case of spillages are a good idea, too.

Final details

The quantities specified should feed 8-10 hungry children quite adequately: either make more of the same for a larger picnic, or fill it out with new (or old) ideas of your own.

The citric and tartaric acid specified for the lemonade can be bought from the home-made wine-making sections of large chemists or department stores. Both are perfectly harmless ingredients occurring naturally in a wide range of fruits.

PICNIC PLANNER

● **One week before:** prepare the cake: it improves with keeping.

● **Two days before:** make the lemonade and leave it to steep. Prepare the jellied stock for the devilled drumsticks.

● **One day before:** strain and bottle the lemonade. Do all the shopping. Make and set the jellies in the refrigerator, and make and bake the flan bases. Grill the chipolatas and bake the drum-

sticks: cool, and wrap tightly in cling film and polythene bags.

● **Final preparation:** prepare the two flan fillings and put them into the flan cases: cover each carefully with cling film. Prepare all the ingredients needed to assemble the salad pittas and wholemeal rolls when you get to your picnic spot. Check that nothing is missing as you pack the hamper, using the suggestions given in the introduction: try to ensure the hamper will not slide around on the journey.

Salad pittas with chipolata sausages

1 Webb's lettuce
30 ml/2 tbls mayonnaise *or* salad cream
5 ml/1 tsp orange juice
6 pitta breads, cut in two
4 medium carrots, grated
3 sticks celery, chopped
450 g/1 lb cherry tomatoes
1 kg/2 lb chipolata sausages

Shred 6-8 of the lettuce leaves,

mix the mayonnaise with the orange juice, and turn the lettuce leaves in this. Spoon into the pitta breads. Packs the carrots and celery into a hollow made in the lettuce; add two or three tiny tomatoes. Brush the chipolata sausages with a little oil and grill on all sides. Allow them to drain of dripping fat and cool. Leave room for one or two chipolatas to be tucked into the sides of the pittas when the picnic food is served: see the photograph overleaf for a suggested sample serving of these pittas.

Crunchy Salad pittas are the perfect foil for spicy Devilled drumsticks and the ever-popular chipolatas: cherry tomatoes fit neatly into the top.

Devilled drumsticks

60 ml/4 tbls jellied stock
50 g/2 oz butter
½ tsp each of salt, freshly ground black pepper, dry mustard, and ground ginger
a dash of Tabasco
8 chicken drumsticks
15 ml/1 tbls soya oil
15 ml/1 tbls tomato ketchup
15 ml/1 tbls Worcestershire sauce
15 ml/1 tbls thick honey

OVEN TEMPERATURE: 200°C/400°F/ Gas Mark 6

Make the jellied stock, some days in advance if possible, according to the recipe in the *Reference Section* on page 138, or use previously made stock from frozen (it freezes well).

Cream together 25 g/1 oz of the butter with the seasonings and Tabasco. Spread this mixture over the drumsticks and leave for a minimum of 2 hours.

Put the oil and remaining butter in a roasting tin and heat in the preheated oven. Add the drumsticks and baste well. Mix the stock and sauces together and add them to the roasting tin. Roast the drumsticks for about 30 minutes, basting every 10 minutes. Add the honey after the second basting, turning the drumsticks in it as you do so. Remove from the oven after 30 minutes and put under the grill to brown and crisp the skin on all sides: this will take between 10 and 15 minutes. Allow to cool fully, then wrap closely.

Cheese crumb flans

For the crumb crusts:

225 g/8 oz cheese-flavoured biscuits
150 g/5 oz butter, melted
100 g/4 oz mild Cheddar cheese, grated
seasoning
Dijon mustard to taste

For the salmon and flageolet filling:

1 large tin (439 g/15½ oz) salmon
1 large tin (397 g/14 oz) flageolet beans
30-45 ml/2-3 tbls mayonnaise
seasoning
4 large tomatoes, skinned and sliced

A mushroom and ham filling on the left and salmon and flageolet on the right are the positive outdoor flavours for these Cheese crumb flans.

For the mushroom and ham filling:

65 g/2½ oz butter	
1 small onion, finely chopped	
100 g/4 oz mushrooms, chopped	
6 eggs, beaten	
30-45 ml/2-3 tbls double cream	
100 g/4 oz lean ham	

OVEN TEMPERATURE: 180°C/350°F/
Gas Mark 4

Crush the biscuits finely, put the crumbs into a bowl and stir in the melted butter, the grated cheese, seasoning, and mustard. Turn equal halves of the mixture into two 23 cm/9 in ovenproof china flan dishes, and press the mixture over the bottom and sides of each with the back of a spoon. Bake in the preheated oven for 10 minutes, then allow to cool. To make the salmon and flageolet filling, drain the salmon, remove any skin and bone and then flake carefully with a fork. Tip the liquid from the beans, turn them into a basin and mix them with the mayonnaise. Season. Add the salmon to the beans and turn the mixture into the prepared flan case. Arrange the tomatoes on top of the filling, and cover with cling film. This flan is quite runny, so have plates ready when serving.

To make the mushroom and ham filling, melt the butter in a shallow pan, add the onion and cook slowly until soft and golden. Add the mushrooms, increase the heat, and cook through until all the liquid they produce has evaporated. Remove from the heat. Beat the eggs and the cream together.

Add the eggs and cream to the mushroom mixture while it is still hot, and stir slowly with a metal spoon until it thickens creamily. (If you have to return to a low heat to get this effect, be very careful not to curdle the eggs.) Cool slightly, then turn the mixture into the crumb crust. Scatter the ham over the top and cover tightly with cling film to exclude the air and keep the ham pink.

Wholemeal salad rolls

For the very young members on the picnic take small round wholemeal or white rolls hollowed out and filled with a very little lettuce and carrot mixture and one small tomato. Tiny mouths will find these easier to manage than the salad pittas.

These small wholemeal rolls, filled with freshly mixed salad and a cherry tomato, are the perfect size for tiny mouths.

Home-made lemonade

1.5 kg/3 lb granulated sugar	
25 g/1 oz citric acid	
15 g/½ oz tartaric acid	
3.6 litres/6 pints boiling water	
6 lemons	

Put the sugar, citric and tartaric acid in a basin and pour over the boiling water, stirring well until the sugar is melted. Add the juice of the lemons and the rinds of three of them cut into very fine strips. Stand overnight and allow to steep.

The next day, thoroughly clean 4 litre-size bottles and rinse out with cold water. Strain the lemonade into a pouring jug, and fill the bottles. Cap firmly.

Home-made lemonade is so much tastier than commercial versions.

Luncheon plum cake

melted lard

350 g/12 oz plain flour	
2.5 ml/½ tsp ground cinnamon	
2.5 ml/½ tsp ground nutmeg	
5 ml/1 tsp mixed spice	
75 g/3 oz butter	
175 g/6 oz soft brown sugar	
175 g/6 oz currants	
225 g/8 oz sultanas	
225 g/8 oz raisins	
50 g/2 oz cherries, cut into quarters	
50 g/2 oz peel, finely chopped	
grated rind of ½ lemon	
150 ml/¼ pint apple juice or cider	
250 ml/8 fl oz milk	
7.5 ml/1½ tsp bicarbonate of soda	

OVEN TEMPERATURE: 180°C/350°F/ Gas Mark 4

Brush a 23 cm/9 in tin with a light coating of melted lard. Line with greaseproof paper and repeat.

Sift the flour with the spices and salt, rub in the butter, and then mix in the sugar, fruit, peel and lemon rind. Make a well in the middle, and pour in the apple juice or cider. Warm 30 ml/2 tbls of the milk with the bicarbonate of soda; when dissolved, add to the rest of the milk. Add the milk and stir all the liquids into the dry ingredients; mix well. Turn the mixture into the tin; leave to stand for 12 hours. Bake in a preheated oven for 1½ hours.

Rich, moist and full of fruit, Luncheon plum cake is a match for healthy appetites and discerning palates alike.

Fresh fruit jelly is always popular, whether served in a plain dish, or unmoulded on the spot from characterful jelly moulds.

Fresh fruit jelly

juice of 4 lemons and the rind of 2, thinly peeled	
600 ml/1 pint water	
100 g/4 oz granulated sugar	
40 g/1½ oz gelatine	
600 ml/1 pint tropical fruit juice	
2 large ripe nectarines	
3 bananas	

Squeeze the juice from the lemons. Put the water, sugar and lemon rind in a pan and scatter the gelatine on top. Stir over a gentle heat until both the sugar and gelatine are dissolved. Cover and let all steep together for 10 minutes, then add the lemon juice and strain. When cool, add the tropical fruit juice and pour into individual moulds. When the jelly is on the point of setting, add the peeled sliced fruit, mix well, cover and chill in the refrigerator until completely cold and set.

Note: This jelly contains quite a large quantity of gelatine to hold the fruit pieces in suspension and keep the jelly firm enough to unmould.

Meadow Flower Group

Children love a picnic, but there's no harm in making it educational once in a while. Suggest they try to find as many different kinds of flowers, seed heads and berries around the neighbouring fields as possible, then they can bring them back for identification and, with a little help and supervision, the flowers can be made into a simple arrangement later. The one illustrated has been made in a shallow bowl, which has then been hidden in an upturned hat.

A number of grasses, hops (*humulus lupulus*), blackberry (*rubus fruticosus*), snowberry (*symphoricarpos rivularis*), hazelnuts (*corylus avellana*), *achillea*, ox-eye daisy (*chrysanthemum leucanthemum*), clover (*trifolium*), lucerne (*medicago sativa*), heather (*calluna vulgaris*), and *senecio* are the main ingredients of this informal group. Start the arrangement with tall thin grasses at the back, then take any curved stems to the sides for width. Single, flat flowers are ideal for the centre, then fill in other shapes and colours to balance and weight the arrangement.

Picking wild flowers

There are certain points that one should always remember when using wild flowers. Never pick rare specimens: these should be left for others to enjoy, and to allow them to multiply. Always cut flowers carefully and take just a little – do not pull at the materials and damage the plant. Place your cut pieces on damp paper in a large black polythene bag and keep airtight and out of the heat until you can get them properly prepared back home. A few wild grasses or hedgerow cuttings will make all the difference to your garden flowers, or to those from your local florist.

Flowers to watch out for on picnics in spring and early summer include primroses (*primula vulgaris*), violets (*viola*), wood anemones (*anemone nemorosa*), bluebells (*endymion nonscriptus*), king cups (*caltha palustris*), buttercups (*ranunculus acris*), dandelion (*taraxacum officinale*), campion (*silene*), cow parsley (*anthryscus sylvestris*), vetches (*vicia*), poppies (*papaver rhoeas*) and willow herb (*ephilobium*), and all of these can be used most attractively in simple arrangements.

PATIO DINNER

A summer's evening offers few more elegant pleasures than that of a leisurely meal taken with friends,
looking quietly out across your own garden.

EATING OUTDOORS REQUIRES special thinking and planning: hot dishes requiring intensive work in the kitchen should be kept to a minimum, and the flavours and textures of the food should be well-defined, so that they can hold their own against the other excitements of the open air. This is, accordingly, a richly-flavoured menu, and most of the dishes can be prepared in advance, with only the main chicken dish needing last minute attention before it comes to table.

Remember to make allowances, too, for changing weather conditions, particularly if you are holding your dinner in late spring or early autumn when the light fades rapidly and evening temperatures change within the hour from warm to cool. Candles can be very romantic on a still evening, but an unexpected dose of chilly air rarely is!

Equipment hints
None of the techniques involved in the menu

MENU

for a party of six

Avocado Sévillienne
with wholemeal rolls

Chicken Suprêmes with Mango
with buttered rice
Cucumber Raita
Apple and Mint Chutney

Strawberry Gâteau

WINES

Alsace Sylvaner or Riesling

is difficult. Avocado dishes are specified for the avocado recipe: these will make presentation perfect, but an attractive result can be obtained with small, plain, shallow bowls. The cake is best made in the French sponge cake tin called 'moule à manqué': a large ordinary sandwich tin will do if you can't find one anywhere. For an extra-light result with the sponge, make the cake batter with an electric whisk.

Uncomplicated wines
This is a light-hearted meal, and the same wine throughout would be a suitably uncomplicated way to accompany the food. A sylvaner or riesling wine from Alsace would be a good choice: remember to chill it well before serving, and if the evening is a very warm one, a wine cooler would help keep the wine at an appropriate temperature (an example of one of these is illustrated in the photograph for our **Summer Dinner** menu, shown on page 14).

MENU PLANNER

● **The day before:** shop for all ingredients. Make the cake; prepare the glaze. Shred the tomatoes and prepare the dressing.

● **The morning:** prepare the apple chutney, raita and rice.

● **Final preparation:** begin the chicken dish; finish, decorate and glaze the cake. Reheat the rice and rolls. Finish the chicken dish and fluff the rice immediately before serving.

Avocado sévillienne

3 large ripe avocado pears

For the dressing:
4 large ripe tomatoes
1 finely chopped shallot
juice and grated rind of 1 orange
30 ml/2 tbls tomato purée
30 ml/2 tbls red wine vinegar
salt and freshly ground black pepper
½ tsp caster sugar
150 ml/¼ pint salad oil, preferably olive

30 ml/2 tbls freshly chopped basil or snipped chives

To serve:
hot wholemeal rolls and butter

Prepare the dressing: begin by scalding and skinning the tomatoes. Cut each tomato into four and scoop out its seeds. Place the seeds in a nylon strainer and press well to extract their juices.

Place the shallot in a basin and add the orange rind and juice, tomato purée, wine vinegar and juice from the tomato seeds.

Season to taste and add the sugar. Whisk in the oil, check the flavour and adjust the seasoning if necessary. Slice the quartered tomatoes into eighths. Mix the herbs into the dressing.

Place a spoonful of the dressing in each avocado dish. Halve each avocado and remove the stone. Skin them by holding cut side down and peeling or slicing off the skin thinly. Place the half avocados in the dishes and fill with the tomato slices: spoon over the remaining dressing. Serve with hot wholemeal rolls.

The combination of fruit and meat is always refreshing, and the accompanying sauce for these Chicken suprêmes with mango is delicately spiced.

Chicken suprêmes with mango

6 chicken breasts, skinned

50 g/2 oz butter, *clarified*

2 onions, sliced

10 ml/2 tsp curry powder

15 ml/1 tbls curry paste

1 clove garlic, crushed

salt

100 g/4 oz coconut cream

150 ml/¼ pint hot water

150 ml/¼ pint natural yoghurt

squeeze of fresh lime or lemon

1 ripe mango, cut into evenly-sized segments

Flatten the chicken breasts by pushing the blade of a heavy knife or cleaver sideways down onto them. Melt the butter in a shallow flameproof casserole, fry the onions until golden brown, then add the curry powder, the curry paste and crushed garlic. Add the chicken suprêmes to the pan, salt, cover and cook gently for 6 minutes, turning them over halfway through.

Meanwhile, melt the coconut cream by breaking it into lumps and stirring it into the hot water; in a separate basin, beat the yoghurt with a fork until smooth. Add the coconut cream mixture and yoghurt to the chicken and cook for 10 more minutes, again turning the chicken halfway through. Check the seasoning, add the lime or lemon juice together with the mango pieces, and continue to cook for a further 4-5 minutes.

Apple and mint chutney: If you wish to serve this chutney with the main course, follow the recipe on page 141 of the *Reference Section.*

Reheating rice: Time can be saved on the day if the rice is prepared in advance: fully cook it in your normal way, and then drain it well. Thickly butter a gratin dish, and fill to the top with rice: do not press the rice down too tightly. Cover closely with thickly buttered greaseproof paper, and store in a cool place overnight. Reheat either slowly or quickly, depending on what else is in your oven: at 180°C/350°F/Gas Mark 4, enough rice for six should reheat in 30-40 minutes.

Cucumber raita

1 medium cucumber

salt

150 ml/¼ pint natural yoghurt

Peel the cucumber, then grate it coarsely. Salt lightly, and leave it for 15 minutes to drain. Strain off the liquid and press or squeeze dry, then mix the cucumber with the yoghurt.

Strawberry gâteau

75 g/3 oz plain flour

½ tsp ground cinnamon

pinch of salt

3 large eggs

100 g/4 oz caster sugar

grated rind of ½ lemon

For the glaze:

225 g/8 oz redcurrant jelly

To finish:

300 ml/½ pint double or whipping cream

10 ml/2 tsp vanilla sugar

700 g/1½ lb strawberries

OVEN TEMPERATURE: 180°C/350°F/ Gas Mark 4

Cut a disc of non-stick silicone paper the same size as the bottom of the cake tin. (This will ideally be a 'moule-à-manqué' tin, 24 cm/9½ in wide and 5 cm/2 in deep, but a large round sandwich tin of the same dimensions will do.) Wipe the sides of the cake tin with softened butter, then coat with caster sugar and dust with sifted flour. Fit the paper.

Sift the flour with the cinnamon, and add a good pinch of salt. Break the eggs into a mixing bowl and add the sugar gradually, beating with an electric whisk, until it is thick and mousse-like. Fold in the sifted flour and the grated lemon rind, and turn into the tin. Bake in the preheated oven for 15-20 minutes. Cool on a rack.

While the cake is baking, prepare the glaze by melting and *reducing* the redcurrant jelly. Test for consistency by glazing a sample strawberry: the glaze should coat the fruit evenly. Whip the cream, add the vanilla sugar and one-third of the strawberries cut into thin slices. Split the cake, sandwich with this mixture and slide onto a serving plate. Brush the glaze over the cake and allow to set. Arrange the remaining strawberries on top, and brush again with the glaze.

Strawberries are delicious in almost any guise, but a slice of this rich Strawberry gâteau is one of summer's finest treats.

Sunflowers in a Half Lantern

This lantern vase is excellent to use where there is only a little space for flowers: anything up on a wall is well out of the way, yet seen from all angles. The flowers are *helianthus*: varieties Italian White and Sunburst.

The vase is in the form of a half lantern made from twisted wrought iron, filled with a metal lining holding plenty of water. Always watch out for the problem of syphoning – when the water leaches out of the container – as this could lead to a marked inside wall.

The container has a piece of oasis in the base which is held firmly in place with a layer of 1 cm/½ in wire netting. This has been clipped over the edge of the lantern frame. Oasis will hold the stems firmly, should there be any chance of a breeze.

Colour alternatives

If a special colour scheme is required, this vase can simply be painted to suit the occasion. It can be used at any time of the year and is fine with all types of flowers and foliage: some other suggestions would be marguerites (*felicia*) and grasses – both in a white vase; carnations (*dianthus*) with their own foliage or silver-grey *senecio*, or evergreens and red flowers for Christmas (in a black vase).

This arrangement was made in three steps. First, 4 stems of helianthus were placed in the vase to give an overall outline coming well out of the framework. Next, the centre foliage was fixed: *helleborus orientalis* leaves hide the oasis and 3 ivy (*hedera*) trails drape down the sides and front. The 3 large, deep yellow sunflowers make the focal point. *Bergenia* leaves or *hosta* could have been used instead of helleborus.

Finally, the flowers and buds are added, each of them differ-ent lengths, to give an effect of wide variation in shapes and sizes. Make sure that all your stems flow from the centre of the container. Do not over-arrange: this vase and this occasion call for a simple approach.

Sunflowers do not always last well so see that your flowers are well prepared before use in a vase. The stems may be woody and should be split or ham-mered and given a good drink for a day before use. You may place the sunflowers in warm water for this period, especially if the flowers are limp when picked after a hot day.

ELEGANT PICNIC

Dappled evening sunlight falls across the finest of outdoor eating:
here are five simple dishes and a picnic posy to delight your closest friends.

MENU

for a party of six

Smoked Trout Mousse

•

Gammon Roulades à la Princesse

Potato Mayonnaise

Salad Platter

•

Gâteau Ganache

WINE

English or German White Wine

A PICNIC IS A MEAL like no other, and preparing and organising a picnic is entertaining of a very special sort. So many factors have to be considered that do not apply when entertaining in the normal way: the food, plates and cutlery for the meal all have to be packed and transported; uncertain weather conditions have to be anticipated, and seating arrangements often repay forethought. This elegant picnic has been designed with adults in mind, so the emphasis is on a few select dishes to please eye and palate alike.

Preparing the picnic

In many ways, overall preparation for this picnic is simpler than for the children's version on pages 74-79: there are only 5 dishes to make ready, and so less cooking has to be done; packing the picnic is simpler (see the tips for this given on page 75); when you get to your picnic spot, emergencies are less likely to occur and activities and games are not in constant demand. Adults, though, will appreciate little touches to add to the mood and atmosphere of the meal, and a straw hat or parasol may prove as useful as it is decorative if you're lucky with the weather.

English wines

We have suggested English wines to accompany the meal: their light, delicate flavours and appealing freshness make them perfect for outdoor summer drinking. More and more English wines are available nowadays, as English winemaking re-establishes itself after centuries of eclipse; and both quality and quantity improve greatly from year to year. A good alternative to English wine would be a German Kabinett wine from the Mosel or the Rheingau, or an Australian or Californian Riesling wine.

MEAL PLANNER

● **Three days before:** do all the shopping. Prepare and bake the cake mixture for the gâteau: store in an airtight container.

● **Two days before:** prepare the roulades and potato salad: cover and refrigerate.

● **One day before:** prepare the smoked trout mousse: cover and refrigerate. Finish the gâteau.

● **Final preparation:** prepare the salad but do not dress. Pack the picnic carefully.

Smoked trout mousse

3 small *or* 2 medium to large
   smoked trout
15 ml/1 tbls horseradish cream
75 g/3 oz butter, softened
175 g/6 oz curd cheese
freshly ground pepper
lemon juice to taste

To finish:
60 ml/4 tbls each of double and
   soured cream
walnut kernels

To serve:
thinly cut brown bread and butter

Remove the skin and all the bones from the trout and pound well with the horseradish cream until you have a smooth paste. This could either be done in a large pestle and mortar, a food processor, or in a pudding basin with a wooden spoon. Work in the butter and curd cheese, then season with pepper and lemon juice. Fill six small ramekins with this mixture, then cover and leave in the refrigerator until firm.

Whisk the double cream until thick and stir in the soured cream. Put a good spoonful onto each ramekin and garnish with the walnuts. Pack the ramekins in a rigid container. Serve with thinly cut brown bread and butter: to make this easier to transport to your picnic, roll each slice of buttered bread up neatly as for the smoked salmon rolls illustrated on page 92.

Note: With the advent of large-scale fish farming, fresh trout are now much more common than they used to be. Smoked trout, though, are still an undervalued delicacy, and the lightly smoky flavour of their flesh, pointed up by a hint of horseradish, makes a delicous and memorable opening to an open-air meal.

The delicate and subtle flavours of Smoked trout mousse, finished with walnut halves, prepares the palate for the fine picnic fare to follow. (Recipe on page 85.)

Gammon roulades à la princesse

1.2 litres/2 pints chicken stock

150 ml/¼ pint mayonnaise

6 chicken breasts, skinned

1 onion

1 carrot

bouquet garni

6 peppercorns

salt

12 spears of asparagus

30 ml/2 tbls double cream

12 thin slices of cooked gammon

For the aspic jelly:

900 ml/1½ pints stock from the chicken breasts

40 g/1½ oz gelatine

150 ml/¼ pint white wine

seasoning

1 large egg white, beaten to a froth

Make the chicken stock according to the recipe on page 138 of the *Reference Section*, and the mayonnaise according to one of the recipes on page 140. Both could be prepared one day in advance if you wish.

Put the chicken breasts into a pan with the sliced vegetables, herbs and peppercorns. Pour in enough stock to barely cover them, salt lightly and simmer gently for about 25-30 minutes. Let them cool in the stock.

Next make the aspic jelly. Take out the breasts, strain the stock and measure out 900 ml/1½ pints. Add the gelatine to the wine and leave to soak. Remove all traces of fat from the stock, pour into a large clean saucepan, and season well. Add the prepared egg white.

Set the saucepan over a moderate heat and whip the egg white down through the stock. When warm, add the soaked gelatine and wine. Continue to whisk until it reaches boiling point. Draw the pan aside, allow the liquid to settle, then boil it up undisturbed. Repeat the process once more, leave for 5 minutes, then pour it through a scalded cloth or jelly bag. Leave to cool.

Trim and cook the asparagus until just tender. Drain and *refresh*. Cut 6 spears in half lengthways for garnishing. Cut each chicken breast into 4 pieces.

Spoon enough aspic into a shallow dish to cover the bottom and leave this in the refrigerator to set. Mix the cream with the mayonnaise, and spread a little on the pieces of chicken.

Place two pieces of chicken and a spear of asparagus on each slice of gammon, roll up and wrap each roulade in cling film or damp greaseproof paper. Chill in the refrigerator for 15 minutes.

Unwrap the roulades and baste with the cool but still liquid aspic and put half a spear of the reserved asparagus on top of each roulade. Carefully lift the roulades into the shallow serving dish and baste again with the aspic, which should by now be on the point of setting. Leave to set fully.

Garnish the dish with any remaining aspic and keep refrigerated until you are ready to pack it in the picnic hamper or – better still – cold box.

Potato mayonnaise

300 ml/½ pint mayonnaise

1 kg/2 lb potatoes

1 small spring onion, finely chopped

5 ml/1 tsp boiling water

To serve:

1 or 2 heads of chicory, sliced

Make the mayonnaise according to the recipe given in the *Reference Section* on page 140, one or two days in advance if you wish. Scrub and boil the potatoes in their skins. Drain well, then peel and slice them while still hot and mix them carefully with about one-third of the mayonnaise and the spring onion. Dilute and lighten the remainder of the mayonnaise with the boiling water: beat it into the mayonnaise bit by bit.

Serve the potatoes mixed with a little crisp chicory and coat on the spot with the remaining mayonnaise.

Note: Waxy potatoes are always best for potato salads: varieties like Kipfler or small new Maris Piper are excellent.

Salad platter

3 'Little Gem' lettuces

1 kg/2 lb cherry tomatoes

350 g/12 oz French beans

225 ml/7½ fl oz vinaigrette

Trim and wash the lettuce and dry well; wipe the tomatoes. Top and tail the beans, then cut them in half both across and lengthwise. *Blanch* them for 2 minutes, then drain and *refresh*. Arrange the salad in a suitable container: this should be flat, with a lid to hold the ingredients in place until you reach your picnic spot.

Quarter each small lettuce and place it around the rim. Put the tomatoes next, and then finish with the French beans in the middle. Cover and keep cool until you are ready to set off, though do not over-chill in a very cold refrigerator. If the salad container has no lid, cover with clingfilm and then wrap in a tea towel.

Make the dressing according to the method given in the *Reference Section* on page 141: use 75 ml/5 tbls white wine vinegar and 150 ml/¼ pint good salad oil (like sunflower oil) rather than the quantities of vinegar and oil given there. Make the dressing in a screw-topped jar or bottle with enough room to allow for shaking to emulsify the dressing. Dress just before serving.

Gammon roulades à la princesse are exceptionally good to eat: Potato mayonnaise and a Salad platter provide the contrasts that make a perfect accompaniment.

Gâteau ganache

4 egg whites
250 g/9 oz caster sugar
1.25 ml/¼ tsp vanilla essence
2.5 ml/½ tsp white distilled vinegar
120 g/4½ oz ground hazelnuts,
  toasted and browned

For the chocolate sauce:
100 g/4 oz sugar
300 ml/½ pint water
175 g/6 oz plain dessert chocolate
250 ml/8 fl oz double cream

OVEN TEMPERATURE: 190°C/375°F/
  Gas Mark 5

Grease the sides of two 20 cm/ 8 in sandwich tins, then place circles of non-stick silicone paper in the bottom of each. Whisk the egg whites until stiff in a perfectly dry bowl, then beat in the sugar a tablespoon at a time. Add the vanilla essence and vinegar and mix in lightly but thoroughly. Fold in the nuts. Divide the mixture equally between the two tins and bake in the preheated oven for 35 minutes. Turn out and cool on a wire rack.

Next make the sauce. Dissolve the sugar in the water, draw the pan aside and add the chocolate, broken into small pieces. Stir until smooth. Allow to simmer gently for 10-15 minutes. Pour into a bowl and allow to cool. Whip half the cream, and fold 30-45 ml/2-3 tbls of the cooled chocolate sauce into it. Spread this on one round of the cake and cover with the other round. Leave for at least 4 hours, or store it, covered, overnight in the refrigerator. (This period of cool storage will make the cake easier to cut when served.) Whip the remaining cream, place on top of the cake, and quickly spread over the top using a palette knife. Put 30 ml/2 tbls more chocolate sauce on top of the cream, and swirl it into the cream with the palette knife to give a marbled effect. Serve the remaining sauce separately.

Alternatively, if you feel that extra chocolate sauce might be too difficult to serve on your picnic, use up to half the chocolate sauce with the cream initially to fill the centre of the cake, and swirl the rest of the chocolate sauce onto the top of the cake to finish. If you can transport the cake to the picnic in a cold box, it will be easier to cut and serve.

Gâteau ganache, based on hazelnuts and chocolate, is rich in the satisfying elegance that the very best picnic food aspires to.

T his round table or picnic centre is reminiscent of a Victorian posy. It is something that can be both quickly made and easily transported, and it looks and smells enchanting.

You will need a round oasis tray, 23 cm/9 inches in diameter, which you must first immerse in water. Don't soak it for too long: 10 minutes is quite enough. If you don't have or can't obtain one of these, a sandwich tin lined with plastic and filled with damp sand will do just as well, though it will weigh slightly more.

Positioning the blooms
The arrangement was begun by placing the central rose bud (*rosa*), variety Sonia, in the middle of the tray or tin. An edging of ivy (*hedera*) leaves was positioned next to soften the hard rim of the plastic lining, and to protect the fragile flower petals in transit.

A few open tuberose flowers (*polianthes tuberosa*) were added next around the central rose, working in a circle. You only need a small number of these to give a magnificent scent. Then came a small row of yellow roses, variety Spanish Sun, and after that a row of cream spray carnations (*dianthus*). At this point, or at the end, a few sprigs of leather fern (*pteris*) can be added to give a touch of green to the centre.

Finishing the perimeter
Five champagne roses which were rather too open to last in an ordinary arrangement were spaced out around the perimeter, and the areas between these blooms were filled with primrose-coloured single daisy type *chrysanthemum* heads. Spray the whole arrangement regularly with a fine mist of water to keep the flowers damp. If the flowers are in good condition when this decoration is made, and if you spray them conscientiously to keep them moist (especially important if they are sited in full sun) they should last for a week or more.

CHRISTENING TEA

A celebration tea and a glass of champagne
combine to give a fine start to a new life.

MENU

for a party of ten

Smoked Salmon Rolls
Egg and Cress Sandwiches
Cucumber Sandwiches

Walnut Sablés
Walnut Bread

Strawberry Tartlets
Orangines
Meringues Chantilly

Coffee Nut Slices
Chocolate Cake
Christening Cake

Tea

Champagne

ALTHOUGH THE GUEST of honour at a christening tea is generally too young to appreciate the efforts made on his or her behalf, the rest of those invited will certainly do so. This is a splendid spread, a tea worthy of the name: while conceived with a christening in mind, it would be equally successful after any afternoon occasion when something celebratory was called for.

Elements for variety

If a tea is to be really memorable, variety must be put first and foremost: try to plan the meal using as many different elements of flavour and shape as you can. Two groups of predominantly savoury items and two groups of sweet, as here, are generally a good mix: people like to sense a natural progression through the meal, starting with a delicate sandwich and finishing with a piece of celebration cake. Different textures and colours are important: a pretty fruit item (like our strawberry tartlets) is much appreciated in this respect, as are feather-light meringues. If children are going to be present, don't forget to include chocolate cakes, fingers or slices: the technique may be timeworn, but it works, and you will enjoy at least 15 minutes of happy silence!

MEAL PLANNER

● **Five days before:** shop for all the ingredients except the bread, salmon, strawberries and cress. Make the meringues, and store in an airtight tin until ready to fill.

● **Four days before:** prepare the pastry dough for the tartlets: chill. Make the orangines and walnut bread: store in airtight tins.

● **Three days before:** make the walnut sablés: store in an airtight container. Prepare and bake the basic cake mixture for the christening and chocolate cakes. *Blind bake* the strawberry tartlet shells.

● **Two days before:** fill and ice the christening and chocolate cakes. Store in airtight containers.

● **One day before:** do the rest of the shopping. Make and ice the coffee nut slices. Fill the meringues.

● **Final preparation:** fill and glaze the strawberry tartlets. Make the sandwiches last of all, and cover them carefully with cling film until the very last moment to keep them as fresh as possible.

Smoked salmon rolls

100 g/4 oz unsalted butter

1 large wholemeal or wheatmeal loaf

225 g/8 oz smoked salmon trimmings

freshly ground black pepper

½ lemon

Cream the butter on a warm plate until it is very soft. Cut the crust off the bottom and sides of the loaf, butter, and cut in thin slices across the length of the loaf. Cover each slice of bread with smoked salmon, then season with pepper and a few drops of lemon juice.

Cut each slice into two lengthwise and roll up. Arrange the rolls on a plate, cover with cling film until you are ready to serve tea, and keep them cool.

The smoked salmon trimmings used for these rolls are often available at a special price.

Note: When preparing a range of sandwiches, the following are helpful points to bear in mind: always try to keep both the breads and the fillings to be used as varied as possible; make or cut your sandwiches into different shapes if you can; keep the bread thin; be generous with the filling but do not overfill; always keep closely covered with cling film until the very last minute.

A variety of sandwiches, a Smoked salmon roll and a savoury Walnut sablé open this celebration tea in fine style.

Egg and cress sandwiches

8 eggs

265 g/9½ oz butter

30 ml/2 tbls single cream

seasoning

1 large white loaf, cut thinly to give about 20 slices

1 box of cress, trimmed, washed and dried

Boil 4 of the eggs for 8 minutes, cool under running water and peel. Scramble the other 4 eggs with 40 g/1½ oz of butter and the cream, and season to taste. Chop the hard-boiled eggs and mix with the scrambled eggs.

Soften the rest of the butter well and spread thinly on the slices of bread. Spread half the slices generously with the egg mixture, cover with a little cress and another slice of bread. Press the sandwiches together gently and stack, 3 rounds at a time, to cut away the crusts. Cut each round into 4 small sandwiches.

Cucumber sandwiches

1 large *or* 2 small cucumbers

seasoning

225 g/8 oz butter

1 large brown loaf, cut thinly to give about 20 slices

Peel and slice the cucumber and season lightly with salt and pepper. Soften the butter, then butter the slices of bread. Fill the sandwiches, as in the preceding recipe, stack, remove the crusts and cut up each round into small sandwiches.

Walnut sablés

75 g/3 oz butter

75 g/3 oz flour

75 g/3 oz grated cheese

seasoning

1 egg, beaten

25 g/1 oz walnuts, coarsely chopped

rock salt

OVEN TEMPERATURE: 190°C/375°F/ Gas Mark 5

Rub the butter into the sifted flour, then add the cheese and seasoning. Press all the ingredients together into a paste. Roll this out thinly and cut into strips about 5 cm/2 inches wide.

Brush the strips with beaten egg, sprinkle with walnuts and a little freshly ground rock salt, and cut each strip into triangles. Bake in the preheated oven for 10 minutes or until golden brown in colour.

Walnut bread

100 g/4 oz sugar

175 g/6 oz golden syrup

250 ml/8 fl oz milk

50 g/2 oz sultanas

225 g/8 oz plain flour

15 ml/3 tsp baking powder

a pinch of salt

50 g/2 oz chopped walnuts

1 egg, beaten

OVEN TEMPERATURE: 180°C/350°F/ Gas Mark 4

Place the sugar, syrup, milk and sultanas in a saucepan over a low heat and stir until the sugar has dissolved. Tip this mixture into a basin, and allow to cool. While it is cooling, grease and flour a 450 g/1 lb loaf tin.

Sift the flour with the baking powder and salt into a mixing bowl and add the walnuts. Then add the beaten egg to the cooled syrup mixture, blend together and pour into the flour. Mix quickly to a smooth batter, and pour immediately into the prepared tin. Bake in the preheated oven for about 1-1½ hours. Turn the oven down to 160°C/325°F/Gas Mark 3 after 45 minutes. When the cake is cooked, turn it out onto a cake rack to cool thoroughly. Store it in an airtight container. Serve thinly sliced and buttered.

Strawberry tartlets

For the pastry:

100 g/4 oz plain flour

50 g/2 oz butter

50 g/2 oz caster sugar

2 egg yolks

2 drops of vanilla essence

For the filling:

50-75 g/2-3 oz cream cheese

vanilla sugar

150 ml/¼ pint double cream

redcurrant glaze

450 g/1 lb strawberries

OVEN TEMPERATURE: 190°C/375°F/ Gas Mark 5

Prepare the pastry dough according to the recipe method for rich shortcrust pastry in the *Refer-*

Fruit and nuts provide the rich flavours of Walnut bread.

Two Orangines, a Meringue Chantilly, and a Strawberry tartlet make a memorably pretty teaplate for your christening guests.

Meringues Chantilly

4 egg whites
225 g/8 oz caster sugar
a little extra caster sugar

For the filling:
150-300 ml/¼-½ pint double cream
5 ml/1 tsp caster sugar
2-3 drops of vanilla essence

OVEN TEMPERATURE: 140°C/275°F/
Gas Mark 1

Line two baking sheets with non-stick silicone paper. Put the egg whites in a dry mixing bowl and whip until they are stiff. For each egg white, add 5 ml/1 tsp of the measured caster sugar and whisk until the mixture looks like satin. Then fold in the remaining sugar. Shape the mixture into small 5 cm/2 in meringues with two spoons, or force through a bag fitted with a plain 1 cm/½ in eclair pipe, onto the prepared baking sheets. Dredge with the extra sugar and leave for 5 minutes before baking.

Bake in the preheated oven for about 45 minutes or until the meringues lift easily from the paper. Hold each one carefully in the palm of the hand and press in its centre; put back in the oven and continue cooking for 15-20 minutes, or until the meringues are completely dry.

Meanwhile whip the double cream until thick, and fold in the other two filling ingredients. When cold, sandwich the meringues together with this flavoured whipped cream.

Note: These quantities will make 12-16 unfilled meringues, or 6-8 filled meringues of the usual Cordon Bleu size. In this case, slightly smaller meringues were made for an even prettier finish, and the quantities above are sufficient for 12-14 filled meringues. If you wish to make the smaller meringues, remember to shorten the baking time by 10-15 minutes: test after 35 minutes as above.

Coffee nut slices

For the sponge:
2 eggs
75 g/3 oz caster sugar
50 g/2 oz plain flour

For the butter icing:
50 g/2 oz butter
100 g/4 oz icing sugar
instant coffee to colour and flavour

To finish:
almonds, blanched, flaked and
   browned
icing sugar

OVEN TEMPERATURE: 180°C/350°F/
Gas Mark 4

To make the sponge, beat the eggs, add the sugar gradually and then whisk over a gentle heat until thick and mousse-like. Remove from the heat and continue beating until the bowl is quite cold. Fold in the finely sifted flour and turn the mixture at once into a greased, lined tin, measuring 23×13 cm/9×5 inches. Bake in the preheated oven for about 10 minutes. The sponge is done when it begins to shrink slightly from the sides of the tin.

Meanwhile, prepare the butter icing. Cream the butter, then add the finely sifted icing sugar in stages, beating well between each addition. Add the coffee (diluted in a tiny quantity of hot water) to taste.

When the sponge is cold, trim it carefully and spread the top and sides thickly and evenly with butter icing, reserving at least a quarter of it to finish. Cut the whole cake into 2.5 cm/1 inch thick fingers, and coat on all remaining sides of with the rest of the butter icing. Press the flaked browned almonds over the top and sides, dredge with icing sugar and put in a cool place to set.

The photograph of these coffee nut slices is found overleaf.

ence Section on page 142. Line some greased tartlet tins with cut rounds of the pastry dough, prick the bottoms and *bake blind*.

Push the cream cheese through a wire strainer and add vanilla sugar to taste. Beat in the double cream. Make the redcurrant glaze according to the recipe in the *Reference Section* on page 143. When the pastry cases are cold, fill them with the cream cheese mixture, cover with the strawberries, and brush carefully with warm redcurrant glaze.

Orangines

40 g/1½ oz plain flour
50 g/2 oz almonds
50 g/2 oz butter
50 g/2 oz caster sugar
50 g/2 oz candied orange peel
10 ml/2 tsp milk

OVEN TEMPERATURE: 180°C/350°F/
Gas Mark 4

Sift the flour. Peel the almonds (the easiest way to do this is by dropping them into boiling water, then rubbing their skins off), then chop them finely. Soften the butter, add the sugar and beat until white. Add the almonds, peel, flour and milk.

Place the mixture, ½ teaspoon at a time, on greased baking sheets. These quantities will make about 24 orangines, so you may need to bake in batches if you have a small oven or only one or two baking sheets. Flatten each orangine with a wet fork and bake in the preheated oven for 7-8 minutes, or until tinged with brown. Leave to cool for 2-3 minutes before removing and cooling fully. When cool, store in an airtight tin until needed.

Chocolate cake

For the cake:
65 g/2½ oz cocoa
150 ml/¼ pint water
3 eggs
120 g/4½ oz caster sugar
65 g/2½ oz flour

For the butter cream:
50 g/2 oz sugar
60 ml/4 tbls water
2 eggs yolks
175 g/6 oz butter
100 g/4 oz good quality plain chocolate, melted

For the glacé icing:
175 g/6 oz good quality plain chocolate
150 ml/¼ pint water *or* syrup

450 g/1 lb icing sugar
5 ml/1 tsp salad oil
4-5 drops vanilla essence

To finish:
apricot glaze
walnut halves
sifted icing sugar

OVEN TEMPERATURE: 180°C/350°F/ Gas Mark 4

Prepare the cocoa for the cake by working it to a paste in a small saucepan with the water, then stirring it over a medium heat until it cooks down to a cream. Allow to cool. When cool, it should be the consistency of light mud; if it is too thick, add a few drops of cold water.

Whisk the eggs a little, add the sugar and then whisk at high speed until thick and mousse-like. If using a hand whisk, set the basin over a pan of hot water to hasten the thickening process. Fold two-thirds of the flour into the mixture, then add the prepared cocoa and the remaining flour. Turn into a greased and floured 23 cm/9 in mould à manqué tin (or a similarly prepared round sandwich tin of the same dimensions) and bake in the pre-heated oven for 45-50 minutes.

Meanwhile prepare the butter cream: dissolve the sugar in the water in a saucepan over a gentle heat, then boil steadily until the syrup forms a 'thread' between finger and thumb, dipped into the syrup quickly and removed (this will be at 102°C/215°F on a sugar thermometer). Take the saucepan off the heat, and when the bubbles subside, pour the syrup onto the egg yolks, whisking thoroughly until the mixture is thick and mousse-like. Cream the butter and add the egg mousse gradually to this, together with the chocolate.

To prepare the glacé icing, break the chocolate into small pieces and place it in a saucepan with the water or sugar syrup. Dissolve over a gentle heat and then bring it just to the boil. Allow it to cool slightly and beat in the finely sifted icing sugar, a spoonful at a time, together with the oil and the vanilla essence. Keep the mixture warm.

When the cake is cool, split it in two and sandwich it with a layer of chocolate-flavoured butter cream, reserving a little for the final decoration. Make the apricot glaze according to the recipe in the *Reference Section* on page 143, and keep warm. Brush over the top and sides of the cake with a thin coating of the glaze.

When it has set, ice with chocolate glacé icing and leave to set. Decorate with rosettes of the reserved chocolate butter cream. Sprinkle half the walnuts with icing sugar and arrange on top of the cake alternating them with unsprinkled walnuts.

Christening cake

350 g/12 oz butter
the rind of ½ lemon, grated
350 g/12 oz caster sugar
6 eggs
350 g/12 oz self-raising flour, sifted
a pinch of salt
a little milk
225 g/8 oz lemon curd
225 g/8 oz apricot glaze
750 g/1½ lb commercial or ready-prepared fondant icing
30-45 ml/2-3 tbls sugar syrup
a little lemon juice, strained

For the royal icing:
1 small egg white
175 g/6 oz icing sugar, sifted

To finish:
1.35 m/1½ yards ribbon

OVEN TEMPERATURE: 180°C/350°F/ Gas Mark 4

Line a greased 26 cm/10½ in moule à manqué or sandwich tin with a disc of greased grease-proof paper. If you can cut this from a butter wrapper or wrappers, so much the better since it is ready-greased.

Beat the butter with a wooden spoon or an electric mixer in a warm bowl until soft. Then add the lemon rind and the sugar gradually, and when the mixture is light in colour start adding the eggs, one at a time; beat thoroughly between the addition of each egg. Then fold in the flour and salt with a large spoon, about a third at a time. Add just enough milk to give the mixture a dropping consistency.

Turn the mixture into the prepared tin, spread quickly with a palette knife, and bake on the middle shelf of the preheated oven for 45-50 minutes. When it is cooked, cool it on a rack, then split and fill with lemon curd. Make the apricot glaze according to the recipe in the *Reference Section* on page 143: reassemble the cake, brush with the apricot glaze, and leave it to set.

Prepare the fondant icing, if

Coffee nut slices provide the background for this superb Chocolate cake, finished with both butter cream and chocolate glacé icing.

necessary, according to the manufacturer's instructions. Prepare a little sugar syrup according to the recipe in the *Reference Section* on page 143 if you do not already have some. Work the fondant icing over a gentle heat in a saucepan with the lemon juice and the 30-45 ml/2-3 tbls of sugar syrup until easy to pour. Tip onto the cake and spread it quickly over the top and down the sides. Leave to set.

To make the royal icing, whip the egg white to a froth and then beat in the icing sugar a little at a time until it has all been absorbed. Then beat well again until the icing will stand in peaks.

Make a paper piping bag according to the instructions below. When ready, cut off the end and drop in a No.1 or 2 writing tube. Put in a small quantity of icing, write the baby's name on a piece of ribbon 20 cm/8 inches long, and leave this to set. (As there will be plenty of royal icing to spare, practice this first on greasesproof paper.) Next, tie two separate bows of ribbon, one a little larger than the other. Either tie a floral garland (ordered from your local florist) or a long length of ribbon round the cake, and place the name ribbon across the top. Fix the prepared bows at each end.

To prepare a paper piping bag:

1. Take a 25 cm/10 in square of greaseproof paper, fold it corner to corner, and cut along the fold into two triangles.
2. Hold one of the triangles with its longest side at the bottom, and fold the right hand point up to meet the centre point. Hold these two points together.
3. Bring the third point of the triangle (the left hand point) across and around the bag so that this point meets the others at the back of the centre point.
4. Fold over the flap formed where all the points meet the top of the cone to prevent the bag from unfolding.
5. Cut the point off the tip of the bag, and fit the nozzle.

Celebration Pedestal Group

A black urn on a mahogany pedestal was used for this formal christening arrangement. The vase has a shallow lining, so when you fill it with wire make sure that the netting is well domed to support the woody stems. Make sure, too, that the pedestal is standing straight and firm on the floor surface before filling the vase with water: top up when the arrangement is complete.

Varieties and outlines
The materials used here are laurustinus (*viburnum tinus*), *mahonia japonica*, *aralia*, trails of ivy (*hedera*), eucalyptus (*myrtaceae*), guelder rose (*viburnum opulus*), white lilac (*syringa*), tuberose (*polianthes tuberosa*), white hyacinths (*hyacinthus*), yellow lilies (*lilium*) variety Connecticut King, and cream and spray carnations (*dianthus*).

Begin by setting the outline points. The first stem should be placed three-quarters of the way back in the vase to give the arrangement balance. When placing the side pieces, let them fall downwards over the sides of the vase. Try to find materials that have natural curves to use in this way. Place a front stem curving low down, approximately half to three-quarters the length of the first tall outline stem placed in the vase initially. Stand well back and check the outline shape before filling in with other materials. Complete any missing outline with lighter coloured materials.

Filling the centre
Begin filling in the centre, next, with heavier or darker material to give the arrangement a focal point. All the materials placed in the centre of the arrangement should radiate out from the base of the first stem.

In this group, the laurustinus, eucalyptus and ivy trails create an outline and the mahonia and aralia have been used to fill in the centre. Always try to use a few of the outline materials through the centre as well so that the overall colouring and pattern doesn't give an impression of being too schematic. One of the basic principles of good arranging is that monotony should be avoided at all costs, and any arrangement that looks too symmetrical or perfect will give one an overall impression of monotony.

Varying shapes and sizes
Make sure that the foliage complements the flowers. Try to find different shapes and sizes of leaves to make the arrangement interesting. Once the foliage is complete, fill in with the flowers, following the outline of the arrangement and grouping heads loosely together.

The white flowers show up particularly well; yellow lilies are positioned in the centre, and the guelder rose has a prominent place thanks to its interesting shape and colour. Make sure the flowers, like the foliage, have different shapes wherever possible, and vary all the lengths of the stems, placing the larger blooms deeper down in the vase.

PASSOVER DINNER

First and foremost, a Passover dinner is a family affair, and these dishes will prove as popular
for any special family meal as they are at Passover time in Jewish homes.

J EWISH PEOPLE ARE renowned for their great sense of family and strong instinct for hospitality, and the Passover meal is the most important of their celebratory family meals. There is, of course, no need for you to be of the Jewish faith to enjoy a special family celebration, any more than you need to be American to tuck into a Thanksgiving turkey. This is, quite simply, a varied and delicious menu.

Ritual elements to the meal

A Passover meal for a Jewish family is also a religious service (the service takes place with everyone sitting around the table before and after the meal) and this explains the various symbolic items seen in the photograph opposite. The silver cup on the sideboard, for example, is called the Elijah cup, and is placed there to provide a symbolic welcome for passers-by and wayfarers; the three matzos biscuits covered and separated by the napkin next to it commemorate the manna that the Israelites received in the desert. Water can be seen in a jug on the sideboard for the father of the family to wash his hands in before, during and after the service. In the centre of the table is a seder plate containing six symbolic items: a white jug full of salt water can be seen, standing for the tears shed by the captive Jewish tribes in Egypt, and next to it parsley, to symbolise a new life

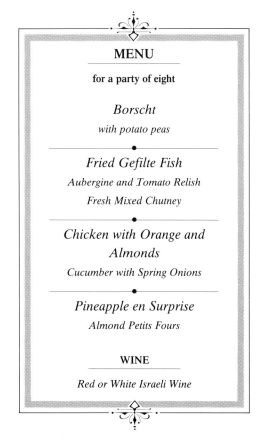

MENU

for a party of eight

Borscht

with potato peas

Fried Gefilte Fish

Aubergine and Tomato Relish

Fresh Mixed Chutney

---

*Chicken with Orange and
Almonds*

Cucumber with Spring Onions

Pineapple en Surprise

Almond Petits Fours

WINE

Red or White Israeli Wine

(Passover is a spring feast). After the parsley comes a roasted egg, a traditional paschal offering, and after that horseradish (both whole and grated) to stand for the bitterness

of slavery in Egypt. The lamb's shankbone symbolises the paschal offering itself, and the charoseth next to it (a mixture of grated apple, nuts, spice and red wine) stands for the clay bricks and mortar used by the Israelites in slavery to build Pharaoh's cities. At each place setting is a haggadah: this is the book from which the passover service is read. To the left of each place setting are sliced hard-boiled eggs in salt water: the salt water symbolises, again, the tears of slavery, while the egg symbolises the first new life. These eggs traditionally are eaten as a first course.

Kosher food

This meal is 'kosher', which means that everything in it fulfills the requirements of Jewish food law. There is nothing 'different' about kosher food: in practical terms, it just means that various food items (like yeast, peas and beans) are *not* used in the meal at certain times of the year.

Israeli wine

Israeli wines are made in accordance with kosher laws, too, and so they are pasteurised to kill off any yeast remaining in the wine after fermentation. This is not as drastic a procedure as it might sound: one of the finest merchant houses of Burgundy is famous for pasteurising its wines in the same way!

MEAL PLANNER

● **Two days before:** do all the shopping except for the fish and watercress. Make the chutney, the aubergine and tomato relish, the petits fours and chicken stock.

● **The day before:** buy the fish and the watercress. Make the soup. Prepare and cook the gefilte fish balls: drain well, and allow to cool fully. Cover and store in the refrigerator overnight.

● **The morning:** prepare the cucumber and spring onions: do not cook yet. Prepare the pineapple, fruit and glacé strawberries for the pineapple en surprise: do not assemble. Make the potato garnish: store in cold water.

● **Final preparation:** Cook the chicken and prepare its garnish. Assemble the pineapple en surprise. Reheat the soup. When the first two courses are eaten, cook the cucumber and spring onions. Finish the chicken dish.

Borscht provides a light, colourful opening for this special evening meal: serve with a simple potato garnish.

Fried gefilte fish

1 kg/2 lb mixed white fish (such as haddock, sea bream or whiting), filleted and skinned

1 small onion

1 egg, beaten

seasoning

45 ml/3 tbls matzo meal

extra matzo meal

vegetable oil

For the garnish:

watercress

Mince the fish and onion together. Add the beaten egg, season well, then mix in the matzo meal. Form the mixture into apricot-sized balls and roll in matzo meal. Fry the fish balls in hot, shallow oil until they are deep brown on all sides. Drain well on paper towels. Serve cold, garnished with watercress.

Aubergine and tomato relish

1 small aubergine

1 shallot, finely chopped

60 ml/4 tbls olive oil

15 ml/1 tbls lemon juice

seasoning

2-3 tomatoes, skinned, cored and deseeded

OVEN TEMPERATURE: 190°C/375°F/ Gas Mark 5

Wrap the aubergine carefully in oiled greaseproof paper and bake in the preheated oven until soft: this will take about 20 minutes. When cool enough to handle, remove the skin, chop the flesh, and put it into a mixing bowl. Add the shallot, oil, lemon juice and seasoning. Dice the tomato and mix into the aubergine mixture.

Borscht

1 kg/2 lb shin of beef

1.75 litres/3 pints water

1 kg/2 lb raw beetroot

50 g/2 oz sugar

30 ml/2 tbls lemon juice

seasoning

For the garnish:

2 large potatoes, peeled

Shred the beef with a sharp knife or chop in a food processor and place in a large saucepan with the cold water. Slowly bring to boiling point then simmer very gently for 2 hours. Remove from the heat and allow to cool.

Peel and grate the beetroot and add to the beef stock with the sugar and lemon juice. Bring to the boil and simmer very gently until the beetroot colour has left the vegetables and passed into the broth. Strain the soup, and season to taste.

Next prepare the garnish. Using a melon scoop, cut out pea-sized pieces of potato, then steam or boil them until tender. Reheat the soup, and serve with the potato garnish.

Fried gefilte fish is perfectly matched by the light, piquant flavours of Aubergine and tomato relish and Fresh mixed chutney.

Fresh mixed chutney

1 sharp eating apple (such as a Granny Smith), peeled, cored and roughly chopped

1 shallot, grated

1 tomato, skinned, seeded and chopped

1 stick celery, chopped

1 small red pepper, seeded, chopped and *blanched*

5 ml/1 tsp chopped mint

5 ml/1 tsp grated horseradish

15 ml/1 tbls sugar

pinch of salt

10-15 ml/2-3 tsp lemon juice

Heat all the ingredients together until they reach boiling point. Cool, and serve cold.

Note: This chutney will keep for up to a week if kept cool, and is very good served with cold meat of all sorts. It would make a good standby for the family refrigerator over the Christmas and Easter periods, or for Passover and the Jewish New Year.

Chicken with orange and almonds

600 ml/1 pint chicken stock

2.75 kg/6 lb roasting chicken

salt

freshly ground black pepper

75 g/3 oz Tomor *or* chicken fat

3 sprigs of tarragon

the rind and juice of 1 large orange

15 ml/1 tbsp potato flour

To finish:

50 g/2 oz flaked almonds

3 oranges, cut in segments

OVEN TEMPERATURE: 190°C/375°F/
Gas Mark 5

Make the chicken stock according to the recipe in the *Reference Section* on page 138, one or two days in advance, if possible.

Season the inside of the bird with salt and freshly ground black pepper, add a nut of the fat, the tarragon and the thinly pared orange rind. Truss the chicken well and place it in a roasting tin. Spread the rest of the fat over the breast and legs, and pour the orange juice and 150 ml/¼ pt of stock around the bird in the tin. Cover with a piece of grease-proof paper and place in the preheated oven.

After 30 minutes, baste well, turn onto one side, and baste again: replace the paper and return to the oven. Baste every 20 minutes, adding extra stock as necessary to prevent the fat and orange juice from burning. After 40 minutes on one side, turn and cook the bird on the other side in the same way.

Carefully turn the chicken breast side up and cut the trussing strings that hold the legs. Baste well and add a little more stock if necessary, but this time discard the greaseproof paper. Turn the oven down to 180°C/350°F/Gas Mark 4 and cook for another 20 minutes.

Check that the bird is cooked by piercing the thigh with a trussing needle or the point of a small sharp knife. The juice that runs

As good to eat as it is to look at, Chicken with orange and almonds is shown partnered by Cucumber with spring onions: a delicate and refreshing combination.

out should be quite clear; if it is pink, cook for a further 15-20 minutes.

Take the chicken out of the oven, remove all the trussing string, cut off the wing pinions with kitchen scissors or poultry shears, and trim the drumsticks with poultry shears. Lift the chicken onto a hot dish and cover with a clean tea towel wrung out in boiling water.

Deglaze the roasting tin by adding the rest of the stock a little at a time, scraping the sides and bottom of the tin and bringing back to the boil each time. When all the stock has been used in deglazing, strain into a saucepan. Add the potato flour, mixed to a paste with a little cold water, to this, and then stir until boiling. Check the seasoning, and add about half the almonds to the sauce. Spoon some of the sauce over the chicken, garnishing the dish with the rest of the almonds and the orange segments. Serve the rest of the sauce separately in a sauceboat.

Note: This is a delicious chicken dish, and it is well worth the effort of acquiring a really first-rate fresh chicken for the recipe. For an even better flavour (though this would not be according to Jewish food laws, and hence not kosher) use butter instead of the Tomor or chicken fat specified.

Cucumber with spring onions

2 cucumbers

2 bunches of spring onions

25 g/1 oz Tomor *or* 15 ml/1 tbls olive oil

seasoning

15 ml/1 tbls chopped parsley

Peel the cucumbers, cut them into round 2 cm/¾ in slices and cut out the seeds with a knife. Cut the spring onions into 4 cm/1½ in lengths.

To cook, *blanch* the cucumber and onions together in boiling water for 2-3 minutes, then drain and return to the pan with the Tomor or olive oil. Season, then cover and cook for 3-4 minutes. Add the parsley and serve.

Pineapple en surprise

1 large ripe pineapple
450 g/1 lb strawberries
caster sugar for dusting
30 ml/2 tbls red Israeli wine

For the garnish:
a few extra strawberries
225 g/8 oz sugar
45 ml/3 tbls water

Use a serrated knife to cut the top off the pineapple. Hollow out the flesh using a grapefruit knife, and remove the tough core from the flesh.

Cut the pineapple flesh into neat pieces. Wipe all the strawberries, and hull them all except for a dozen or so of the most handsome, to be reserved for the garnish. Mix the hulled strawberries with the pineapple pieces, then dust all with sugar and sprinkle with the wine. Cover and leave for about 1 hour in the refrigerator.

Meanwhile prepare the garnish, using the previously reserved berries. Dry them well. Place the sugar in a small pan with the water and dissolve it over a low heat, keeping the sides of the saucepan free of sugar crystals by washing them down with a clean pastry brush dipped in cold water. Increase the heat under the pan and boil until the syrup just begins to look straw coloured at the sides of the pan (154°C/310°F on a sugar thermometer). Immediately remove the saucepan from the heat, dip the base in cold water to check the cooking, and then stand it in a small bowl of hand-hot water.

Hold the reserved strawberries by their hulls and dip them one at a time into the syrup. Place them on an oiled dish or marble slab and leave them to set.

When ready to serve, place the pineapple shell on a glass plate and fill with the sweetened pineapple and strawberries. Surround it with the glacé strawberries and serve, if you wish, with almond petits fours.

Note: This is a splendidly handsome dessert, always popular with children, and ideal to finish a special late spring or summer menu. If you omit the glacé strawberries it can be prepared very quickly and easily.

Almond petits fours

225 g/8 oz ground almonds
175 g/6 oz caster sugar
4 egg whites
15 ml/1 tbls icing sugar, sifted
almond essence
split almonds
glacé cherries
angelica

OVEN TEMPERATURE: 180°C/350°F/ Gas Mark 4

Mix the almonds and sugar together and pass all through a wire strainer. Reserve 5 ml/1 tsp of the egg white and place it in a small bowl with the icing sugar. Whisk the rest of the egg whites until stiff, add the sifted almond and sugar mixture and almond essence, and put in a nylon forcing bag fitted with an 8-cut vegetable rose pipe or star nozzle.

Pipe the mixture into various shapes onto a baking tin lined with non-stick silicone paper, and decorate each one with an almond, cherry or piece of angelica. Bake in the preheated oven for about 12-15 minutes. As soon as the petits fours are cooked and pale brown in colour, add 5 ml/1 tsp of water to the reserved egg white and icing sugar mixture and quickly brush this over the tops of the petit fours with a pastry brush.

Strawberries and pineapple dressed in red wine make a Pineapple en surprise, and Almond petits fours accompany the fruit in suitably elegant style.

Note: These petits fours keep well in an airtight tin. They are always welcome on their own or with mid-morning coffee, and make very pretty presents at any time of the year.

Mixed Spring Stems For A Sideboard

For our Passover meal, we have chosen an appropriately seasonal spring arrangement. A chalice-shaped Italian pottery vase has been chosen to stand on the sideboard. It is always a good idea to use a tall vase on a stem when space is short: low trails and sprays can then be tucked in under the flowers, as some of our varieties have been here, to give an impression of spaciousness.

Using spring stems
Spring flowers are not the easiest to arrange, as many of them have such straight stems. Simplicity is the key to this arrangement: keep the overall lines flowing smoothly and easily.

Hazel catkins (*corylus avellana*) and *forsythia* form the outline: set these in place first of all. Ivy leaves (*hedera*) are put in place next, and are used to hide the wire netting and break up the hard rim of the vase. The flowers in this spring group are narcissi (*narcissus*), varieties Soleil d'Or, Primo and Ice Follies; tulip (*tulipa*), variety Apricot Beauty; and hyacinth (*hyacinthus*), variety Myosotis.

Arranging spring flowers
The hyacinths go into the vase next, so that their thick stems are held firmly by the netting. As they tend to be short in the stem and rather heavy-looking, keep them to the centre of the vase. Narcissi look best with their own foliage, so add some of these green spikes to the flower stems, held to them with an elastic band so that they go into the netting easily. Fill in any remaining gaps with the tulips, but do not overfill: the group should look light and delicate overall, so space is needed between the flower heads.

ST. VALENTINE'S DAY DINNER

Something very special is in the air on St. Valentine's Day:
this intimate dinner for two will nourish romance as only the finest food can.

A DINNER FOR TWO ON St. Valentine's Day is a unique occasion. It gives you a chance to cook something lighthearted yet very delicious: something that will say what you'd like to say, while prompting what you'd like to hear. It is a personal meal, though at the same time traditional; it is highly romantic, though it should satisfy the appetite, too!

Our menu takes all these points into account, looking to the practical side of things for the cook, as well as ensuring a romantic atmosphere for the lucky guest. Several of the dishes can be prepared in advance, and the cooking techniques need only a little extra care and attention, rather than advanced know-how.

Setting the atmosphere
This is a dinner where candles are of great importance. Romantic pinks and pastels pro-

MENU

for a dinner for two

Spinach Creams

•

Lobster au Gratin Cordon Bleu
Paprika Rice
Mixed Salad

•

Gâteaux à la Reine

WINE

Champagne

vide natural colour themes, and flowers should be much in evidence: try making the simple flower holder napkins shown (see the *Reference Secton*, page 147). Champagne suggests itself as the wine of the evening: it will accompany any of the courses happily.

MEAL PLANNER

● **Two days before:** do all the shopping, except the lobsters. Prepare the choux pastry and praline.

● **One day before:** Make the spinach creams and their sauce. Buy the lobster and prepare the rice, if you wish. Prepare the filling for the choux hearts, and finish them.

● **The day:** prepare the lobster: grill when you are ready to eat. Reheat or prepare rice and spinach. Grill bacon; prepare salad.

Spinach creams

150 ml/¼ pint béchamel sauce
450 g/1 lb fresh spinach
1 egg
150 ml/¼ pint double cream
seasoning
freshly grated nutmeg
pinch of paprika
lemon juice

For the garnish:
4 rashers thin cut unsmoked
    streaky bacon

OVEN TEMPERATURE: 180°C/350°F/
    Gas Mark 4

Prepare the béchamel sauce according to the recipe in the *Reference Section* on page 140: place a butter wrapper on the surface to prevent a skin forming and allow to cool.

Wash the spinach and then *blanch* the leaves for 3 minutes in a large saucepan of boiling water. Drain, *refresh*, then spin in a salad dryer or carefully press the leaves between 2 plates to remove any excess water. Use 4-8 spinach leaves (depending on their size) to line 4 buttered aluminium dariole moulds. (If you do not have dariole moulds use large ramekin dishes.)

Place the remaining spinach and cold béchamel sauce in a blender or food processor and process until smooth. Add the egg and 15 ml/1 tbls of the cream. Season with salt, pepper and freshly grated nutmeg. Spoon the mixture into the prepared moulds and cover each with a small piece of buttered greaseproof paper.

Stand the moulds in a bain marie, and cook them in the preheated oven for 15-20 minutes. (If you do not have a bain marie, put them in a roasting tin and fill with water half-way up the sides of the moulds.)

Boil the remaining cream, with a pinch of paprika, until it begins

to *reduce* and thicken. Season with a little salt and lemon juice. Remove the rind from the bacon, and flatten out the rashers with the blade of a heavy knife. Cut each piece into two and grill until crisp and brown. Drain on kitchen paper and keep warm.

Remove the dariole moulds from the bain marie or roasting tin and allow them to stand for 2-3 minutes. Turn onto individual plates, but do not remove the moulds yet. Wipe away any moisture from the plates.

Just before serving, lift off the moulds, pour a ribbon of cream around each spinach parcel and garnish with the crisp bacon.

Spinach creams are garnished with small slices of thin, crisp bacon and served with a lightly seasoned cream sauce. (Recipe on page 103.)

Lobster au gratin Cordon Bleu

2 small lobsters, cooked
450 g/1 lb ripe tomatoes
30 ml/2 tbls olive oil
1 shallot, finely chopped
65 ml/2½ fl oz dry sherry
10 ml/2 tsp tomato purée
5 ml/1 tsp chopped fresh tarragon
5 ml/1 tsp chopped fresh chervil
seasoning
150 ml/¼ pint double cream
22.5-30 ml/1½-2 tbls Cheddar cheese, grated
30 ml/2 tbls melted butter

Split the lobsters, remove the sack from the top of the head and the dark thread running through the tail. Crack the claws and remove the meat from the body, tail and claws; chop coarsely and set aside.

Scald and skin the tomatoes, cut them into quarters, remove the seeds and shred the flesh. Heat the oil in a small frying pan, add the shallot and cook very

gently for 3-5 minutes. Draw the pan aside, *flame* with the sherry and add the shredded tomatoes, tomato purée, herbs and seasoning. Return to the heat and simmer for 10 minutes. Take the pan off the heat, and add the cream and lobster flesh. Mix gently and adjust the seasoning.

Spoon the mixture into the lobster shells, sprinkle the tops with the grated cheese and melted butter. Heat and brown under the grill, then serve immediately.

Mixed salad

a little vinaigrette dressing
radicchio leaves
chicory leaves

Make the vinaigrette dressing according to the recipe in the *Reference Section* on page 141. Lightly dress some radicchio and chicory leaves with the dressing, and arrange in individual bowls.

Paprika rice

Note: Paprika is generally sold as one of two types: sweet or hot. Sweet is best for this recipe, as it will colour the rice without making it very hot to eat. The best paprika comes from Hungary; Spanish paprika can also be good.

150 g/5 oz long grain rice, dry weight
15 g/½ oz butter
10 ml/2 tsp sweet paprika

Put the rice into a pan of boiling salted water and cook for between 12 and 20 minutes, or until almost soft. Drain, and allow the rice to steam dry.

Heat the butter in a frying pan, add the paprika, and fry very gently for a few seconds. Add the rice, and fork the paprika through to give a uniform colour.

Reheating rice: If you wish to save time, you could prepare the rice in advance and then reheat it as described on page 82. Add butter and paprika at the last minute.

Gâteaux à la reine

choux dough made with 2 eggs
1 egg, beaten
15 ml/1 tbls icing sugar

For the praline:

65 g/2½ oz unblanched almonds
75 g/3 oz caster sugar

To finish:

150 ml/¼ pint double cream
vanilla sugar
65 ml/2½ fl oz thick custard
225 g/8 oz strawberries
icing sugar

OVEN TEMPERATURE: 190°C/375°F/ Gas Mark 5

Prepare the choux pastry according to the recipe in the *Reference Section* on page 142. Lightly butter 4 heart-shaped moulds and half fill with the prepared choux

Sherry, tomatoes and freshly chopped herbs distinguish Lobster au gratin Cordon Bleu: Paprika rice and a Mixed salad provide the perfect foil.

pastry. Smooth the tops with the back of a metal spoon, dipped in beaten egg. Sprinkle lightly with icing sugar.

Place the moulds in the pre-heated oven, and after 10 minutes increase the temperature to 200°C/400°F/Gas Mark 6 and bake for a further 15 minutes until crisp. Meanwhile, make the praline: begin by lightly oiling a shallow metal baking tin. Next, place the unblanched almonds and sugar in a small heavy pan over a gentle heat. When the sugar has become a light liquid caramel, stir gently with a metal spoon to brown the nuts on all sides. Turn the hot caramel/nut mixture out onto the baking tin and allow it to cool. When cold, crush the praline with a rolling pin or grind in a food processor.

Split the choux pastries and remove and discard any soft dough-like mixture from the centres. Whip the cream with the vanilla sugar. Make the custard (using custard powder) to double its normal thickness, and beat it well as it cools. Stir the custard and crushed praline into the cream. Use this mixture to fill each pastry. Halve the strawberries, and put the halves on top of the cream filling. Replace each top and dust with icing sugar.

The pale shades of our St. Valentine's Day arrangement have been chosen to complement both the food and the occasion. Artichoke (*cynara scolymus*), *helichrysum petiolatum, senecio greyi* and *eucalyptus* provide the foliage, with blooms of chincherinchee (*ornithogalum thyrsoides*), hyacinths (*hyacinthus*), orchids (*dendro-bium*), *anemones*, carnations (*dianthus*), and heather (*erica*) providing delicate pastel colours.

Begin the arrangement by taping a little netting to the top of the cherub vase. Position the foliage: fan the artichoke leaves out from the centre, and place the helichrysum on the left hand side at the bottom. Fix senecio above this, bringing more leaves across the top. Set the width with the eucalyptus on the right and at the front.

Begin arranging the blooms with the chincherinchee at the top and the sides, and the hyacinths for weight at the centre. Set the orchids in a diagonal from top right to bottom left, and fill out with anemones, carnations, and a little heather.

CHRISTMAS ENTERTAINING

Warmth, generosity and the festive spirit are part and parcel of the traditional family Christmas:
new and well-loved ideas mingle in three balanced, memorable meals.

Christmas comes but once a year, the saying runs, and so often it's the only occasion when all the family can be together to enjoy one another's company. Cooking successfully for large numbers over a period of two or three days can be trying for the cook, though: advance preparation wherever possible is the best way to cope, and our **Meal Planner** will be a great boon here. Make sure that your store cupboards are well-filled, so that you are able to cater for the unexpected: a spell of snowy weather, surprise guests, or a day out with packed lunches to prepare. Check that you have enough large serving plates to accommodate all the food for the meals you plan; and if possible arrange some overlap on stocks of ordinary plates, bowls and cutlery to tide you over, if need be, from one meal to the next. Get the family to help in the kitchen if they will; if not, making the garlands and swags described on page 113 could be great fun for everyone, from oldest to youngest.

Christmas Eve and Boxing Day
The Christmas Eve and Boxing Day meals described and illustrated on pages 111 and 112 have been designed to complement the main Christmas Day meal. The food for Christmas Eve is appropriately simple to prepare and light to eat, and our Boxing Day meal draws inventively – though by no means exclusively – on the rest of the turkey.

At Christmas, the food itself is the centre-piece, and time is generally too short for finely detailed flower arrangements. Candles, though, quickly establish the right atmosphere, and your best plates and cutlery will be recognized and enjoyed by the whole family.

Wines for the Christmas period
The Christmas period is a time for favourite wines, and sherry and port will open and

MENU

for a party of ten

Grilled Grapefruit

Roast Turkey
with Chestnut and Sausage Stuffing
and Apple and Raisin Stuffing

Fondant Potatoes
Brussels Sprouts
Cranberry Sauce
Bread Sauce

Christmas Pudding
with Brandy Butter

Croquembouche
of Chocolate Meringues
Fresh Fruit Salad
Mince Pies

WINES

Fino Sherry

Claret (red Bordeaux)

Port

close the meal perfectly. A cabernet sauvignon wine, like claret, will accompany the turkey well, and is always popular. Not everyone will want to drink on Christmas Eve, so we have not suggested a wine, though a favourite white would be an obvious choice. Provencal rosé is just the thing for Boxing Day.

MEAL PLANNER

● **Early November:** make the Christmas puddings and boil them. Make and freeze any of the following: mince pies, cranberry sauce, brandy butter, relishes, Christmas Eve dishes, angel cake.

● **One week before:** do all shopping for the non-fresh ingredients and salt beef. Make the chocolate meringues: freeze them if cream-filled, or store in an airtight tin if unfilled. Begin spicing the beef.

● **Three days before:** shop for the basic fresh ingredients. Make mince pies if not already frozen. Prepare brandy butter and cranberry sauce. Remove the giblets from a fresh turkey and make the turkey stock. Make the tomato and rice soup. Make and bake the angel cake if not already frozen.

● **Two days before:** begin defrosting a frozen turkey at room temperature. Make the stuffings. Cook, drain and press the beef.

● **Christmas Eve:** do last minute shopping. Make the fruit salad, omitting strawberries and bananas. Make the gravy; prepare the sprouts and potatoes. Serve the Christmas Eve Dinner. Stuff the bird.

● **Christmas Day:** prepare the grapefruit, croquembouche mound, and fruit salad. Begin cooking the turkey. Steep the milk for the bread sauce, and begin the final boiling of the pudding. Begin cooking the vegetables and sauces. Let the turkey rest while you grill and eat the grapefruit, then finish the vegetables and sauces while the bird is being carved.

● **Boxing Day:** fill and decorate the angel cake. Prepare the relishes and fricassée.

Grilled grapefruit

For each half grapefruit allow:

15 ml/1 tbls sweet sherry

10 ml/2 tsp soft light brown sugar

10 g/¼ oz butter

Prepare the halved grapefruit carefully, removing the core and pips and slicing between each segment. Sprinkle each half with the sherry (this can be done several hours before the meal) and set the grapefruit halves in a flameproof dish ready for grilling.

Preheat the grill to high. Sprinkle the sugar over the grapefruit halves and dot each with butter, then grill them in the flameproof dish until the sugar on top of the fruit is lightly caramelized. Serve immediately.

Roast turkey

1 × 6.5 kg/14 lb fresh turkey, *or*
1 × 4.5 kg/10 lb frozen turkey, defrosted

175-225 g/6-8 oz butter

1.2 litres/2 pints turkey stock

30 ml/2 tbls flour

To garnish:

225 g/8 oz rashers of streaky bacon, rolled

450 g/1 lb chipolata sausages

watercress

OVEN TEMPERATURE: 180°C/350°F/ Gas Mark 4

Make the stuffings and stock (see recipes below) for the bird one or two days in advance. Late on Christmas Eve, stuff the bird: place the chestnut and sausage stuffing in the vent end. Truss the legs together with string. Loosen the neck skin and push the apple and raisin stuffing well into the breast cavity from the neck end. Pull the skin gently over the stuffing and fasten in under the wing tips, using a skewer to hold it firm. Refrigerate overnight.

On Christmas morning, rub half the butter over the bird and the rest of the butter over a large double sheet of greaseproof paper or a single sheet of foil. Lay the buttered sheet over the bird and pour round 300 ml/½ pint of stock. Cook in the preheated oven for 4½ hours, beginning the roasting of the bird on its back, turning and basting every hour, and finishing the roasting of the bird the right way up. After 1½ hours, when the bird is breast upwards, cut the string holding the legs together. At the end of 4 hours, remove the foil or paper to brown the bird.

To check if the bird is cooked, pierce the thigh with a thin skewer: if the juice runs out clear and not pink, the bird is ready. Plan to remove the turkey from the oven half an hour before you carve.

Set the turkey on a serving dish, remove any remaining trussing strings and the skewer and cover the bird with a clean tea towel wrung out in very hot water. Put it in a warm place for at least half an hour.

Meanwhile drain the juices from the roasting tin, and skim off some of the fat. Mix this fat with the flour. Place the cooking juices in a saucepan with the remaining turkey stock, reserving a little to mix with the fat and flour paste. Heat, add the fat and flour mixture and stir until boiling. Check the seasoning and simmer for 5-10 minutes. Serve, garnished with the bacon rolls and sausages: these may be cooked in a separate baking tin with the turkey for the last hour of its

cooking period. Finish the garnish with the watercress. Serve with Brussels sprouts and fondant potatoes, prepared according to the recipes given in the Autumn Dinner, page 20.

Note: Time can be saved on Christmas Day if the gravy is prepared beforehand, using turkey stock. Add the cooking juices when ready.

Chestnut and sausage stuffing

600 ml/1 pint veal stock

225 g/8 oz dried chestnuts *or*
450 g/1 lb fresh chestnuts

1 stick celery, chopped

seasoning

1 large onion

50 g/2 oz butter

225 g/8 oz pork sausage meat

50 g/2 oz fresh breadcrumbs

Make the veal stock according to the recipe in the *Reference Section* on page 138, well in advance if possible. If you wish to use dried chestnuts, cover them with boiling water and soak overnight. Remove the shells from fresh chestnuts, if using, with a sharp knife, then blanch and peel off the inner skin.

Place the prepared chestnuts in a saucepan with enough stock to cover them; add the chopped celery and seasoning. Cook for about 30 minutes until the chestnuts are quite tender, then *reduce* away any remaining stock; tip into a bowl to cool. If you prefer a smooth-textured stuffing, mash the chestnuts well.

Meanwhile, chop the onion finely, and cook in the butter until soft. When cool, add to the sausage meat. Work in the chestnuts and enough breadcrumbs to bind. The stuffing is now ready to use in the turkey.

Roast turkey with two stuffings takes centre stage at Christmas lunch. The garnishes are traditional – and all the better for being so, the family will say.

Apple and raisin stuffing

2 medium onions
75 g/3 oz butter
225 g/8 oz breadcrumbs
1 stick celery, finely chopped
2 dessert apples, diced
50 g/2 oz raisins, chopped
15 ml/1 tbls chopped parsley
5 ml/1 tsp dried mixed herbs
salt
freshly ground black pepper
15 ml/1 tbls milk

Chop the onions finely, and cook in the butter until soft but not coloured. Mix the breadcrumbs, celery, apples, raisins, parsley and dried mixed herbs together, and add the cooked onions. Season well with the salt and pepper, and bind with a little milk. The stuffing is now ready to use.

Turkey stock

1 large onion
10 g/¼ oz butter
all the turkey giblets, except the liver
1.2 litres/2 pints water
bouquet garni
1 stick celery, chopped
¼ tsp salt

Slice the onion and brown it slowly in the butter. Increase the heat under the pan, add the cleaned giblets and brown well. Pour on the water, add the bouquet garni, the chopped celery stick and salt. Bring to the boil, cover, and simmer very slowly for 1 hour. Sieve, cool and store until needed in the refrigerator or freezer.

Cranberry sauce

450 g/1 lb cranberries
175 ml/6 fl oz cold water
100 g/4 oz granulated sugar (or to taste)
a strip of orange rind

Wash the cranberries, put them in a saucepan, cover them with the cold water and bring to the boil. Simmer, bruising the cranberries with a wooden spoon, until reduced to a pulp.

Add the sugar and the strip of orange rind. Cook very gently until all the sugar is dissolved. Remove the rind before serving.

Bread sauce

600 ml/1 pint milk
1 small onion, stuck with 2-3 cloves
½ bay leaf
approx. 75 g/3 oz fresh breadcrumbs
seasoning
25 g/1 oz butter

Bring the milk to the boil, add the onion and bay leaf, cover, and leave on the side of the stove for at least 15 minutes to infuse. Remove the onion and bay leaf, add the breadcrumbs and seasoning and return to the heat. Stir gently until boiling, then remove from the heat. Beat in the butter, a small piece at a time. Serve hot.

Christmas pudding

Note: This quantity will fill 1 × 1.2 litre/2 pint pudding basin – enough to serve 10 – plus 2 × 600 ml/1 pint pudding basins. Christmas puddings are best prepared 1½-2 months ahead.

225 g/8 oz self-raising flour
a pinch of salt
10 ml/2 tsp mixed spice
½ nutmeg, grated
350 g/12 oz breadcrumbs
450 g/1 lb Demerara sugar
350 g/12 oz beef suet
500 g/1¼ lb currants
500 g/1¼ lb sultanas
500 g/1¼ lb stoned raisins
100 g/4 oz candied peel, finely chopped
100 g/4 oz almonds, finely chopped
1 cooking apple, grated
juice and grated rind of 1 orange
6 eggs
150 ml/5 fl oz brown ale

Richly flavoured with fruit and brown ale, our Christmas pudding, and Brandy butter, are matchless. Serve with a glass of port.

To flame:
30 ml/2 tbls brandy

Sift the flour with the salt and spices into a large mixing bowl and stir in the breadcrumbs and sugar. Finely chop the suet, dusting it with a little flour to prevent it from sticking. Roughly chop the currants, sultanas and raisins and add them to the suet; add all to the flour and mix well.

Add the candied peel and almonds to the grated apple, orange rind and juice. Beat the eggs to a froth, and pour into the dry ingredients with the ale. Add the peel, almonds, apple and orange mixture, and stir thoroughly to mix.

Turn into well-buttered pudding basins of the size you wish to use, cover with buttered paper and foil and tie securely. If you wish, use boilable plastic basins with snap-on lids, covering with buttered paper first.

To cook the large (1.2 litre/2 pint) pudding, prepare a large saucepan containing enough fast boiling water to completely cover the basin: cook for 6 hours, replenishing the water from time to time. At the end of this period, allow the pudding to drain and cool. Store. Boil again, as above, for 2 hours on Christmas Day.

To cook the smaller puddings, cook for 5 hours for the first cooking and 1 hour on the day you wish to eat the pudding.

For the flaming of the pudding, gently heat 30 ml/2 tbls of brandy to blood heat. Pour over the pudding, and light.

Brandy butter

225 g/8 oz unsalted butter, softened
225 g/8 oz caster sugar
60-90 ml/4-6 tbls brandy

Cream the butter thoroughly in a bowl, gradually beat in the sugar and continue to beat until white and smooth. Then gradually add the brandy, beating well after each addition.

Pile up in a small dish or serving bowl and chill until firm.

Croquembouche of chocolate meringues

5 egg whites

275 g/10 oz caster sugar

30 ml/6 tsp cocoa

For the filling:

300 ml/½ pint double cream

15 ml/1 tbls caster sugar

5 ml/1 tsp vanilla essence

To finish:

icing sugar

OVEN TEMPERATURE: 140°C/275°F/
Gas Mark 1

Prepare the meringue mixture: whisk the egg whites until very stiff, then beat in the caster sugar and then fold in the cocoa lightly with a large metal spoon. Pipe small 5 cm/2 in meringues on to a baking sheet covered with non-stick silicone paper, and bake in the preheated oven for about 1 hour. After 40-50 minutes, lift the meringues from the paper and press them in very carefully on their bottoms. (This is to create space for the cream to fit inside the meringue and hold the pyramid together.) Turn them onto their sides and return them to the oven to finish cooking and dry out thoroughly.

Whip the cream, and flavour it with the sugar and vanilla essence. When the meringues are quite cold, fill them with two thirds of the cream and mound them into a pyramid using the remaining cream to hold them in place. Chill well. Just before serving, dust with icing sugar and serve with the fresh fruit salad.

Fresh fruit salad

1 large pineapple

2 mangoes

6 clementines

225 g/8 oz strawberries *or* raspberries

4 bananas

For the syrup:

175 g/6 oz granulated sugar

300 ml/½ pint water

juice of 1 lemon

a strip of lemon rind

Begin by making the syrup. Dissolve the sugar in the water over a gentle heat, then add the lemon juice and rind and boil rapidly for 1 minute. Strain and cool.

Prepare the fruit by cutting it into fairly large pieces, leaving the strawberries and bananas until last. Turn all the fruit into a glass bowl and pour over just enough syrup to moisten. Cover, using a plate that is a little smaller than the bowl: this will hold the fruit under the syrup, to stop it discolouring. Chill.

Mince pies

Note: This quantity will make 18 mince pies.

45 g/1 lb rich shortcrust pastry dough

For the filling:

Approx. 700 g/1½ lb mincemeat

15-30 ml/1-2 tbls brandy, rum or sweet sherry

caster sugar

OVEN TEMPERATURE: 200°C/400°F/
Gas Mark 6

Make the pastry dough according to the recipe in the *Reference Section* page 142, and chill well.

On a lightly floured surface, roll out just over half of the pastry dough fairly thinly, and stamp into rounds with a 6 cm/2½ in cutter. Put the rounds to one side. Add the trimmings to the second half of the pastry dough, and roll out a little thinner than the first half. Stamp into rounds as before.

Turn the mincemeat into a bowl, and mix in the brandy, rum or sherry. Put the thinner pastry rounds into greased patty tins, and put a good spoonful of mincemeat into each to fill well. Place the thicker pastry rounds on top, pinch the pastry edges together, brush lightly with cold water and dust with caster sugar.

Cook for 15-20 minutes in the preheated oven until pale brown. Cool slightly before removing from tins.

Note: Mince pies are always a great standby at Christmas. They can be made well in advance and frozen, as suggested in our **Meal Planner**, or if you find you have the time nearer Christmas, they can be made freshly. They reheat well. For a special treat, ease off the tops of hot mince pies, put in a little brandy butter, then replace the tops and serve.

Croquembouche of chocolate meringues and Fresh fruit salad provides a light alternative to the traditional Christmas pudding.

Christmas Eve Dinner

Tomato and rice soup

900 ml/1½ pints chicken stock

1 medium onion, finely chopped

25 g/1 oz butter

30 ml/2 tbls tomato purée

10 ml/2 tsp patna rice, rinsed

seasoning

4 tomatoes, skinned and seeded

5 ml/1 tsp rice flour

Make the chicken stock according to the recipe in the *Reference Section* on page 138, in advance if possible. (If you don't have time, and don't have any stock in the freezer, use a good commercial stock or chicken consommé.)

Cook the onion in the butter until soft and golden, then add the stock, purée and rice. Season, and stir until boiling. Cover and simmer for 20-30 minutes. Meanwhile chop the prepared tomatoes. Add them to the soup after the first cooking period: simmer for 10 more minutes. Check seasoning. Mix the rice flour with 10 ml/2 tsp cold water, add this to the soup, boil gently for 2 more minutes and serve.

Fillet of plaice with mushroom duxelles and mornay sauce

4 large fillets of plaice, about 175 g/6 oz each

a little butter

seasoning

15 ml/1 tbls water

225 g/8 oz mushrooms, very finely chopped

15 g/½ oz butter

10 ml/2 tsp chopped fresh mixed herbs (5 ml/1 tsp parsley and ½ tsp each thyme and marjoram)

Seasoning

For the white sauce:

25 g/1 oz butter

25 g/1 oz flour

150 ml/¼ pint milk

seasoning

a pinch of ground mace

For the mornay sauce:

25 g/1 oz butter

25 g/1 oz flour

300 ml/½ pint milk

50 g/2 oz mature Cheddar, grated

¼ tsp made English mustard

seasoning

To finish:

15 ml/2 tbls finely grated Parmesan cheese

4 slices French bread, fried golden in butter

OVEN TEMPERATURE: 160°C/325°F/ Gas Mark 3

Skin the fillets of plaice and fold them in half. Place them in a buttered dish, season lightly, and sprinkle with the water. Cover with a sheet of buttered foil or buttered greaseproof paper and bake in the preheated oven for 7-10 minutes. Turn off the oven but leave the fillets there to keep warm until you are ready to use them.

Make the white sauce next. Make a *roux* with the butter and flour, then blend in the milk and stir until boiling. Season lightly, add a pinch of ground mace, and simmer for 2 more minutes.

Sauté the mushrooms in the butter until the purée is free of excess water and lifts in a body off the sides of the pan. Add the herbs, season, mix with the white sauce and set aside.

Now make the mornay sauce: melt the butter, add the flour, pour on the milk and stir until boiling. Draw aside, beat in the cheese and add mustard and seasoning to taste.

Reheat the mushroom duxelles mixture and spread it down the centre of a serving dish. Arrange the plaice fillets on the top and coat with the mornay sauce. Sprinkle with Parmesan cheese and brown lightly under the grill. Garnish with the slices of fried French bread.

Serve the plaice with petit pois peas. Use good quality frozen petit pois: cook them quickly in a small quantity of boiling water, then toss them in a little butter.

Freezer tip: As indicated in the **Meal Planner**, the whole of this dinner could be prepared in advance and frozen until needed. Complete the plaice recipe in a freezer-to-oven serving dish, wrap well, and freeze. Fry the French bread very lightly (it will cook further when reheated) and freeze separately. Freeze the soup as usual. Remove the soup the night before, and the bread and plaice in the morning: defrost at room temperature. Reheat the soup in a saucepan, and the plaice in a preheated 180°C/ 350°F/Gas Mark 4 oven for 25-30 minutes. Put the bread into this oven on a baking tin for 10 minutes.

Boxing Day Lunch

Fricassée of turkey

1 cooked turkey drumstick

1 cooked turkey thigh

6 slices of cooked turkey breast
meat

For the devilling mixture:

25 g/1 oz butter

30 ml/2 tbls tomato ketchup

45 ml/3 tbls Worcester sauce

30 ml/2 tbls mushroom ketchup

15 ml/1 tbls anchovy essence

10 ml/2 tsp prepared mustard

seasoning

For the white sauce:

25 g/1 oz butter

25 g/1 oz flour

300 ml/½ pint milk

seasoning

65 ml/2½ fl oz cream

To garnish:

6 thin rashers of streaky bacon

3 large tomatoes, skinned

salt, sugar and black pepper

25 g/1 oz butter

175 g/6 oz small flat mushrooms,
trimmed and peeled

½ bunch watercress, trimmed

Begin by preparing the devilling mixture: melt the butter in a large, shallow flameproof dish, then add the bottled sauces, essence, mustard and seasoning. Mix together well. Slice the dark meat off the bones, cut into chunky pieces, and put into the devilling mixture. Baste frequently. Cut the white meat into thin strips 5 cm/2 in long.

Make the white sauce: melt the butter, add the flour away from the heat, blend in the milk and stir until boiling. Season lightly, and add the thin strips of white meat. Remove the saucepan from the heat, carefully pour the cream over the top and cover.

Next, remove the rind from the bacon, and flatten out the rashers with a knife blade. Cut the toma-

toes into thick slices and season with salt, sugar and black pepper.

About 40 minutes before you wish to eat, stand the saucepan containing the white meat and sauce in a larger saucepan containing gently simmering water. Melt half the butter for the garnish in a frying pan and fry the mushrooms. Remove them, and fry the slices of tomato in half the remaining butter. Remove and keep all warm. Put the devilled dark meat into the frying pan with the last of the butter, and fry it quickly to a golden brown. Pour in any remaining devilling sauce, and simmer all together for a minute or two. Grill the bacon.

Arrange the dark meat at each end of the ovenproof serving dish, put the hot white meat and sauce in the centre and finish with the bacon, mushrooms and tomatoes. Keep warm. Garnish with watercress before serving.

Spiced beef

2 bay leaves, dried

4 cloves

3 blades of mace

12 black peppercorns

50 g/2 oz brown sugar

10 ml/2 tsp coarse rock salt

2 kg/4½ lb salt beef brisket

1 onion, sliced

2 large garlic cloves, peeled

2 bouquet garnis

mock glaze

Cut up the bay leaves, and separate the clove heads from their 'tails', discarding the tails. Put the bay leaf pieces, the clove heads, the mace, 6 of the peppercorns, the sugar and salt into a food processor or mortar and blend or grind to a fine dust. Rub three-quarters of this mixture into the beef, and rest the beef on the remainder. Refrigerate for 5 days: rub spices into the meat daily.

After 5 days, wash off the mixture. Put into a large saucepan, and cover with water. Add the other ingredients and bring to the boil. Simmer for 5 hours, then cool the beef in the liquid. Drain.

The meat should then be pressed between two large dishes, with a heavy weight resting on the upper dish. Refrigerate. Make the mock glaze according to the recipe in the *Reference Section* on page 139: glaze at least an hour before serving.

Angel cake Cordon Bleu

100 g/4 oz plain flour

175 g/6 oz caster sugar

10 large, size 1 egg whites

a pinch of salt

¼ tsp cream of tartar

165 g/5½ oz caster sugar

¼ tsp vanilla essence

¼ tsp almond essence

For the filling:
275 g/10 oz raspberries
450 ml/¾ pint double cream
vanilla sugar to taste

To decorate:
225 g/8 oz redcurrants
1 egg white
caster sugar

OVEN TEMPERATURE: 190°C/375°F/
Gas Mark 5

Sift the flour and the first quantity of caster sugar together. Repeat this sifting process twice more. Place the egg whites with the salt and cream of tartar in a large, dry mixing bowl, and whisk with a thin wire whisk until foamy. Add the second quantity of caster sugar, 30 ml/2 tbls at a time, and the essences to the mixture and continue mixing until the egg whites stand in peaks.

Carefully fold the sifted flour and sugar into the egg whites. Turn the mixture into a clean, dry angel cake tin, level the surface, and draw a knife through the mixture to break any air bubbles. Bake the cake in the preheated oven for about 50 minutes, or until no imprint remains when a finger lightly touches the top. Turn off the oven and leave the cake for a further 10 minutes.

Turn the cake out onto a wire rack and leave for at least 1 hour.

Rub 225 g/8 oz of the raspberries through a nylon strainer. Whip 300 ml/½ pint of the cream and flavour it with this raspberry purée: sweeten lightly with vanilla sugar to taste. Cut the cake into three, and reshape, sandwiching each third together with the raspberry cream.

Use the remaining whole raspberries to fill the cavity in the middle of the cake. Frost the redcurrants by brushing them with lightly beaten egg white, and then rolling them in caster sugar. Dry on a sieve. Whip the remaining 150 ml/¼ pint cream, and add vanilla sugar to taste.

Decorate the angel cake with rosettes of vanilla cream, and top with the frosted redcurrants.

Festive Garlands and Swags

Space is at a premium at Christmas, and garlands and table swags make attractive decorations without taking up important space. The materials you need are traditional Christmas varieties: holly with berries (*ilex*), ivy with berries (*hedera*), *cotoneaster*, sugar pine or hemlock (*tsuga*), and any other evergreen material that you have readily available.

Making a garland
To begin a garland, set a spiral line to work to. Fix a strong piece of nylon string very firmly around the highest point you wish the garland to hang from on your column, then drop 2 perpendicular strings down either side of the pillar (see figure 1 right). Mark one of these strings with knots every 38 cm/15 in, starting from the top, and the other string in the same way, starting the knots 19 cm/7½ in from the top. Twine the guide

Fig 1.

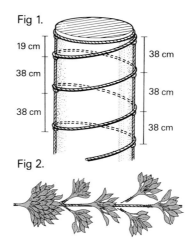

19 cm
38 cm
38 cm

38 cm
38 cm
38 cm

Fig 2.

string around the column using the knots as markers.

Next, make the garland. Work with the correct length of strong nylon string flat on a table. Sort the materials into groups of colour and shape, and fix sprigs to the string using

single leg mounts (see page 155) about 6-7.5 cm/2½-3 in long. Attach to the string in a staggered V-shape, adding pieces to fill out the centre (figure 2). Fix the whole garland to your pillar, attaching it to the guide string. It will be heavy, so fix firmly to the top circle of string with wire.

Making swags
Swags are thicker than garlands, and are made individually and hung in separate units, before being joined in the middle with ribbon.

Measure the table length and work out carefully how many swags you will want, and how long each one should be. (If they are uneven in length, put the largest ones in the middle.) Finish each table corner with a hanging end drop: these should be a third of the length of the adjacent swag.

To make the swags and drops you will need pieces of 5 cm/2 in wire mesh netting, up to 90 cm/3 ft in length and not more than 45 cm/18 in in width, and a quantity of teased-out moss (available from garden centres or florists), as well as the same materials as those used for the garlands. Form the netting for each swag into an open sausage shape about 7.5-10 cm/3-4 in thick, and stuff the moss into the netting. As you stuff each section of the sausage, seal the netting around it. Taper each end of the swag.

When this is complete, insert the foliage. Mount it on double leg mounts (see page 155), and proceed as for the garland, using the zig-zag and filling method shown in figure 2.

When the swags and drops are complete, attach them firmly to the table with wire or strong string. Fix the ribbon to finish the decoration, tying a large bow in the centre and smaller bows on the outside.

ITALIAN DINNER

Bright colours and simple, lively flavours are two of the outstanding features of Italian cooking,
and they set the style for our exciting Italian dinner.

ITALIANS LOVE EATING, as anyone who has been to Italy will know, and the simple, wholehearted pleasure they take in consuming food characterises their approach to preparing it as well. The Italian way with ingredients, indeed, can be summed up in one word: simplicity. The best ingredients, treated in the simplest possible way – that is the principle common to all of the finest Italian dishes. An example of this is the first course melon served here with Parma ham: two stunning ingredients to which no more is done than to bring them together. The combination is still better than each ingredient on its own.

Italian inspiration

In this menu, as with the other menus in this section of the book, the aim has been to convey some of the tastes and techniques of a country's cooking, without necessarily being too literal about the precise origins of each dish. The veal, for example, is inspired by the happy Italian way of combining béchamel sauce with cheese and meat, and the dessert is another simple but stunning combination – of raspberries and cream, in this case. No Italian meal would be complete without pasta, and a richly flavoured tomato sauce points up the tagliatelle used here.

MENU

for a party of six

Melon and Parma Ham

Tagliatelle alla Romagnola

Braised Veal Italienne
Buttered Courgettes

Raspberry Parfait
with Cigarette Russe Biscuits

WINE

Dry Italian White Wine

When giving a meal based around a national theme, try to find one or two 'props' that will help to establish the right atmosphere: this is much appreciated by guests. Even if the blue skies of Tuscany aren't always available, little touches like a simple decorative bowl of lemons, or some grissini (breadsticks) to nibble with apéritifs, will soon remind everyone of a relaxed Italian meal. Obviously your tableware and linen can reinforce this mood, if you have a suitable selection to draw on.

Ripening melons

Whichever variety of melon you buy, it is important to eat it when it is exactly ripe – and this can sometimes be difficult to gauge. Buy the melon well in advance, and speed or slow its ripening by placing it in a warm place or in the refrigerator. It is ripe when under gentle pressure at the stalk end, the melon gives a little.

Italian wines

There is a good and ever-increasing range of quality wines exported from Italy (look for DOC or DOCG on the label) and any dry Italian red or white quality wine should go well with this meal. The one shown in our photograph opposite is Lugana, a dry white wine from Lombardy (where, incidentally, the best Italian veal comes from): other suitable white wines would include Frascati, Orvieto secco, Soave and Gavi. If you wished to drink red wine, Barbaresco, Chianti classico or Vino nobile di Montepulciano would all be good choices: they are dry Italian reds in the lighter, more elegant style.

MEAL PLANNER

● **One week before:** buy the melon.

● **Two days before:** do all of the shopping. Make the jellied stock and the tomato sauce: cover closely, and store in the refrigerator.

● **The day before:** make the cigarette russe biscuits, and store in an airtight tin. Make the raspberry parfait, and store in the freezer or freezing compartment of the refrigerator.

● **The morning:** prepare the courgettes but do not cook yet. Prepare the vegetables for the veal.

● **Final preparation:** slice and arrange the melon and Parma ham. Transfer the raspberry parfait from the freezer to the refrigerator: beat well before spooning into glasses. Cook the veal and prepare its sauces, then grill and brown: keep all warm while you serve the first two courses. Prepare the courgettes before serving the veal. The tagliatelle should be cooked and the tomato sauce reheated after the first course has been served and eaten. This should take no longer than 5 minutes to do. Do not put the cigarette russe biscuits into the parfait until the last minute.

The haunting perfume and flavour of a perfectly ripened melon brings out the best in Parma ham. It makes a delicate start to a summer dinner.

Melon and Parma ham

1 ripe melon
100 g/4 oz Parma ham, thinly sliced

To serve:
black pepper
lemon wedges

Cut the melon into six wedges. Remove the seeds and, if you wish, cut the flesh from the skin in one piece. Arrange the wedges and slices of ham alternately around the plate. Roll one piece of ham into a cornet and position in the centre of the dish.

Provide your guests with freshly ground black pepper and lemon wedges when you serve the dish so that they can garnish their portions as they wish.

Note: There are a number of different melons available nowadays: cantaloup melons (like *charantais*, Tiger or Ogen) or honeydew melons will be ideal with Parma ham.

Tagliatelle alla romagnola

350 g/12 oz dried tagliatelle

For the sauce:
1 medium onion, thinly sliced
90 ml/6 tbls olive oil
2 cloves garlic, crushed
1 kg/2 lb ripe tomatoes, skinned, seeded and sliced
salt
freshly ground black pepper
30 ml/2 tbls chopped fresh parsley or 10 ml/2 tsp dried basil

To serve:
30 ml/2 tbls olive oil
50-75 g/2-3 oz freshly grated Parmesan cheese

Begin by making the sauce: brown the onion in the oil, then add the garlic and tomatoes. Season well, add the parsley or basil, and cook until soft and pulpy: this will take between 15 and 20 minutes.

Meanwhile, cook the tagliatelle in a large quantity of boiling salted water until tender and *al dente*. Drain, *refresh* and turn back into the saucepan. Add the serving quantity of olive oil and shake well over a medium heat. Turn into a large single serving dish or into individual serving bowls and spoon over the sauce. Sprinkle on the Parmesan cheese and serve immediately.

Note: Always grate Parmesan cheese freshly: its flavour is incomparably better than ready-grated versions.

Buttered courgettes

25 g/1 oz butter
750 g/1½ lb courgettes, sliced
salt
freshly ground black pepper

Heat the butter in a small frying pan, add the courgettes, cover with a tightly fitting lid and cook over a high heat for 3 minutes. Hold the lid of the pan on firmly and toss the courgettes once or twice during cooking. When ready, they should be tender but not over-soft or broken. Season with salt and pepper and turn into a warmed serving dish.

Braised veal italienne

300 ml/½ pint jellied stock
15 g/½ oz butter
2-3 rashers of streaky bacon
2 carrots, sliced
2 onions, sliced
1 stick celery, sliced
1-1.25 kg/2-2½ lb shoulder of veal, boned and rolled
250 ml/8 fl oz white wine
15 ml/1 tbls tomato purée
bouquet garni
seasoning

For the sauce:
25 g/1 oz butter
25 g/1 oz flour
450 ml/¾ pint milk, infused with ½ bay leaf, a slice of onion and 6 peppercorns
seasoning
45 ml/3 tbls cream
75 g/3 oz freshly grated Pecorino or Parmesan cheese

OVEN TEMPERATURE: 160°C/325°F/ Gas Mark 3

Make the jellied stock according to the recipe in the *Reference Section* on page 138, in advance

Tagliatelle alla romagnola combines a heady tomato and herb sauce with strips of plain tagliatelle. Freshly grated Parmesan tops the sauce.

The veal shoulder used for Braised veal italienne is casserole roasted in stock and white wine, then finished with béchamel and cheese.

if possible. Put the butter and the bacon rashers on the bottom of a flameproof casserole, then place the vegetables on top of the bacon. Cover and cook gently on top of the stove for 6-7 minutes. Place the veal on top of the vegetables, cover the casserole with the lid and cook over a very gentle heat or in the preheated oven for 15-20 minutes, until small 'beads' of juice begin to appear on the meat. Neither the meat nor the vegetables should

colour in any way. Add the wine to the casserole and cook uncovered over a moderate heat on top of the stove until the liquid is *reduced* by half. Add the stock. If the level of the stock comes well above the vegetables, *reduce* slightly. It should cover the vegetables, and just touch the bottom of the meat. Add the tomato purée, bouquet garni and seasoning. Cover with greaseproof paper and a tightly fitting lid, and cook in the preheated oven

for 1½-2 hours, until very tender.

Meanwhile, prepare the sauce: melt the butter, add the flour, blend to a smooth paste and stir in the infused, strained milk. Season and bring to the boil. Cook for 3 minutes, and then add the cream. Draw away from the heat and gradually beat in two-thirds of the cheese. Cover the surface of the sauce with buttered paper or cling film, put the lid on the saucepan and set to one side.

Lift the veal from the casserole and leave it to rest, covered, in a warm place. Strain the juices from the casserole into a saucepan and *reduce* to a syrupy texture. Reheat the cheese sauce if it has cooled. Slice the meat thinly and arrange in a flameproof dish, spoon the syrupy cooking liquor over and then pour over the sauce. Sprinkle the remaining cheese over the top of the slices and then brown in a hot oven or under the grill.

Raspberry parfait brings the meal to a leisurely close: the fresh flavour of fruit and cream linger in the mouth long after the glass is empty.

Note: The raspberry parfait can be made, as suggested in the **Meal Planner**, one or two days in advance – but make sure that you beat it well several times as it softens in the refrigerator to ensure that it has a smooth texture, free from ice crystals. If you are able to make it on the morning or afternoon of the dinner itself, so much the better: this problem will not then arise.

Cigarette russe biscuits

2 egg whites
100 g/4 oz caster sugar
50 g/2 oz butter
50 g/2 oz plain flour
2-3 drops vanilla essence

OVEN TEMPERATURE: 190°C/375°F/ Gas Mark 5

Break the egg whites into a dry basin; add the sugar and beat until smooth with a fork. Melt the butter over a very low heat and add it to the egg white together with the sifted flour. Flavour the mixture with a little vanilla. Spread it in 15 × 9 cm/6 × 3½ in oblongs on several shallow greased, floured baking tins. Bake each tin in the preheated oven for 5-6 minutes, or until the oblongs are pale golden in colour. The most convenient way to do this is to put one tin into the oven 3 minutes after the other tin, so that no two tins of biscuits are ready at the same time.

When the biscuits are baked, allow them to rest in the tins for a second or two, then remove them with a sharp knife and place upside down on a table or other flat surface. Wind each biscuit tightly around a wooden skewer or pencil. Remove at once and cool quickly. Store in an airtight tin. Remember only to remove one tin at a time from the oven so that the biscuits do not harden before you can roll them up.

Note: As the texture of the biscuit dough is very important if they are to be formed into cigarette shapes successfully, bake one oblong on its own first, to test the mixture. If it is very soft and difficult to handle after it comes out of the oven, add a pinch of flour; if it is too firm and hard, add 5 ml/1 tsp more melted butter and then try again.

Something crisp, light and sweet goes well with a creamy dessert, and Cigarette russe biscuits fit this bill perfectly.

Raspberry parfait

1 kg/2 lb fresh *or* frozen raspberries
4 egg whites
225 g/8 oz caster sugar
300 ml/½ pint double cream
300 ml/½ pint whipping cream

To serve:

langue de chat or cigarette russe biscuits

Rub the raspberries through a nylon sieve. Place the resulting purée in a rigid plastic container and freeze. Transfer to the refrigerator 3-4 hours before you wish to make the rest of the dish.

About 2 hours before serving, whisk the egg whites until stiff, gradually add the sugar and continue whisking until the mixture stands in peaks. Whisk the two creams together until they are thick and bulky but not stiff. Fold them lightly and thoroughly into the egg white mixture.

Beat the chilled raspberry purée to break down any ice particles. Fold it into the cream and egg white mixture.

Pile the parfait into chilled glasses or a glass bowl. Chill well before serving. Serve with langue de chat or cigarette russe biscuits.

An Italian Summer Vase

The Italian theme of this dinner is carried through into our flower group: a large, simple vase, filled with a wide assortment of vibrant, boldly coloured flowers and foliage suggests the exuberance of an Italian summer.

The vase is practical as well as decorative: a large group like this needs a sturdily-weighted vase, and to save on oasis and add weight, the bottom third of the vase has been filled with gravel. Put a block of oasis on top of this: enough to protrude about 2.5 cm/1 inch above the rim of the vase.

Beginning the arrangement

First, set the height of the arrangement with the *cupressus arizonica glauca*, then use *sansevieria* to set the width. Two different types of ornamental *asparagus* have been used to fill in on each side: *mayerii* on the left and *plumosus* on the right. Croton (*codiaeum*) brings foliage colour to the centre of the arrangement, and a young *dracaena* shoot is used with this for contrast. A large *strelitzia* leaf dominates the back right.

Next, begin to bring the floral varieties into the arrangement: *bougainvillea* on the left and jasmine (*jasminum*) on the right at the front, then *mimosa* at the back on the right. Fill in with other varieties: *bouvardia*, carnations (*dianthus*) and, centre right, a single bird of paradise flower (*strelitzia*).

Garden flower alternatives

The arrangement as photographed uses a number of houseplants and hothouse flowers; *agapanthus*, *geranium*, *clematis* and *antirrhinum* would make good garden flower alternatives, using *coleus* and *thalictrum* for foliage.

SCOTTISH HIGH TEA

Homely and nourishing Scottish dishes make a convenient meal for the late afternoon
– or for those who'd like a taste of the hills.

THE TRADITIONAL SCOTTISH high tea has no peer in this book: it is, like the American brunch, one of those meals that combines in one the best of two. In this case, that means the wholesome savouriness of a supper dish can be followed by the sweeter delights of teatime fare, and – again like brunch – the meal can be taken more or less when you please. For example, it would be perfect as a satisfying meal after a hectic day that left little or no time for lunch, while being no less ideal as a nutritious stopgap before a long, busy evening. Adaptability is the hallmark of the high tea.

Tastes of Scotland

This meal is adaptable in another sense, too: it provides a number of uniquely Scottish tastes, all or any of which could be taken out and used in other contexts. The oatcakes are an obvious example: in addition to their use

MENU

for a party of six

Whiting with Brown Butter
with Bacon and Grilled Tomatoes
Sauté Potatoes

Scotch Oatcakes
Crowdie
Scotch Pancakes
with butter and honeycomb
Plain Scones
with butter and raspberry jam
Dundee Cake

here, they are excellent with most cheeses, particularly hard ones, and they are very good, too, with many of the thicker vegetable soups. The Dundee cake is a wonderful fruit cake, and would prove popular in any teatime or picnic setting. Scotch pancakes are a particular favourite of children, and just the thing for keen after-school appetites; while plain scones are loved by all, whenever served. The main course whiting is a lovely country dish, perfect on its own or with the potatoes for a late-night supper after a long journey or a day out.

Although tea is our only counsel as far as teatime drinking is concerned, the observant will have noticed one or two bottles of malt whisky on the sideboard. No truly Scottish occasion would be complete without whisky, and it would make an excellent digestive after the meal. Oatcakes, by the way, make an excellent accompaniment to whisky!

MEAL PLANNER

● **A week before:** make the Dundee cake.

● **One day before:** do the remaining shopping. Make the crowdie if possible. Make the oatcakes.

● **The morning:** make the scones.

● **Final preparation:** prepare the pancake batter. Make the pancakes and wrap to soften while you prepare and serve the main course dishes.

Whiting with brown butter

6 × 175 g/6 oz whiting fillets
6 rashers of streaky bacon
6 tomatoes, halved, rind removed

To finish:
40 g/1½ oz butter
15 ml//1 tbls lemon juice
15 ml/1 tbls chopped mixed herbs
  (½ parsley, the rest a mixture of
  chives, thyme and chervil)
seasoning

OVEN TEMPERATURE: 190°C/375°F/
Gas Mark 5

Trim and wash the fish and place in an ovenproof dish without draining it. Season, cover with a butter wrapper and poach in the preheated oven for about 8-10 minutes.

Meanwhile, grill the bacon and tomatoes under a preheated moderate grill, until the bacon is crisp and well browned, and the tomatoes cooked through. Drain the fish fillets and transfer to a large warmed serving dish. Place a bacon rasher between each fillet, and garnish with the toma-

toes. Keep warm.

Put the butter into a small saucepan and heat it until it is nut brown. Draw the pan aside and add the lemon juice, mixed herbs, and seasoning to taste. Pour over the fish while it is all still foaming together.

Note: If Scottish whiting is not available use small fillets of haddock or lemon sole. This dish gives particularly good results if the fish is poached in a microwave cooker: follow the manufacturer's instructions for timing and power level.

Whiting with brown butter, colourfully garnished by grilled bacon and tomatoes, is served with Sauté potatoes. Scotch oatcakes and Crowdie follow.

Sauté potatoes

750 g-1 kg/1½-2 lb potatoes

30 ml/2 tbls salad oil

40 g/1½ oz butter

seasoning

10 ml/2 tsp chopped parsley

Boil the potatoes until just tender. Drain, cool slightly, then peel and roughly slice while still warm. Heat the oil and butter together until foaming, then slide all the warm potato slices into the pan. Season and *sauté* the slices carefully, turning each one from time to time until every slice is golden brown and crisp on both sides. Remove the pan from the heat and sprinkle over the chopped parsley. Serve the potatoes immediately.

Scotch oatcakes

100 g/4 oz medium oatmeal

a pinch of salt

a pinch of bicarbonate of soda

15 ml/3 tsp bacon fat *or* butter *or* dripping

300 ml/½ pint boiling water

25 g/1 oz fine oatmeal

OVEN TEMPERATURE: 200°C/400°F/ Gas Mark 6

Mix together the oatmeal, salt and bicarbonate of soda. Melt the fat in the water and mix with the oatmeal to a stiff dough. Turn out onto a board sprinkled with fine oatmeal and knead quickly for 1 minute. Roll out as thinly as possible, then cut into rounds. Rub the cakes with fine oatmeal,

then place them on a lightly greased baking sheets. Cook them in the preheated oven for 8-10 minutes, or until the edges begin to curl. Serve immediately, or warm through before serving.

Crowdie

Crowdie can only be made at home if you can obtain unpasteurised milk (TT tested). If you cannot, genuine Scottish crowdie may sometimes be obtained from good delicatessens or cheese shops.

Pour 1.2-1.75 litres/2-3 pints of fresh raw (unpasteurised) milk into a mixing bowl and leave in a cool larder for about 3-4 hours to allow the cream to rise and settle. Skim off the cream into a small bowl, cover and keep in the refrigerator. Leave the milk in the kitchen until it sours and sets to a gel, then turn it into a basin lined with muslin. Tie this up and leave the milk, suspended, to drip through the muslin for about 4-5 hours or overnight. Mix in the reserved cream and a little extra, lightly whipped fresh cream.

Scotch pancakes

225 g/8 oz flour

5 ml/1 tsp salt

10 ml/2 tsp cream of tartar

5 ml/1 tsp bicarbonate of soda

1 egg

250 ml/8 fl oz milk and water, mixed

Sift the dry ingredients together, then drop in the egg and a little of the milk and water. Mix quickly to a smooth paste, then add enough liquid to make a thick batter. Grease a large sturdy frying pan, then spoon on tablespoons of the mixture to make rounds. Cook about 4-6 pancakes at a time, turning them to make sure they are cooked on both sides.

Place the pancakes between the folds of a clean tea towel to keep them warm and moist, and leave until soft before serving.

Plain scones

225 g/8 oz plain flour

a large pinch of salt

5 ml/1 tsp bicarbonate of soda

10 ml/2 tsp cream of tartar

10 ml/2 tsp caster sugar

50 g/2 oz butter *or* margarine *or* shortening

150 ml/¼ pint milk

OVEN TEMPERATURE: 230°C/450°F/ Gas Mark 7

Sift the flour with the salt, bicarbonate of soda, cream of tartar and sugar into a mixing bowl. Rub in the fat lightly, and mix quickly with the milk to a pliable dough. Roll the dough out onto a floured board to a thickness of 1-2 cm/½-¾ in, and cut into 5 cm/2 in rounds with a pastry cutter.

Place the scones on an ungreased baking sheet, brush with milk and bake in the preheated oven for 12-15 minutes.

Note: Excellent variations can be made to this basic scone recipe: the addition of 50 g/2 oz sultanas and 25 g/1 oz mixed peel will make **Sultana scones** and 50 g/ 2 oz chopped preserved ginger and 25 g/1 oz chopped walnuts will give you **Ginger and walnut scones.**

Scotch pancakes and scones are highland teatime favourites.

Dundee cake

225 g/8 oz plain flour

225 g/8 oz self-raising flour

a pinch of salt

225 g/8 oz butter

the rind of 1 lemon, finely grated

225 g/8 oz caster sugar

3 large *or* 4 small eggs

50 g/2 oz ground almonds

225 g/8 oz currants

225 g/8 oz sultanas

75 g/3 oz candied peel, finely
   chopped

30 ml/2 tbls milk

To finish:

50-75 g/2-3 oz Valencia almonds,
   skinned, blanched and split

OVEN TEMPERATURE: 160°C/325°F/
   Gas Mark 3

Line a 20 cm/8 in round cake tin with a double thickness of greased greaseproof paper. Sift the two flours together with the salt. Cream the butter until soft, then add the lemon rind and sugar, and beat until it becomes pale in colour. Add the whole eggs, one at a time, beating very thoroughly between the addition of each egg. Fold in a third of the flour.

Mix the ground almonds with the fruit and candied peel and add lightly to the mixture. Fold in the remaining flour, adding 15 ml/ 1 tbls milk to give a mixture that will just drop from the spoon when lightly shaken.

Turn into the prepared cake tin. Smooth the top and cover with the almonds. (If you use ready-blanched almonds, pour boiling water over them for 10 minutes to soften them first.) Brush with the rest of the milk and bake on the middle shelf of the preheated oven for 2½-3 hours. Cover the cake with greaseproof paper when coloured, and test to see if it is done after 2¼ hours with a fine skewer or trussing needle. If the skewer comes out clean, with no trace of moist uncooked cake mixture adhering to it, then the cake is done.

A Mixed Fresh and Dried Group

This informal arrangement uses mostly dried materials, with just one or two sprays of fresh *chrysanthemum* (variety Bonny) for colour and interest. The materials are arranged in a pewter fruit dish, and held on a pinholder with a little wire netting. The vase is shallow, but it allows enough water for the fresh flowers; the dried mate-rials have the tips of their stems painted with varnish to prevent them rotting in the water.

Dried stem varieties

The dried group is made up of alder (*alnus*); larch (*larix*) with cones; artichokes (*cynara scolymus*); blackthorn (*prunus spinosa*) with lichen; *echinops*; *eryngium*; heather (*erica*); pine cones and other assorted stems of dried materials. To make the arrangement, begin by setting the height and width with your longest dried stems. Fill in the centre with the remaining dried materials, grouping large heads and cones low down in the vase. Add the colourful fresh stems last of all, placing the heads together in small groups of two or three.

CREOLE DINNER

Rich flavours and dark colours entice your guests to table
under the light of a waxy southern moon.

A CREOLE DINNER IS A MEAL that brings together the old and the new in a unique way: longstanding French cookery traditions meet the wealth and diversity of ingredients the New World has to offer, and the result is an exciting mix of original flavours in traditional forms. The pecan pie of this meal is a case in point: richly flavoured, soft and moist to eat, it represents Louisiana French cooking (from which Creole cooking stems) at its best.

Creole options
As the photograph opposite perhaps suggests, this menu is one well-suited to outdoor eating during the summer months: it would make an excellent alternative to the **Patio Dinner** described on pages 80-83. It might also provide an enchanting birthday dinner for a friend: help along the atmosphere with some pretty paper lanterns and use an appropriate number of tiny wax tapers in the flower arrangement. Another possibility is that of a special celebration evening meal for teenagers, who will love the bright

MENU

for a party of six

Prawn Bisque

Sauté of Veal Creole
Spinach en Branche

Pecan Pie

WINE

Californian White Wine

colours and striking flavours of the meal: for those in their early teens, you may wish to omit the bisque and simply serve the main course and dessert on their own.

The slow boat home
Different entertaining occasions require different approaches. This is not only a question of mood and atmosphere, but also springs from practicalities such as the speed with which one course follows another, and how quickly or slowly you pace the evening. To some extent this is a question of personal choice and intuition – you learn to 'feel' when your guests are ready for the next course – but to some extent it also relates to the nature of the meal. The leisurely, calm, relaxed atmosphere of the Deep South pervades this dinner in a way that would obviously not be appropriate for an after-theatre supper or pasta meal.

American wine
American wines – with their positive, exciting flavours – make excellent partners for Creole food. We have shown a white Californian Chardonnay wine whose full, dry taste matches both the bisque and veal perfectly. Other good Chardonnay wines are made both in Oregon and New York State – though not, as yet, in Louisiana!

MEAL PLANNER

● **Two days before:** buy all ingredients except prawns.

● **One day before:** buy the prawns. Make the prawn bisque and the pecan pie. Cook the sauté of veal until the meat is tender, but do not finish.

● **Final preparation:** prepare the pilaff and finish the sauté. Reheat the bisque. Cook the spinach; warm the pie before serving.

Prawn bisque

1.5 litres/2½ pints fish stock
50 g/2 oz butter
2 medium onions, chopped
1 kg/2 lb ripe tomatoes
3 'caps' of tinned pimento, chopped
10 ml/2 tsp tomato purée
seasoning
40 g/1½ oz flour
225 g/8 oz peeled prawns, chopped
150 ml/¼ pint whipping cream

Prepare the fish stock according to the recipe on page 139 of the *Reference Section*: this need not necessarily be done in advance, as fish stock takes no longer than ½ an hour to prepare.

Melt half the butter, add the onions and cook until soft and golden. Skin the tomatoes, cut in half and squeeze to remove the seeds; add them to the pan and cook slowly until pulpy.

Add the pimento, tomato purée and stock, season, cover and simmer for 10-15 minutes.

Blend the soup in a liquidiser and reheat in the rinsed pan.

Work the flour into the remaining butter, add to the soup a small piece at a time and stir until thickened. Check the seasoning, add the prawns and warm through. Pour the soup into a hot tureen and swirl in the cream.

Note: UHT (longlife) cream is a handy commodity to have in your store cupboard, and it could substitute perfectly for fresh cream in this recipe.

Prepare the veal or chicken stock according to the recipe in the *Reference Section* on page 138, a day in advance if possible. Cut the meat into 4 cm/1½ in cubes. Heat the oil and butter in a sauté pan, and when foaming add the meat, about a quarter of it at a time, and brown well. Reduce the heat under the pan, add the onion and dust with flour; stir for 5-6 minutes until the onion and flour are a rich golden brown.

Add the wine and stock and stir well to blend in the *roux* while bringing to the boil over a brisk heat. Turn down the heat, add the seasoning, garlic and bouquet garni. Cover and place in the preheated oven, where the meat should simmer steadily for 1½ hours. (You can, if you prefer, cook it on top of the stove, turning the meat occasionally and regulating the heat so that the sauté never cooks faster than a simmer.)

Meanwhile, trim the mushrooms and *sauté* them in a small pan with a nut of butter. At the end of the meat cooking time, use a slotted spoon to remove the meat: place it in a serving dish and keep it warm. Boil down the sauce in the sauté pan until it is reduced to about 900 ml/1½ pints, then add the mushrooms and shredded red pepper and bring back to the boil. Spoon the sauce over the meat.

To prepare the pilaff, crush the tomatoes. Remove the core and seeds from the pepper, slice thinly, and *blanch* in boiling water for 1 minute. Drain and *refresh*. Melt half the butter, add the whole mushrooms, season and cook gently for 3 minutes, then add tomatoes, pepper and the rest of the butter. Cook for a few minutes longer and fork into the rice.

Tomato and seafood meet memorably in Prawn bisque.

Sauté of veal Creole

1.2 litres/2 pints veal *or* chicken stock

1 kg/3 lb oyster (boned shoulder) of veal

30 ml/2 tbls oil

45 ml/3 tbls *clarified* butter

1 large onion, finely chopped

15 ml/1 tbls flour

250 ml/8 fl oz white wine

salt

freshly ground black pepper

2 cloves of garlic, crushed

bouquet garni

225 g/8 oz button mushrooms

a nut of butter

¼ red pepper, shredded and *blanched*

For the pilaff:

4 large tomatoes, skinned, cored and seeded

1 green pepper

50 g/2 oz butter

175 g/6 oz button mushrooms

seasoning

275 g/10 oz long-grain rice (dry weight), cooked, drained and kept warm

OVEN TEMPERATURE: 180°C/350°F/ Gas Mark 4

Moist and inviting, this Cordon Bleu Pecan pie is distinguished by its use of pecan nuts in pastry as well as filling.

Sauté of veal Creole is served with a vegetable pilaff, and Spinach en branche makes for a classic combination.

Spinach en branche

1.5-1.75 kg/3-4 lb spinach

25 g/1 oz butter

seasoning

Pick over the spinach, remove any excess stalk and wash it in three changes of water. Lift the spinach into a colander to drain after each washing.

Cook the spinach, uncovered, in boiling salted water for 1-2 minutes, then drain and *refresh*. Remove all the water in a salad spinner, or by pressing the spinach firmly between two plates. Just before serving, toss in hot butter, and season.

Pecan pie

For the pastry:

75 g/3 oz pecan nuts
225 g/8 oz flour
100 g/4 oz butter
25 g/1 oz shortening
75 g/3 oz caster sugar
2 egg yolks
15 ml/1 tbls water

For the filling:

25 g/1 oz butter
225 g/8 oz golden syrup
225 g/8 oz black treacle
the grated rind of 1 lemon
2 eggs
90 ml/6 tbls double cream
75 g/3 oz pecan nuts

OVEN TEMPERATURE: 190°C/375°F/
Gas Mark 5

First prepare the pastry. Grind the nuts and toast them until golden brown. Leave them to cool. Sift the flour into a bowl, add the butter and shortening, then cut and rub the fat into the flour as you would when making shortcrust pastry. Stir in the sugar and prepared nuts. Beat the egg yolks with the water, and mix all together to make a firm dough. Roll out the pastry to a circle the same size as the base of a 24 cm/9½ in flan dish. Line the flan dish and press the pastry up the sides of the dish with your fingertips. Chill for 1 hour.

Meanwhile, prepare the filling. Melt the butter, add the syrup, treacle and lemon rind and warm slightly. Beat the eggs and double cream together with a fork and stir into the treacle mixture.

Cover the pastry with foil: it will not need beans in it. *Bake blind* in the preheated oven for 8-10 minutes or until the pastry looks dry but not brown. Remove the foil, place 25 g/1 oz of the nuts broken in pieces on the pastry, pour in the filling, then place the rest of the nuts on the top. Bake for 35-40 minutes in the same oven until the pastry is brown and the filling soft. Serve the pie luke-warm or cold.

A Candlelight Surround

Branches of magnolia in flower make a lovely background for this exotic evening meal, as illustrated in the opening photograph on page 124. The flowers around the candlelight above reflect the ivory colour of the magnolia blooms with subtle white and cream shades. They are set in a small, well-soaked oasis wreath frame. If you don't have one of these, a ring mould or savarin tin could be used, filled with pieces of soaked oasis or wire netting to hold the materials in place.

Fronds of *asparagus plumosus* and leather fern (*pteris*) are the two varieties of foliage used to provide greenery. With these we have selected white roses (*rosa*), variety Carte Blanche, together with their own foliage; white sim carnations (*dianthus*), and white single *chrysanthemum* heads, variety Bonny Jean.

Working in sections

To make the arrangement, work section by section around the candlelight. Start by placing large flower heads high up (though not more than half way up the glass), and then fill in with green foliage. Make sure that each head faces directly outwards, and that each section curves gradually from top to bottom. Fill in with tiny flower buds at the bottom, and use heads of fern to fill in any remaining gaps or spaces in the arrangement.

Wax Tapers

For a thoroughly celebratory effect, finish the arrangement with some slender wax tapers. These are non-drip, so they shouldn't pose any stain or fire risk, but to be on the safe side try to keep them upright or at a shallow angle.

AUSTRIAN DINNER

Generosity and tradition are two of the cornerstones of Central European cooking
and our Austrian meal memorably emphasizes both.

G EMÜTLICHKEIT IS PERHAPS the most famous of all Austrian words: its nearest English meaning is somewhere between 'hospitality', 'kindness' and 'cosiness', though any true Austrian will protest at the inadequacy of this translation. Hospitality is a way of life in Austria, and the Austrian dishes shown opposite and on the following pages illustrate at least part of the meaning of *gemütlichkeit* more successfully than mere words can. Lavish and rich, this is a meal to serve to your oldest – or your dearest – friends.

Practical considerations

This menu has the advantage of being one of the least seasonal in the book. Farmed trout of a good standard are now available year-round, and red cabbage, too, is nearly always available. The kartoffelknödeln (potato dumplings) are best made with old potatoes: if you are only able to buy new ones, then serve

MENU

for a party of six

River Trout

with Brown Butter

Roast Loin of Pork

Kartoffelknödeln

Braised Red Cabbage

Plum and Almond Torte

with whipped cream

WINE

Austrian White Wine

those instead, finished with butter and fresh parsley. If fresh plums are not available, the torte could also be made with ready-soaked apricot halves.

Trout can either be served with their heads on or removed. There is no reason why the heads should not be left on (in fact it makes cooking easier: the trout are done when their eyes turn white) but some people find this unattractive, and you may wish to remove them for this reason.

Austrian wine

Austrian white wines can be excellent – fuller and stronger than the German wines with which they are so often compared – and nothing could be more appropriate to serve with this meal. For a special treat, serve one of the delicious and inexpensive Austrian dessert wines (look for the word *beerenauslese* on the label) with the torte: your guests will appreciate the final, *gemütlich* touch.

MEAL PLANNER

● **Four days before:** order the chined loin of pork from your butcher, if it is not something normally stocked by him.

● **Two days before:** do all of the shopping except for the trout. Make the soured cream pastry and chill it. Fully complete the braised red cabbage: store in the refrigerator.

● **One day before:** make and bake the plum and almond torte. Cover closely with cling film and store in an airtight container overnight.

● **The morning:** buy the trout. Whip the cream to serve with the torte. Prepare all the ingredients for the pork dish and dumplings.

● **Final preparation:** Put the pork on to roast. Make the dumplings and reheat cabbage. Bake the trout and keep warm; make the sauce. After the first course is eaten, cook the potato dumplings, check the cabbage is fully reheated, and finish the sauce for the pork.

River trout with brown butter

6 trout
120 ml/4 fl oz dry white wine
300 ml/½ pint water
seasoning

To finish:
50 g/2 oz butter
seasoning
juice of ½ lemon
10 ml/2 tsp chopped parsley
10 ml/2 tsp fresh mixed herbs
wedges of lemon for serving

OVEN TEMPERATURE: 160°C/325°F/ Gas Mark 3

Trim, wash and dry the trout. Lay them in an ovenproof dish, pour over the wine and water, and season lightly. Poach the fish in the preheated oven for 20-25 minutes, basting occasionally.

Lift out the trout and place on a hot serving dish. Heat the butter slowly in a small pan until nut brown in colour, then season and add the lemon juice and herbs. Pour the brown butter over the fish. Garnish with lemon wedges and serve at once.

River trout with brown butter makes a simple but sophisticated start to a traditional meal. Garnish with a wedge of lemon.

Roast loin of pork

75 g/3 oz butter *or* bacon fat	
1.5-1.75 kg/3½-4 lb loin of pork, chined and scored	
2 shallots, finely chopped	
2 bay leaves	
2 cloves garlic, crushed	
300 ml/½ pint stock	
150 ml/¼ pint white wine	
½ lemon, peel and pith removed, thinly sliced	
1 small sweet apple, cored, peeled and sliced	
freshly ground rock salt	
150 ml/¼ pint white wine *or* cider	
10 ml/2 tsp softened butter	
85 ml/3 fl oz double cream	

OVEN TEMPERATURE: 190°C/375°F/ Gas Mark 5

Melt the butter or bacon fat in a flameproof roasting tin, then put in the meat and baste well. Add all the other ingredients to the roasting tin down to and including the apple. Grind a little rock salt over the pork rind. Put into the preheated oven and cook, basting frequently, for about 2 hours. If the liquid in the roasting tin reduces too much, add extra stock or water so that the amount is never less than a teacupful.

After the meat has cooked, rest it on a warm dish while you finish the sauce. Strain the cooking juices into a small saucepan, and press the contents of the strainer to extract all the juice. *Deglaze* the roasting tin with the second quantity of wine or cider and add it to the sauce. Add the softened butter to thicken the sauce slightly, bring to the boil and add the cream. *Reduce* rapidly for 2 minutes, then pour into a sauce boat, reserving a little to pour around the meat for serving.

Kartoffelknödeln

1 kg/2 lb old potatoes	
25 g/1 oz butter	
salt	
2 egg yolks	
175 g/6 oz flour	
100 g/4 oz semolina	

Wash the potatoes well but do not peel them. Place in a sauce- pan of cold water, cover and bring to the boil. Simmer until tender.

When cooked, peel the pota- toes and pass through a mouli- sieve or potato ricer, or mash very finely. Add the butter, salt and yolks to the potato purée, mix well and add the flour and semolina. Knead together to form a firm dough. Divide the mixture into twelve pieces and roll into balls. Place in boiling salted water and simmer very gently for 10 minutes. When cooked the dumplings will rise to the top of the saucepan. Lift out, drain and serve, cutting each dumpling and pouring sauce from the pork over it.

Braised red cabbage

1 red cabbage, weighing 750 g-1 kg/ 1½-2 lb	
1 onion	
25 g/1 oz butter	
2 cooking apples, peeled, cored and sliced	
30-45 ml/2-3 tbls wine vinegar	
30-45 ml/2-3 tbls water	
15 ml/1 tbls sugar	
seasoning	
25 g/1 oz butter	
15 g/½ oz flour	

OVEN TEMPERATURE: 160°C/325°F/ Gas Mark 3

Quarter the cabbage and cut out the centre stalk. Shred the cab- bage finely. *Blanch* then drain.

Slice the onion and soften it in a large flameproof casserole with the butter. Add the apples and cook for 5 minutes: turn out onto a plate. Add the blanched cab- bage to the saucepan, layering it with the apple mixture, and final- ly sprinkling with the vinegar, water, sugar and seasoning. Cover with thickly buttered greaseproof paper or foil and the saucepan lid and cook in the preheated oven for about 1½ hours or until very tender. Stir from time to time and moisten with extra water if necessary. While the cabbage is cooking, make a *beurre manié* with the butter and flour and at the end of the cooking period stir it through the cabbage to 'bind' its texture.

Roast loin of pork is served with Kartoffelknödeln (potato dumplings) and Braised red cabbage in this popular Central European dish.

Plum and almond torte

450 g/1 lb Victoria plums
30 ml/2 tbls sugar

For the soured cream pastry:
175 g/6 oz flour
75 g/3 oz butter *or* margarine
40 g/1½ oz caster sugar
45 ml/3 tbls soured cream

For the almond cream:
1 egg
50 g/2 oz caster sugar
10 ml/2 tsp arrowroot
100 ml/3½ fl oz soured cream
45 ml/3 tbls whipping cream
50 g/2 oz ground almonds
2 drops vanilla essence

To serve:
whipped cream

OVEN TEMPERATURE: 190°C/375°F/
   Gas Mark 5

Butter a 20 cm/8 in springform mould. Prepare the soured cream pastry: sift the flour, rub in the butter, add the sugar and mix with the soured cream. Knead lightly and chill well.

Halve and stone the plums, sprinkle with the sugar and cover with cling film. Work the egg and sugar for the almond cream together until thick and light in colour, then blend in the arrowroot. Stir in the two creams, the almonds and the essence.

Roll out the pastry dough and use it to line the prepared tin, both bottom and sides. Place a piece of foil over the pastry and bake in the preheated oven for 8 minutes. Remove the foil and arrange the plums cut side down on the pastry. Pour the almond cream over the plums, return the flan to the oven and bake until set and golden brown (allow 40-45 minutes for this). Leave it to rest in the tin for 10 minutes, then release the clip and let it cool on the base of the springform tin. Lift onto a serving plate when firm. Serve with whipped cream.

Classic Silk Flower Arrangement

Silk flowers are nowadays so realistic that they can be used to great effect without anyone making adverse remarks – and sometimes without people even noticing. When silk flowers are as beautiful as the German ones shown in the photograph, then the initial expense of acquiring them seems worthwhile, for they can be arranged and rearranged indefinitely.

In addition to their potential for artificial arrangements pure and simple (as above), they can also take the place of pot plants in positions where the light or growing conditions are too poor for real ones to survive. It is possible to mix artificial with real, using silks with both pot plants and freshly cut flowers.

Working with silks
Treat your silks just as you would fresh flowers as far as shape and colour is concerned. The only advantage silks have is that you can adjust the stems at will by carefully bending them to the required shape.

This mixed flower group has been arranged in a heavy iron vase which has at its base a block of oasis sec. You could also use sand or moss.

Start by setting the height with *iris*, and then set the width with *laburnum* and lilac (*syringa*). Next place a group deep down in the centre of the arrangement: an *aphelandra* and a pink *hydrangea* have been used here. All the stems should flow out from the centre of the vase, and should seem to fit 'comfortably'. Complete the rest of the arrangement using this principle of filling in from the centre outwards, using broad, fluid lines.

A final touch
As a final touch in the main photograph on page 128, you will see a small vase containing typically Austrian varieties. This little group shows how well art can blend with nature: some of the flowers are real, some are silk, and some are handmade paper flowers.

ENGLISH SUNDAY LUNCH

The roast beef of Old England reigns unchallenged at Sunday lunch,
and a choice of desserts to finish will please the entire family.

AN ENGLISH SUNDAY LUNCH needs no introduction: it is as time-honoured and well-loved an institution as the changing of the guard. This shouldn't obscure its merits as a meal: first-class raw ingredients, treated with inspired simplicity, shine through in the main course, while the opportunity to try two different desserts (dishes which the English excel at creating) is much relished in English homes from Newcastle to Penzance.

Traditional English entertaining

This is a meal where the traditional virtues of English hospitality are much in evidence. A generous number of dishes, presented with classic simplicity; an atmosphere of calm, unhurried enjoyment: these are the things that distinguish the occasion. The food, like the hour, responds well to your best china and cutlery, and the younger members of the family might like to have a go at making the 'bishop's mitre' napkins (see pages 146-147). One of the great secrets of a successful

MENU

for a party of eight

Roast Sirloin

with Horseradish Cream

Yorkshire Pudding

Roast Potatoes

Spring Greens

Braised Leeks

—•—

Gooseberry Plate Pie
English Trifle

WINE

Australian Red Wine

Sunday lunch is last-minute coordination, and the recipes contain full instructions to help you bring everything to table piping hot.

Red Australian wines are an appropriate choice for the meal: their big, muscular character responds superbly to the challenge offered by prime English beef. Look out for those made from Shiraz or Cabernet Sauvignon grapes.

MEAL PLANNER

● **Two days before:** do all of the shopping. Prepare the pastry dough for the plate pie: refrigerate. Make the horseradish cream.

● **One day before:** prepare the trifle. Parboil the potatoes in the evening.

● **Final preparation:** prepare the sirloin, potatoes, leeks, spring greens and Yorkshire puddings as outlined in the recipes. Finish and cook the plate pie.

Roast sirloin

Note: If you wish to impress visitors and give the family a rare treat, order a joint from the chump end of the sirloin, with undercut, and on the bone. Ask the butcher to 'set it up' for you, i.e. the chine bone will be released but not removed.

For a party of 8, order a joint weighing anything from 3.2-5 kg/ 7-10 lb. This will be easy to carve and plenty will be left for the next two or three days.

If you would prefer to buy a piece of boned, rolled sirloin, this would be best spit-roasted (if you have the facility in your oven). If you cannot spit roast, place a boned, rolled joint on a grill or cake rack in the roasting tin to prevent the cut side getting hard or overcooked.

4 kg/9 lb joint of sirloin
50-75 g/2-3 oz beef dripping

For the gravy:
a dusting of flour

600 ml/1 pint brown stock
seasoning

OVEN TEMPERATURE: 220°C/425°F/
Gas Mark 7

Make the stock for the gravy according to the recipe in the *Reference Section* on page 138, or, if time is short, use a good beef consommé.

Remove the meat from the refrigerator at least 1 hour before roasting. Place the shelves in the required position in the oven

before preheating it: the top shelf should have space for the potatoes, and there should be plenty of clearance underneath for the meat to sit comfortably on the second shelf. A low third shelf will be necessary for the leeks.

A joint of this cut and weight should stand well as the chine bone will support it. If you think it might topple over, have a grid handy to avoid disasters.

Put the roasting tin in the oven with the dripping, and when it is smoking hot take it out, put in the meat and baste well. Return the tin to the oven and baste regularly every 20 minutes until the meat is done. If you like your beef rare, calculate 15 minutes per 450 g/1 lb, plus an extra 15 minutes; if you like it well done, 20 minutes per 450 g/1 lb, plus 20 minutes. After the first 15 minutes, turn the oven down to 200°C/400°F/Gas Mark 6. When the meat is done, place it on a serving dish and stand it in the warming drawer of the cooker, or a warm place in the kitchen. Leave the oven on at the same temperature to make the Yorkshire puddings in.

To make the gravy, tilt the roasting tin and gently pour off the dripping, leaving behind the meat juices and sediment. Dust in just enough flour to absorb the juices, and allow this paste to colour slowly over a low heat. When it is brown, draw the pan aside, pour on the stock, blend and bring to the boil. Season and *reduce*. Strain into a gravy boat and serve very hot.

Horseradish cream

| 30 ml/2 tbls white wine vinegar |
| ½ tsp dry mustard |
| seasoning |
| 60 ml/4 tbls freshly grated horseradish |
| 150 ml/¼ pint double cream |
| 5-10 ml/1-2 tsp caster sugar |

Mix together the vinegar, mustard, seasonings and horseradish. Whip the cream until it just leaves a trail on itself and then carefully fold in the horseradish mixture and the sugar. Adjust seasoning and sugar to taste.

Note: Horseradish cream freezes well, so it is worth making a large quantity when you can find fresh horseradish, and freezing what you do not immediately need. Bought varieties make good substitutes: improve them with a pinch of sugar and a little lightly whipped double cream.

A family meal to remember is provided by Roast sirloin of beef, served in the traditional English way, with Yorkshire pudding, Roast potatoes, Spring greens, Braised leeks and a little Horseradish cream.

Yorkshire pudding

Note: The quantities given below are sufficient for 12 small puddings.

100 g/4 oz flour
salt
1 large egg
scant 300ml/½ pint equal parts milk and water
30 ml/2 tbls dripping

Sift the flour with a good pinch of salt into a mixing bowl. Make a well in the centre, and drop in the egg. Gradually add the liquid to the egg, drawing in the flour a little at a time. When half the liquid has been added beat the mixture thoroughly until air bubbles begin to break on the surface. Whisk in the remaining milk and water. (If using a blender, place the ingredients in the blender jar in the same order and proceed in the same manner.)

Cover the batter and leave it in a cool place for at least 1 hour. After the meat has cooked, and while the gravy is being made, check the oven is still at 200°C/400°F/Gas Mark 6. Put ½ teaspoon of dripping, or fat skimmed from the gravy, in the base of each 12 deep bun tins and heat the tins until the fat is just beginning to smoke. Gently rotate the tray to coat the sides of the moulds with the fat.

Pour the batter into the piping hot moulds and place near the top of the oven for 10-15 minutes until the puddings are well risen, golden brown and crisp. Serve immediately.

Note: The key to success with Yorkshire pudding is to pour the batter into a very hot tin or tins, and to put it immediately into a very hot oven. The quicker these steps can be accomplished, the better will be the result.

Roast potatoes

1.5 kg/3½ lb evenly sized potatoes (allow 2-3 per person depending on size)
dripping *or* oil
salt

Peel, then boil the potatoes for 7-10 minutes: drain. Scratch the surface of each potato with a fork to roughen it.

Have ready a roasting tin filled to a depth of 1 cm/½ inch with smoking hot dripping or oil. Put in the potatoes and baste at once.

Roast on a shelf above the meat but at the same oven temperature for 30-40 minutes or until the potatoes are brown and crisp, turning and basting them from time to time. Drain on kitchen paper and salt lightly before serving in a vegetable dish.

Note: If you wish (and have room) some of the potatoes could be roasted around the joint of meat.

Spring greens

1.5 kg/3 lb spring greens
salt
15-25 g/½-1 oz butter
seasoning

Trim the stalks and remove any coarse or damaged outside leaves. Put the greens in plenty of fast boiling water and cook, uncovered, for about 8 minutes. Drain in a colander and *refresh*.

When the other vegetables have all been placed in their dishes, turn the greens into a large shallow saucepan and heat quickly to drive off any moisture. Add the butter and toss until it melts. Season and serve.

Braised leeks

16 large leeks
butter
seasoning
30 ml/2 tbls stock
15 ml/1 tbls single cream

The fruit purée used in Gooseberry plate pie is encased in a delicious almond pastry. (Recipe on page 136.)

Trim off the root of the leeks, and cut away the 'scruffy' half of the green part of each leek. Wash them very thoroughly to remove any grit or sand, then *blanch* them in boiling water for 1 minute and drain well. Reserve 2 or 3 of the most tender leeks for the garnish: shred these finely.

Place the rest of the leeks in a buttered casserole with salt, freshly ground black pepper and stock (use a little of the same stock that you will be using for the beef gravy), cover and cook on a shelf under the meat for about 45 minutes, basting the leeks at least twice at 20 minute intervals.

To finish the leeks, scatter the shredded reserved leeks over the top of the dish, baste the whole dish once again, and then add the cream. Return to the oven on the shelf below the Yorkshire puddings to heat through fully before serving.

Note: Leeks are notoriously difficult to wash, particularly if you are using home-grown ones. A good principle to remember is that grit or earth is heavy and will naturally sink, so always lift the leeks out of rinsing or soaking water (leaving the grit behind) rather than pouring the water off the leeks. Alternatively, split the leeks down their green part, hold them under running water, and flick out the grit.

Gooseberry plate pie

450 g/1 lb green gooseberries
150 ml/¼ pint water
175 g/6 oz sugar

For the almond pastry:
275 g/10 oz flour
150 g/5 oz butter
40 g/1½ oz shortening
65 g/2½ oz caster sugar
65 g/2½ oz ground almonds
3 drops of almond essence
1 large egg yolk
45 ml/3 tbls cold water

To finish:
1 egg white, beaten
15 ml/1 tbls caster sugar
85 ml/3 fl oz double cream,
 whipped (optional)

To serve:
whipped cream

OVEN TEMPERATURE: 190°C/375°F/
Gas Mark 5

The day before you wish to make the pie, gently simmer the gooseberries in the water until the skins are soft. Add the sugar, allow it to dissolve, then bring to the boil and cook quickly for about 15-20 minutes. Stir frequently until the gooseberries have turned slightly pink and are well reduced. Turn into a bowl and leave to cool. Cover closely, and store in the refrigerator overnight.

Prepare the pastry as for rich shortcrust pastry, using the recipe method given in the Reference Section on page 142. Add the ground almonds with the sugar and the almond essence with the egg yolk and water. Wrap the dough and store it overnight in the refrigerator.

Roll out just over half the dough and use it to line a 24 cm/9½ in flan dish: *bake blind* in the preheated oven. Then fill the flan with the gooseberry purée, cover with the rest of the rolled dough, seal and decorate the edge. Mark out a circle in the centre of the top crust with a pastry cutter, but do not cut out yet. Bake for about 30-40 minutes.

Brush the top with a little egg white, dust with the sugar and return to the oven for 2-3 minuets to frost the top. Allow to cool a little and then cut out the previously marked central disc of pastry. Fill, if you wish, with the optional whipped cream. Serve just warm, with more whipped cream.

Note: The gooseberry pulp used for this pie freezes very well: make a larger quantity with fresh fruit in the summer for use during the winter months.

English trifle

150 ml/¼ pint sugar syrup
3 nectarines *or* peaches
3 macaroons
8 small trifle sponge cakes
85 ml/3 fl oz medium or sweet
 sherry
225 g/8 oz raspberries

For the custard:
2 strips of orange rind
900 ml/1½ pint warmed milk
60 ml/4 tbls custard powder
150 ml/¼ pint cold milk
150 ml/¼ pint natural yoghurt

English trifle is known and loved the world over – but nowhere more so than around the family Sunday lunch table.

150 ml/¼ pint double cream,
 lightly whipped

To finish:
150 ml/¼ pint double cream
a few almonds, blanched and split
a few glacé cherries
a little angelica
a few ratafias

Make the sugar syrup according to the recipe on page 143 of the *Reference Section*, and then poach the nectarines or peaches in this. Drain the fruit, and return the syrup to the saucepan. Keep warm. Cut the macaroons in half and arrange them in the bottom of a glass bowl. Cover them with the poached fruit, and put the sponge cakes, split in half, on top. Moisten all with the sherry. Pour the hot sugar syrup onto the raspberries and leave them to steep in the syrup while you make the custard.

Infuse the orange rind in the warmed milk for 10 minutes, then bring to the boil. Mix the custard powder to a smooth paste with the cold milk, then blend the boiling milk into this. Mix well and return to the saucepan: stir until boiling.

Beat the hot custard with an electric mixer until cold, then add the yoghurt. Mix well and fold in the double cream. Spoon the raspberries over the sponge cakes, pour on the custard, then cover with foil and keep in the refrigerator overnight.

The next morning, finish the trifle: whip the cream and pipe a thick lattice of it over the custard. Decorate with the almonds, cherries, angelica and ratafias to give the trifle a pretty finish.

Note: Sherry is the most traditional fortified wine to use for making trifle, but if you wished to intensify the almond kernel flavour already suggested by the macaroons, use the same quantity of an Italian amaretto instead.

Flowers For The Dining Room

Mantelshelf Freesias

On the mantelshelf for this sweet-smelling arrangement of *freesias*, we have used a narrow flat container with mirrored sides. The vase was designed by Constance Spry herself: it is also made in stainless steel, and provides an excellent centrepiece for the table.

A framework of three different ivies (*hedera*) has been used for the foliage, to hide the mechanics and provide a suitable background for the flowers. Keep the more open and deeper-coloured flowers to the centre to give visual weight to the arrangement, and use taller buds for the outline. Any curved stems will be most useful over the front of the vase. As the first flower heads fade, these should be carefully removed to encourage the buds underneath to open out and provide colour and aroma for a longer period.

Semi-Permanent Arrangment

During the winter, a large, semi-permanent arrangement in mixed green is a practical and attractive idea. It provides a quiet pool of restful monochrome colours during the most expensive time of the year for flowers and the varieties used are unusual in both shape and texture.

A marble tazza

The mixed group has been arranged in a large marble tazza. Marble is a hard, heavy stone which will hold water without deteriorating. It is similar in appearance to alabaster – though alabaster is very fragile and cannot be used without a lining to hold the water.

The mechanics explained

The materials are arranged in oasis with wire netting for extra support. It will last for many weeks, providing the oasis is always moist. Some will root.

Begin by setting the height with yellow/green dogwood (*cornus stolonifera*), then on the left with a branch of hemlock (*tsuga*) with some small cones attached, and then alder (*alnus*). Violet willow (*salix daphnoides*) on the right, with its lovely red bark and silver grey/pink downy flower buds, goes in next. Then position the centre succulent: in this instance, we have used *echeveria*. Three fronds of *mahonia japonica* and two *aralia* leaves, making a dark green patch around the centre, are positioned together with an adult form of variegated ivy (*hedera canariensis*) with berries. The narrow pointed leaf is *sansevieria trifasciata* and the wider variegated leaf on the left is from a pot of parlour fern (*aspidistra*). The greyish brown, felty-looking leaf is from a *kalanchoë beharensis*. Finally fill in remaining gaps with the materials you have left.

Reference Section

This reference section summarises the background information needed to make your entertaining as smooth and successful as you would wish. The section opens with six pages of Basic Recipes; a section on The Well-Stocked Kitchen follows. Successful Entertaining contains information about invitations, seating plans, place settings, napkin folding, menu planning and glasses, while Entertaining With Wine is full of information on buying, storing and serving wine. The Wine Glossary helps you decode even the most abstruse wine label. Four pages on Entertaining With Flowers and a Directory Of Cooking Terms complete the information to be found in the section.

Basic Recipes

Jellied (brown) stock

This recipe will make about 2.25 litres/4 pints of stock.

1.25 kg/2½ lb small beef bones
1 calf's foot *or* pig's trotter, split in half, *or* 1 knuckle bone of veal
1 large onion, thickly sliced
1 large carrot, thickly sliced
3 litres/6 pints water
½ tsp salt
6 peppercorns
bouquet garni

OVEN TEMPERATURE: 200°C/400°F/ Gas Mark 6

Wipe the bones with a damp cloth and place them in a roasting tin with the vegetables. Brown bones and vegetables in the preheated oven: this will take about 30 minutes.

Lift the bones and vegetables from the roasting tin with a slotted spoon and place them in a large saucepan with the water, salt, peppercorns and bouquet garni. Half cover the pan with the lid and simmer continuously for 3-4 hours or until the stock is reduced by about one third. Skim well every hour.

Strain the stock off into a large bowl and cool quickly. Remove any fat from the surface, set aside the stock needed for immediate use, and refrigerate or pack and freeze the remainder of the stock until needed.

Veal stock

This recipe will make about 2.25 litres/4 pints of stock.

1.5 kg/3 lb veal bones, cracked, including 1 knuckle bone
3 litres/6 pints water
½ tsp salt
1 large onion, thickly sliced
1 large carrot, thickly sliced
6 peppercorns
bouquet garni

Place the wiped bones in a large saucepan with the water and salt, then bring slowly to the boil and skim well. Add all the other ingredients and simmer continuously for 3-4 hours or until the stock is reduced by about one third. Skim well every hour.

Strain the stock off into a large bowl and cool quickly. Remove any fat from the surface before setting aside what you need and refrigerating or freezing the rest for use later.

Chicken giblet stock

This recipe will make about 900 ml/1½ pints of stock.

1 set of chicken giblets (see *Note* below)
10 g/¼ oz butter
1 onion, washed but not peeled, and cut in half
1.2 litres/2 pints water
bouquet garni
small stick of celery (optional)
large pinch of salt
3-4 black peppercorns

Scald the chicken feet: place them in a basin, and cover with boiling water. Put a saucer on top to keep the feet submerged, and leave them for 8-10 minutes. Remove the feet, and take off their scales with a small sharp knife.

Smear the fat onto one side of the giblets and the two cut sides of the onion. Place them fat side down in a heavy saucepan and cover with the lid. Cook over a high heat until lightly browned, then draw the saucepan aside, pour on the water, and add the remaining ingredients. Simmer gently for 1-2 hours. Strain, and cool quickly. Freeze or keep refrigerated and use the stock within 2 or 3 days.

Note: The giblets used for this stock should ideally include the neck, gizzard, heart and feet of a good chicken. Never use the liver for stock, as it can give it a bitter flavour: freeze livers individually and keep until you have enough to use for chicken liver pâté.

Chicken stock

This recipe will make about 1.75 litres/3 pints of stock.

1 boiling chicken *or* carcass and bones from 2 raw chickens
1 set of giblets (excluding the liver)
water to cover, about 2.5 litres/4½ pints
1 onion, stuck with 1 clove
1 medium carrot, cut in half
2 sticks celery
bouquet garni
½ tsp salt
6 black peppercorns

If you are using a boiling chicken, remove any fat from the inside of a bird. (This can be rendered down and used as dripping for roasting other poultry; it is also good for cooking pilaff and risotto with.) Place the bird or carcasses and bones, together with the giblets, in a large saucepan. Cover with the water. Bring to the boil and skim well. Add all the other ingredients and simmer for 2-2½ hours.

The flesh of the boiling chicken (if used) can now be removed and used to fill pancakes, vol-au-vents or bouchées, or in any other way that you wish. Return the boiling chicken's carcass, wing tips and knuckle joints to the stock in the pan and simmer for a further 45 minutes. If you used chicken carcasses to start with, carry on simmering for a further 45 minutes. Strain, and cool quickly. Freeze or keep refrigerated and use within 3 days.

Fish stock

This recipe will make about 1 litre/ 1¾ pints of stock.

750 g/1½ sole *or* plaice bones, *or* a large turbot head
1 medium onion, sliced
10 g/¼ oz butter
bouquet garni
6 white peppercorns
juice of ½ small lemon
pinch of salt
1.2 litres/2 pints water

Wash the fish bones or head and drain well. *Blanch* the onion, drain, and *refresh*. Melt the butter in a large saucepan, put in the prepared onion, cover with the fish bones, bouquet garni, peppercorns, lemon juice· and salt. Put the lid on the pan and place over a very gentle heat for 10 minutes to 'sweat' the ingredients. Add the water, bring to the boil, and skim well. Simmer very gently for 20 minutes, then strain through a fine nylon strainer.

Leave the stock to cool. Freeze or keep refrigerated and use within 2 or 3 days.

Vegetable stock

This recipe will make about 2.75 litres/5 pints of stock.

15 g/½ oz butter
450 g/1 lb carrots
450 g/1 lb onions
½ head of celery
a small piece of turnip
a few peppercorns
10 ml/2 tsp salt
bouquet garni
4 litres/7 pints hot water
5 ml/1 tsp Marmite (optional)

Melt the butter in a very large saucepan. Peel and wash the vegetables, dry, and slice them into big pieces. Add them to the pan and shake over a low heat until brown. Add the peppercorns, salt, bouquet garni and hot water. Bring to the boil, half cover the pan and simmer for 3 hours or until the stock has a good flavour: it should be reduced by about a third. Marmite may be added if liked to improve both colour and flavour. Strain before use.

Mock glaze

A mock glaze can be made in one of two ways. The first is to use a commercial aspic mixture prepared to double strength (by using only half the quantity of water specified on the packet). The second is to dissolve 5 ml/1 tsp gelatine, soaked in 15 ml/1 tbls cold water, in a ramekin dish: stand the ramekin dish in a larger dish of hot water. When dissolved, mix the gelatine into half a tin of a good commercial consommé, warmed through.

Let the aspic or consommé mixture cool, and spoon it over the meat you wish to glaze as it begins to thicken.

The chart on the right shows, in diagram form, all the steps needed in the making of basic kitchen stocks. Points to remember when making stocks include the caution that stocks in preparation should never be boiled, as fat and scum will then dissolve into the stock itself, making it cloudy or sometimes even making it taste bitter. Always skim stock regularly during its preparation, and always leave stock half-covered or uncovered as it cooks. This will aid the reduc-tion of the stock (concentrating its flavour) and also stop stock souring, as it can when cooked in an airtight saucepan. Remember, too, that you can stop cooking stock at any time and continue later (cool and reheat quickly): a great help as long simmering is the basis of most good stock.

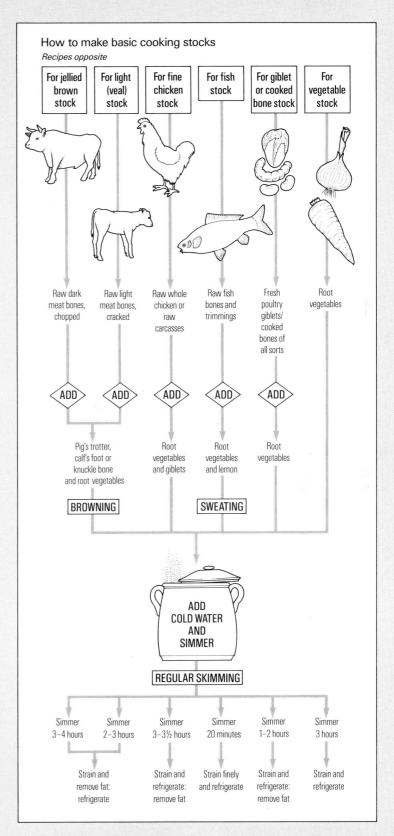

How to make basic cooking stocks
Recipes opposite

| For jellied brown stock | For light (veal) stock | For fine chicken stock | For fish stock | For giblet or cooked bone stock | For vegetable stock |

Raw dark meat bones, chopped — Raw light meat bones, cracked — Raw whole chicken or raw carcasses — Raw fish bones and trimmings — Fresh poultry giblets/ cooked bones of all sorts — Root vegetables

ADD — ADD — ADD — ADD — ADD

Pig's trotter, calf's foot or knuckle bone and root vegetables — Root vegetables and giblets — Root vegetables and lemon — Root vegetables

BROWNING — SWEATING

ADD COLD WATER AND SIMMER

REGULAR SKIMMING

Simmer 3–4 hours — Simmer 2–3 hours — Simmer 3–3½ hours — Simmer 20 minutes — Simmer 1–2 hours — Simmer 3 hours

Strain and remove fat: refrigerate — Strain and refrigerate: remove fat — Strain finely and refrigerate — Strain and refrigerate: remove fat — Strain and refrigerate

Béchamel sauce

This recipe will make about 300 ml/½ pint of béchamel sauce. To make more or less sauce, increase or decrease the quantities taking care to keep all the ingredients in proportion.

a slice of onion
6 peppercorns
a blade of mace
a small piece of bay leaf
a small sprig of thyme
300 ml/½ pint milk

For the roux:
25 g/1 oz butter
25 g/1 oz flour
salt and white pepper

Add the onion, spices and herbs to the milk, cover the pan and stand on a low heat to infuse for 5-7 minutes; do not allow the milk to boil. Pour all the ingredients into a bowl and rinse out the saucepan. Make a white *roux* with the butter and flour, then strain on a good third of the milk, and blend thoroughly. Add the remainder of the milk. When all is thoroughly mixed, season lightly, return to the heat and stir continually until boiling. Boil for 1-2 minutes and adjust seasoning.

Note: These quantities will give a sauce of the right consistency for coating vegetables, fish and eggs.

Béchamel sauce variations

A quick and easy version of a béchamel sauce is basic **White sauce**, made in exactly the same way as a béchamel, save for the fact that the milk is not flavoured with onion, herbs and spices first.

An **Egg sauce** can be made by adding 2 finely-chopped hard-boiled eggs to a finished quantity of béchamel: serve with vegetables or fish.

For a **Mushroom sauce**, chop 50 g/2 oz of mushrooms finely. Melt half the butter for the *roux* and cook the mushrooms in this until dry. Then add the rest of the butter and proceed with the béchamel recipe as above: serve the sauce with egg, fish or chicken dishes.

A recipe for **Cheese** or **Mornay sauce** is given on page 111, using a white sauce base: it can also be made, using the same quantity of cheese, with a béchamel sauce base.

Hollandaise sauce

The quantities used in this recipe will make about 300 ml/½ pint of hollandaise sauce. To make a larger or smaller amount of hollandaise, use more or fewer egg yolks and adjust the other ingredients in proportion (i.e. 20 ml/1 tbls and 1 tsp wine vinegar, and 25-50 g/1-2 oz butter for every large size 1 egg yolk.)

60 ml/4 tbls white wine vinegar
6 peppercorns
½ bay leaf
a blade of mace
150-175 g/5-6 oz butter
3 large size 1 egg yolks
seasoning

Put the vinegar, peppercorns, bay leaf and mace in a small saucepan and *reduce* to 10 ml/2 tsp; set aside.

Work the butter until slightly soft. Cream the egg yolks in a small bowl with a nut of the butter and a small pinch of salt. Strain on the vinegar liquor, set the bowl in a bain-marie or large saucepan half-filled with warm water over a gentle heat, and stir the mixture until thick using a sauce whisk or wooden spatula.

Add the rest of the butter in small pieces about the size of a hazelnut, stirring continually. When all the butter has been added, season delicately and, if the sauce is too sharp, add more butter. It should be lightly piquant, barely holding its shape, and lukewarm rather than hot.

To make a spooning sauce to accompany a dish, hollandaise may be diluted slightly with a spoonful or two of cream.

Note: The water in the bain-marie or saucepan should be lukewarm to begin with, gradually increasing in temperature until very hot — about 76-82°C/170-180°F — but on no account to boiling point. If the sauce is thickening very quickly, remove the bowl from the bain-marie and continue to add the butter away from the heat.

Hollandaise sauce variations

Two basic variations of hollandaise sauce are **Béarnaise sauce**, for serving with steaks and cutlets, and **Mousseline sauce**, a more delicate hollandaise for serving with vegetables and fish, particularly salmon.

Béarnaise is made by adding a single slice of onion to the vinegar mixture for reduction at the start of the recipe. At the end of the recipe, when the sauce is complete, stir in a generously rounded teaspoonful (6-7 ml) of meat glaze or jellied stock, together with a level teaspoonful (5 ml) each of chopped tarragon, chervil and parsley and a pinch of snipped chives or grated onion.

To make the mousseline sauce, omit the first stage of the hollandaise recipe above, and add the juice of half a lemon to 2 creamed egg yolks (instead of the reduced vinegar to the 3 yolks indicated above). Use 75 g/3 oz butter to make the sauce. After the sauce is finished, remove from the heat and beat in 60 ml/4 tbls of lightly whipped double cream.

Mayonnaise

This recipe will make 300 ml/½ pint of mayonnaise. To make a larger quantity of mayonnaise, use more egg yolks and increase the other ingredients in proportion (i.e. another 120 ml/4 fl oz oil, and 15 ml/1 tbls white wine vinegar for every extra egg yolk). To make an especially thick mayonnaise, use 1 extra egg yolk without increasing the quantity of the other ingredients.

2 egg yolks
a pinch each of salt, pepper and dry mustard
250 ml/8 fl oz salad oil
30 ml/2 tbls wine vinegar
10 ml/2 tsp hot water (optional)

Work the egg yolks and seasonings with a small whisk or wooden spoon in a bowl until thick. Then start adding the oil drop by drop. When 30 ml/2 tbls of oil have been added, the mixture will be very thick. Stir in 5 ml/1 tsp of the vinegar.

The remaining oil can then be added a little more quickly, either 15 ml/1 tbls at a time and beaten thoroughly between each addition until it is absorbed, or in a thin steady stream if you are using an electric beater. When all the oil has been absorbed, add the remaining vinegar to taste and check the seasoning.

Note: The eggs used for mayonnaise should be at room temperature. If the oil is chilled and cloudy, it can be warmed slightly to lessen the chances of the eggs curdling by putting the oil bottle in a pan of hot water for a short time.

If the mayonnaise curdles, start with a fresh yolk in another bowl and work well with the seasoning and mustard, then add the curdled mixture to it very slowly and carefully. When the curdled mixture is completely incorporated, add more oil.

Blender mayonnaise

This recipe, quicker and easier than ordinary mayonnaise but with a less fine flavour, will make about 350 ml/12 fl oz finished mayonnaise.

2 whole eggs

a pinch each of salt, pepper and dry mustard

30 ml/2 tbls white wine vinegar *or* 15 ml/1 tbls lemon juice and a pinch of caster sugar

300 ml/½ pint salad oil

Put the whole eggs and seasonings in the liquidiser with the vinegar, and switch to high speed for 1-2 seconds. Remove the central cap from the lid and pour in the oil in a thin, steady stream, keeping the machine on high speed.

Check the seasoning and use within two or three days.

Vinaigrette

This recipe will make 150 ml/¼ pint of vinaigrette. To make a smaller or larger quantity, increase or decrease the ingredients taking care to keep all the quantities in proportion.

a large pinch of salt

freshly ground black pepper

30 ml/6 tsp white *or* red wine vinegar

120 ml/4 fl oz salad oil

a squeeze of lemon (optional)

a tiny pinch of caster sugar

Mix the salt and about five twists of black pepper with the vinegar, and whisk in the oil. Sharpen with lemon juice if liked and add a little sugar to taste.

Demi-glace sauce

This recipe will make about 450 ml/¾ pint of finished sauce.

45 ml/3 tbls oil

30 ml/2 tbls diced onion

30 ml/2 tbls diced carrot

15 ml/1 tbls diced celery

30 ml/2 tbls flour

600 ml/1 pint jellied stock (see page 138)

5 ml/1 tsp tomato purée

a few mushroom peelings

bouquet garni

Heat the oil gently, add the diced vegetables and cook slowly until the onion is transparent, the carrot and celery begin to shrink and all three are about to brown.

Stir in the flour with a metal spoon or small wire whisk, and cook very slowly to a good russet brown. Draw the pan off the heat, allow to cool a little, then pour on three-quarters of the stock and add the remaining ingredients. Season very lightly, return to the heat and, stirring constantly, bring slowly to the boil. Half cover the pan with the lid and simmer very gently for about 30 minutes.

Skim off any scum that rises to the surface. Add half the reserved stock, bring to the boil again, skim, and simmer for 5 minutes. Repeat this process with the remaining stock, then strain through a fine-meshed strainer, pressing the vegetables gently to extract any juice. Rinse and wipe the pan and return the sauce to it; partly cover and continue to simmer the sauce until it is very glossy and has the consistency of syrup.

Rich tomato sauce

This recipe will make about 900 ml/1½ pints of tomato sauce.

2 shallots *or* 1 small (pickling) onion, chopped

15 g/½ oz butter *or* 15 ml/1 tbls olive oil

2 × 400 g/14 oz tins of tomatoes in tomato juice

seasoning

90 ml/6 tbls tomato purée

1 clove of garlic, unpeeled

1 carrot, finely grated

600 ml/1 pint vegetable stock

To finish:

about 40 g/1½ oz butter

Cook the shallots or onion in the butter or oil until golden, then add the tomatoes and crush well with a wooden spoon. Season, then add all the other ingredients and

simmer for about 30 minutes. Strain through a nylon seive and discard the garlic and tomato seeds. Return to the rinsed saucepan, then *reduce* until the sauce is thick enough to coat the back of the spoon. Adjust the seasoning and finally beat in a walnut-sized nob of butter to finish the sauce.

Raspberry vinegar

450 g/1 lb raspberries

300 ml/½ pint white distilled vinegar

preserving or granulated sugar

Bruise the raspberries with a wooden spoon in an earthenware crock or basin with the vinegar. Stir well every day for 3-4 days. Strain into a large measuring jug through a jelly bag or muslin.

Measure the juice and add 450 g/1 lb preserving or granulated sugar per 600 ml/1 pint juice. Stir over a gentle heat until the sugar is dissolved, then boil rapidly for 10-15 minutes. Skim well. Cool, and bottle in clean, screw-top bottles.

Note: If you wish to use commercial raspberry vinegar, check first whether it is sweetened or not. If it is not, sweeten it with granulated sugar before using: 15 ml/1 tbls of sugar will be sufficient for 150 ml/5 fl oz of vinegar. Dissolve thoroughly.

Apple and mint chutney

1 large Granny Smith apple

15 ml/1 tbls white wine vinegar

15 ml/1 tbls chopped mint

5 ml/1 tsp snipped chives

salt

cayenne pepper

Peel and grate the apple coarsely. Mix at once with the wine vinegar, chopped mint and snipped chives. Season with salt and cayenne pepper. Cover closely; keep chilled until required.

Cranberry and orange relish

225 g/8 oz cranberries

1 medium cooking apple, peeled, cored and sliced

300 ml/½ pint water

75 g/3 oz sugar

a strip of orange peel

1 orange, peeled and segmented

2 sticks celery, finely diced

Put the cranberries and other ingredients down to and including the orange peel into a saucepan and cook until the cranberry skins have popped and the apple is soft and pulpy. Allow to cool.

Meanwhile, carefully peel the skin off each orange segment, and cut each segment into three. When the relish has cooled, stir in the orange and celery.

Note: If you have left-over cranberry sauce to finish up, simply add the orange segments and celery (both prepared as above) to it, together with the flesh of a finely diced sweet eating apple.

Beetroot and horseradish relish

225 g/8 oz freshly cooked beetroot, peeled

salt

5 ml/1 tsp sugar

20 ml/4 tsp wine vinegar

freshly ground black pepper

a pinch of dry English mustard powder

10 ml/2 tsp finely grated horseradish, mixed with a little cream

150 ml/¼ pint double cream

Coarsely grate the beetroot into a large bowl; lightly season it with a little salt, the sugar and 10 ml/2 tsp of the wine vinegar, then mix well. Mix a further pinch of salt, the pepper and mustard powder into the remaining wine vinegar, then add the horseradish. Lightly whip the cream and add it to the horseradish mixture, then combine with the beetroot.

Shortcrust pastry

This recipe will make about 450 g/1 lb of pastry dough. To make more or less pastry, in this and the following pastry dough recipes, increase or decrease the amounts of flour, fat and water used, taking care to keep all the ingredients in proportion.

225 g/8 oz plain flour

pinch of salt

100-175 g/4-6 oz butter, margarine, lard or shortening

about 45 ml/3 tbls cold water

Sift the flour and salt into a mixing bowl, then cut the fat into the flour until the pieces are small and well coated. Now rub the fat into the flour with your fingertips until the mixture resembles breadcrumbs. Make a well in the centre, add the water and mix the dough together quickly with a knife. Press into a ball with the fingers, adding extra water if necessary to give a firm dough. Turn onto a floured marble slab or board, knead lightly until smooth, then chill for 15-20 minutes before using.

Rich shortcrust pastry

This recipe will make about 450 g/1 lb of pastry dough.

225 g/8 oz plain flour

a pinch of salt

175 g/6 oz butter

15 ml/1 tbls caster sugar (for sweet pies and flans only)

1 egg yolk

15-30 ml/1-2 tbls cold water

Sift the flour and salt and rub in the butter as described in the recipe above, then stir in the sugar if you are making a sweet dish. Beat the egg yolk with 15 ml/1 tbls of the water, and stir this into the mixture, together with the other 15 ml/1 tbls of water if needed. Press the dough into a ball and knead lightly before chilling.

Puff pastry

This recipe will make 450 g/1 lb of puff pastry.

225 g/8 oz plain flour

a pinch of salt

225 g/8 oz butter

150 ml/¼ pint ice-cold water

a squeeze of lemon juice

Sift the flour and salt into a mixing bowl (1), rub in a piece of the butter about the size of a walnut, and mix to a firm dough with the water and lemon. Work lightly until smooth (2) and leave in a cool place for 15 minutes.

Place the butter between two sheets of greaseproof paper and beat it with a rolling pin two or three times (3) to make a flat, pliable cake; dust this lightly with flour. Roll out the dough to a rectangular shape, then place the butter in the middle (4). Fold the two ends of pastry dough over the butter like a parcel (5) and turn the whole package over.

Roll out to an oblong shape, then fold in three (6) and give the package a quarter turn so that the open edge is in front of you (7). Repeat this procedure once, then wrap the dough in greaseproof paper or a tea towel, and leave it in a cool place for 10-15 minutes.

Continue in this way until the dough has had six rollings or 'turns'. If, after the sixth turn, the pastry looks at all streaky, give it one extra turn but no more or it will not rise to its full capacity.

Chill for 10 minutes after shaping or cutting, before baking in a hot oven.

Rough puff pastry

This recipe will make about 450 g/1 lb of pastry dough.

225 g/8 oz flour

a pinch of salt

175 g/6 oz butter

about 120-150 ml/4-5 fl oz cold water

Sift the flour with the salt into a

mixing bowl. Cut the fat into even walnut-sized pieces and drop them into the flour. Stir carefully with a round-bladed knife so that each 'nut' of fat is covered with flour. Mix quickly and lightly to a pliable dough with the cold water. Set the dough in a cool larder or refrigerator for 10 minutes.

Roll the dough out into an oblong shape, and fold it into three by turning the bottom one third upwards and bringing the top portion one third downwards. Turn the folded dough a quarter turn to the left so that the folded hinge is on your left side and the open layers face you. Roll out into an oblong again, and repeat the folding procedure. Turn as before. Repeat the whole process twice more, and the pastry is then ready to be given a final roll and shaped as required.

Choux pastry

This recipe will make enough choux pastry for a main course for 4-6 people; for 3-4 people, or for a starter, sweet or savoury for 4-6, use 150 ml/¼ pint of water with 50 g/2 oz butter, 65 g/2½ oz plain flour, and 2 eggs.

150 ml/¼ pint water

75 g/3 oz butter

95 g/3¾ oz plain flour

a pinch of salt

3 eggs

Put the water and butter into a large saucepan over a gentle heat. Sift the flour and salt onto a piece of paper. Once the butter has melted, bring it rapidly to the boil and, when bubbling, take it off the heat. As soon as the bubbles have subsided, pour in all the flour and start stirring vigorously until a paste has formed. When this leaves the sides of the pan, the flour is cooked; set aside to cool.

Break the eggs, whisk them lightly and add them to the paste about a third at a time, beating thoroughly. The finished paste

should be smooth, shiny and hold its shape, so add the last portion of eggs particularly carefully if the eggs are larger than standard. The paste is then ready for use.

Choux pastry is baked in a hot oven and on a rising temperature scale, starting at 190°C/375°F/Gas Mark 5, and then — after 5 minutes for small pastries, or 10 for a single, large pastry — increased to 200°C/400°F/Gas Mark 6. Bake until really brown and firm to the touch: failure to do this will result in the choux falling and becoming soft when taken out of the oven.

After removing the choux pastries from the baking sheet, make a small hole with a skewer in the side to release any steam. Cool on a cake rack.

Note: The water, butter and flour paste is made initially by hand but it can be beaten with an electric mixer when eggs are added.

Raw choux pastry can be stored in the refrigerator for a day or two, but it is really best baked straight away. Once baked, it should be eaten the same day, as cooked choux pastry does not store well. It provides the foundation for many puddings, both baked and fried, and when well made it is as light as the proverbial feather. It is baked for eclairs and small choux with a variety of fillings, and fried for beignets.

Lining a flan ring

Roll out the dough to make a round 5 cm/2 in larger than the flan ring. Lift the dough on the rolling pin and lay it over the flan ring on a baking sheet. Ease the dough into the flan ring, taking care not to stretch it, and filling in the corners of the flan ring carefully with loose dough. Cut off the excess by rolling over it with a floured rolling pin. Press the dough firmly against the sides of the ring and decorate the top edge by pinching it between finger and thumb, or by using a pastry cutter.

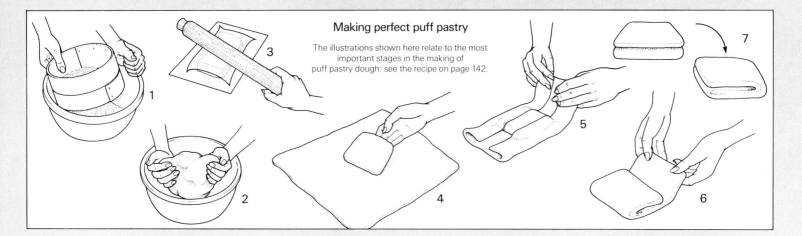

Making perfect puff pastry

The illustrations shown here relate to the most important stages in the making of puff pastry dough: see the recipe on page 142.

Pancake batter

This recipe will make about 20 thin pancakes. Remember to keep all ingredients in proportion to make a greater or lesser number of pancakes.

100 g/4 oz plain flour
a good pinch of salt
1 egg
1 egg yolk
300 ml/½ pint milk
15 ml/1 tbls oil *or clarified* butter

Sift the flour with the salt into a mixing bowl, make a well in the centre and drop in the whole egg and the extra egg yolk. Start adding the milk to the egg and gradually draw in the flour. When half the milk has been added, beat well and add the oil or clarified butter.

Whisk in the rest of the milk, cover and leave in a cool place for 30 minutes before using.

Heat a heavy 15 cm/6 in frying pan. Grease very lightly with oil or clarified butter and put a good tablespoon of batter in the middle; roll the pan to coat the surface evenly, then keep over a brisk heat until the pancake is brown on the underside. Loosen around the edge with a palette knife, and toss or turn over to brown the other side. Slide the pancakes onto a wire cake rack or plate, and pile them up until ready to use.

Sugar syrup

450 g/1 lb preserving *or* granulated
  sugar
300 ml/½ pint water

Dissolve the sugar in the water and boil it steadily, without stirring, to 104°C/220°F. Allow it to cool a little and then pour it into a clean, dry screw-top jar to store.

Note: This is a useful commodity in the kitchen and the only way to sweeten a fresh fruit salad.

Apricot sauce

100 g/4 oz dried apricots
300 ml/½ pint hot water
a strip of lemon rind
50 g/2 oz sugar

Soak the apricots overnight in the hot water, then cook them with their soaking liquid and the lemon rind over a low heat until tender. Allow about 15 minutes of cooking time for the flavour to develop, then add the sugar and continue cooking for 5 more minutes. If you'd like the sauce to have a smooth texture, rub through a nylon strainer or purée in a liquidiser. If you prefer a sauce containing pieces of apricot, only sieve or blend half of the fruit with the cooking liquor, leaving the other half whole or cutting the fruit into large pieces.

Apricot compote

75 g/3 oz sugar
300 ml/½ pint water
a strip of lemon rind
450 g/1 lb fresh apricots

Dissolve the sugar in the water, add the lemon rind and boil for 2-3 minutes. Split the apricots in half and remove the stones. Place them in the syrup and bring slowly to the boil. Allow the syrup to boil up over the fruit, then reduce the heat and cover the pan, simmering very gently until tender. Put the fruit into a serving dish. If necessary, *reduce* the syrup a little before pouring it over the apricots. Cool and serve.

Melba sauce

225 g/8 oz raspberries
60-75 ml/4-5 tbls icing sugar, finely
  sifted

Rub the raspberries (defrosted frozen ones may be used) through a nylon sieve or strainer, then add the icing sugar spoonful by spoonful, beating well.

Apricot glaze

This recipe will make about 450 g/1 lb of glaze. Glaze keeps well: store it in a jam jar with its lid on until you need it.

450 g/1 lb apricot jam
juice of ½ lemon

Turn the jam into a thick saucepan, add the lemon juice and bring slowly to the boil. Simmer for 5 minutes. Strain through a wire strainer, and then return to the saucepan. Boil for a further 5 minutes. The glaze can now be stored in a jar or jars; if it is for immediate use, boil for a few more minutes until slightly thickened, then brush over the fruit or cake. (Test the glaze on a sample slice of fruit first, if you wish.)

Redcurrant glaze

This recipe will make about 450 g/1 lb of glaze.

450 g/1 lb redcurrant jelly

Beat the redcurrant jelly (homemade is best as its sharpness of flavour points up the sweet fruit perfectly) well with a fork or small whisk until it liquifies, then rub through a strainer into a saucepan. Heat gently without stirring until the glaze is clear and runny, but do not boil (as this will spoil the colour and flavour of the glaze). Brush over the fruit with a soft brush, working from the centre outwards towards the edge of the flan or tart you are glazing. Allow to cool slightly before pouring back into a clean jar to store until needed again.

The Well-Stocked Kitchen

Every well-stocked kitchen, and every well-prepared cook, needs a good range of basic equipment. This does not have to run to hundreds of items, but there are perhaps thirty or forty without which many dishes cannot be made – and many more cannot be well-made. Some of those that follow you will already have; others perhaps not. All will repay the effort of acquisition.

Baking sheets: Get two or three of the right size for your oven (i.e. leaving all-round room for air circulation). Buy sturdy ones, preferably with a lip along one edge for easier handling.

Cake tins: Start with three basic tins: a 20 cm/8 in diameter round cake tin, preferably with a loose bottom; a 5 cm/2 in deep rectangular tin for slab cakes, which can also be used for roasting joints; and a 20 cm/8 in diameter sandwich tin.

Flan rings: A set of flan rings in various sizes, about 4 cm/1½ in deep, used in conjunction with baking sheets give great flexibility when baking.

Scissors: Have an ordinary kitchen pair for snipping herbs, cutting off bacon rinds, etc., and a large pair of poultry shears with one serrated blade and a notch for cracking bones.

Kitchen Knives: In general, choose knives with carbon steel blades rather than stainless steel as they are easier to sharpen and keep a better edge. Carbon steel does, however, corrode easily so care must be taken to clean them promptly and dry them immediately. They are also unsuitable for use with acid fruit and other items which will react with them and discolour. Get at least three, with blades ranging in size from 7.5-18 cm/3-7 in.

Palette Knife:
Buy one with an 18 cm/7 in blade. Make sure that it is evenly flexible along its full length, and ensure that the edges are blunt so that you can use it for easing cakes off tins and pans without scratching their surfaces (particularly important with non-stick tins).

Fruit Knife:
A stainless steel, serrated blade slices fruit with ease. Have one with a 7.5-10 cm/3-4 in blade and a sharp tip for piercing tough fruit skins.

Swivel peeler:
Have one that pivots both ways to serve for left- and right-handed use. Stainless steel is best as it can be used for citrus fruits and other acid items.

Saucepans:
In general, the heavier the better as heat is then conducted uniformly. Look for pans with bottoms that are quite flat (both inside and out) with sturdy handles that are easy to grip, and closely fitting lids. It is essential to use the right-sized pan for the job, so buy at least 4, all about 10-13 cm/4-5 in deep, and ranging in capacity from 1.2 litres/2 pints to 6 litres/10½ pints. Lipped saucepans are very useful – make sure they are lipped on both sides.

Sauté pan
The straight sides of this pan allow for greater control over the sautéing action and later reduction of sauces. Buy two: a large one about 30 cm/12 in in diameter and a smaller, about 20 cm/8 in across, both with lids for gentle stewing.

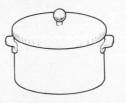

Casseroles
A large casserole is best, but do make sure that it is not too large to fit in your oven! Metal casseroles are better than earthenware in that they are flameproof and can be used over direct heat.

Wooden Corner Spoon
One of these is essential when making scrambled eggs, sauces, custards and other mixtures where you will need to stir into the corners of saucepans. Some spoons have a hole punched through the centre to cut down the turbulence caused by stirring and thus minimize spillages.

Spatula
The flexibility of the blade of a long-handled rubber spatula permits quick and efficient scraping out of bowls. Do not use them with hot liquids.

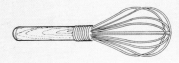

Balloon whisk
The construction of these wire whisks incorporates the maximum air when beating. Buy one with a wooden handle as it is easier to grip than the all-wire version.

Rolling pin
Wooden pins are preferable and the heavier the better! Get one about 50 cm/20 in long. Those without handles give a greater working surface area and are easier to wash.

Colander
This should be large and sit steadily when both empty and full, with no holes near the handle.

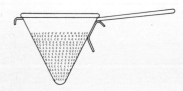

Conical strainer
Intended for straining sauces, the pointed construction produces a narrow stream so that the flow is directed easily.

Strainer
Have at least two: one large one with a double mesh of stainless steel wire for straining and sifting and a smaller nylon one for sieving fine dry ingredients.

THE WELL-STOCKED STORE-CUPBOARD

A well-stocked storecupboard is as important to the cook who does a lot of entertaining as good basic equipment is. Don't forget that not all entertaining is planned as such; often friends or family drop by and a meal has to be conjured up out of nowhere, and this is when your storecupboard will come into its own.

Meals in reserve

Ideally, one should be able to produce several pleasant meals using your storecupboard ingredients alone, or in conjunction with an egg or two and some milk. Tuna fish pancakes, tagliatelle with tomato sauce, a lentil soup: these are the sort of simple but delicious dishes that a storecupboard such as the one listed opposite can provide you with at any time.

The other main use of your storecupboard, of course, is to help you in your general entertaining, and it is important in this respect to check its contents regularly, so that you don't find yourself caught out when an ingredient you relied on being there is absent.

The organizing principle

Keep your storecupboard neat and tidy at all times: this will pay great dividends when you're in a hurry and need to find things at short notice. A tidily organized storecupboard should also help you to keep a careful check on what needs replacing, and it will prevent items getting 'lost', only to reappear months later in a sorry state.

Try to keep savoury ingredients separate from sweet in the cupboard, or, if space is short, use a colour-coding system on your storage jars to help you differentiate between groups of ingredients. Labelling, finally, is a must in a well-organized storecupboard: clear simple labels are best, though make sure they're detachable so that you can use and re-use your storage jars for different items.

INGREDIENT	STORAGE/HOW LONG	USAGE
Dried herbs: bouquet garni; mixed French herbs (*fines herbes*); basil; tarragon; sage; bay leaves	Buy in small quantities, keep tightly sealed and use quickly	From day to day. Use towards the end of the cooking period for best results
Sauces: chilli sauce (or paste); fruit sauce; soy sauce; tomato ketchup; Worcestershire sauce	Indefinitely	Useful ingredients for a wide range of flavoured sauces such as barbecue or devilled sauce
Essences: anchovy essence or paste; pure extract of vanilla	Keep for up to 2 years	Anchovy essence can be used in many Italian dishes; vanilla in desserts, sauces and baking
Oils: good virgin olive oil; a light cooking oil such as sunflower oil	1-2 years. Keep cool	Olive oil is best for salad dressing and mayonnaise, and sunflower oil for day to day use
Vinegars: white and red wine vinegar; white distilled vinegar	Indefinitely	White distilled vinegar is useful in tiny quantities for meringues
Jams and jellies: apricot jam; redcurrant jelly; clear honey; black treacle; golden syrup	Jam, syrup and treacle keep indefinitely; honey up to a year	Useful for glazes and fruit sauces, as well as in baking
Tinned soups & stocks: your own choice; include a good consommé	Indefinitely	Snack meals, and for gravies, stock, sauces and aspic
Tinned fish: salmon; tuna; anchovies	Indefinitely	Salads, mousses, pancake fillings
Tinned vegetables: sweetcorn; kidney beans; whole plum and ready chopped tomatoes	Indefinitely	Sweetcorn and kidney beans in salads or soups. Tomatoes for sauces and casseroles
Milk & cream: powdered skimmed milk; longlife whipping or double cream	Refer to use-by date on packet	Invaluable in emergencies. Longlife cream is economical and can be used in many sauces
Rice: any fine long-grain rice plus a short-grain pudding rice	6 months to 1 year	For sweet and savoury rice dishes. Arborio is the best risotto rice
Dried pasta: noodles; spaghetti or tagliatelle plus one other shape; lasagne; fine semolina	Keep for about 2 months (in small quantities)	For quick meals. As well as in desserts, semolina can be used in savoury dishes like gnocchi
Pulses: lentils, split peas, kidney beans	These take longer to cook as they get older, so buy small amounts	Casseroles, salads and vegetarian cooking
Dried fruit & nuts: raisins, sultanas, dried apricots; hazelnuts; whole, flaked and ground almonds	Dried fruits up to 1 year; nuts up to 3 months	For baking, desserts, sauces and stuffings
Flours: plain, self-raising, cornflour, arrowroot and potato flour	Keep dry: up to six months	From day to day. Use arrowroot for an attractive finish and texture
Sugars: granulated, caster and soft brown or demerara sugar	Keep dry: stores indefinitely	Brown sugars are excellent in fruit cakes and baking. Also for vanilla sugar (with vanilla pod)
Seasonings: table and rock salt; black and and white peppercorns; English dried or ready-made mustard; a good Dijon mustard; bouillon powder or mix; tomato purée (in a tube)	Salt will keep indefinitely in a dry place. Made mustards keep about 6 months. Keep tomato purée in the refrigerator once opened	From day to day. Bouillon powder is a preferable alternative to stock cubes, as you can use exactly the amount you need
Whole spices: allspice (Jamaican pepper); cloves; cinnamon; nutmeg	Kept whole, these spices will last for about a year	Used in desserts and many dishes with a foreign flavour
Ground spices: allspice, cinnamon; cumin; ginger; turmeric; paprika (sweet and hot); cayenne pepper	Ground spices do not last as long as whole. Paprika, in particular, deteriorates rapidly. Keep in airtight jars and use within 6 months	These are useful spices for a wide range of dishes. Use the hotter and stronger spices with discretion

Successful Entertaining

Mr. and Mrs. Christopher Roberts

David and Celia Chandler
at home
Tuesday, January 10th

R.S.V.P.
11, Heyford Avenue   Sherry
London SW8 5NP   6.30 - 8.30 pm

Michael Sedgewood

*Dr and Mrs Stephen Andrews
request the pleasure of your company
at a Dinner to celebrate their*

Silver Wedding

on Saturday 27th May

RSVP   *7.30 for 8 pm*
104 Rosary Road   *Informal Dress*
Norwich
NR4 7PE

How To Make The Bishop's Mitre

1. Fold a square napkin in half, bringing the top down so that both edges are at the bottom edge nearest you. Find the centre by folding it in half again, along the dotted edge marked 'fold' in diagram 1. Crease and re-open.

2. Bring the upper right-hand corner down to bottom centre and the lower left-hand corner up to top centre, as indicated by the arrows in diagram 1 to give you the result illustrated in diagram 2.

3. Turn the napkin completely over onto its reverse side and round so that it looks like diagram 3.

4. Bring the bottom edge upwards to meet the top edge, halving the shape horizontally along the fold as in diagram 3 so that it looks like diagram 4.

5. From beneath the right-hand side pull down the napkin point as shown by the arrow in diagram 4, so that the napkin shape now resembles diagram 5.

6. Now lift up the napkin point at bottom right to meet the top edge as shown by the arrow in diagram 6 (this fold will act as a guide point for the next fold). Bring the far left-hand point over to mid-right along the line marked 'fold'. The napkin shape will now resemble diagram 7.

7. Pull down the napkin point on the right as indicated by the arrow in diagram 7. The napkin shape will now ressemble diagram 8.

8. By holding the top straight edge with both hands turn the whole napkin over onto its reverse side so that the straight edge appears along the base of the napkin as in diagram 9.

9. Bring the right-hand point over to the left along the line marked 'fold'. As you do so, tuck the right-hand point into the fold on the left-hand side so that the napkin shape ressembles diagram 10.

10. With both hands holding the bottom of the napkin, turn it over left to right and tuck the right-hand point as far as it will go into the fold on the left-hand side as in step 9.

All entertaining begins with an invitation, and this can be as informal or as formal as you like. A telephone call, for example, will suffice for an informal dinner party for up to 6 people. If you want a touch more formality than this, an 'At Home' card (available from most newsagents and stationers) is ideal: see the example above left. Simply fill in the name of your guests in the top left-hand corner, together with the date, occasion, time and address or telephone number for replies.

If the party is to be larger and for a specific occasion, you may think it merits a specially printed invitation card (see the example above right). This kind of invitation is always written in the third person and is never signed.

It should ideally be sent out a month in advance. When invitations state the time as 7.30 for 8.00 pm, this means that drinks will be served from 7.30, and dinner will be served at 8.00 pm.

Seating plans
When seating guests, you may, of course, be modern and informal and let guests sit more or less where they please. However precise guidelines do exist, and the diagram below left illustrates most of these. Host and hostess always sit at opposite ends of the table, and the female guest of honour sits to the host's right, while the male guest of honour sits to the right of the hostess. Seat other guests according to a principle of alternation between

male and female, and make sure no two halves of a couple sit together. Serve the female guest of honour first, then the other ladies, and then the men, beginning with the male guest of honour and finishing with the host. A hostess serves herself last. Serve the wine, too, in this way, and remove the plates in the same order.

Place setting
The rules for setting a place at table are simple: always place those items of cutlery and glasses to be used first on the outside, and those to be used last on the inside, as illustrated in the diagram below. This is also the order in which you, when a guest, should use glasses and cutlery.

Seating plan
for a party of ten

If you have no obvious guests of honour, substitute either the most senior couple invited, or a couple you have never entertained before.

If entertaining single people rather than couples, merely adhere to the principle of male/female alternation.

Setting a place at table

1. Butter knife
2. Soup spoon
3. Fish knife
4. Dinner knife
5. Fish fork
6. Dinner fork
7. Dessert spoon
8. Dessert fork
9. Sherry copita (soup)
10. White wine glass
11. Red wine glass
12. Champagne flute (dessert)

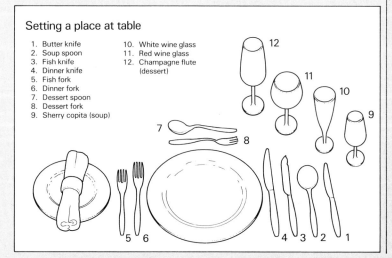

Bishop's Mitre Napkin

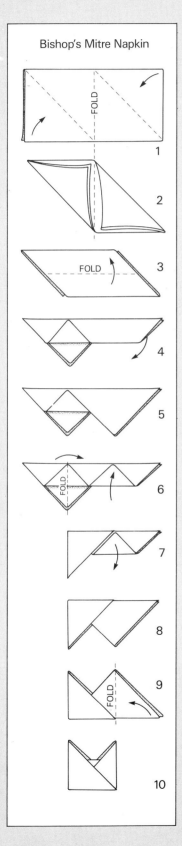

11. Stand the mitre up and open out its base so that the napkin shape is free-standing. Smooth the folds carefully for a good finish.

How To Make The Fan-Shaped Napkin

Note: This shaped napkin is best made with a dressed cotton fabric which will hold the fan folds firmly.

1. Fold a square napkin into two vertical halves as shown in diagram 1.

2. Starting at the bottom edge, accordion pleat upwards gathering pleats about 2.5 cm/1 in deep until you have reached just past the half-way mark as shown in diagram 2.

3. Fold the napkin in half back along the line marked 'fold' in diagram 2. The napkin shape will now resemble diagram 3.

4. Fold the whole top right-hand corner down along the dotted line as shown in diagram 4.

5. To secure the fan shape, allowing it to stand freely, fold the left-hand overlap back along the fold line as in diagram 5.

6. Place the fan on the table as in diagram 6 and allow the fan to unfold as in diagram 7.

7. Position the fan on the table and check that all the creases have been firmly pressed into the napkin fabric; creases may otherwise ease out between napkin folding and the start of the meal.

How To Make The Flower Holder Napkin

1. Fold a square napkin in half and then half again so that all four corners are pointing away from you as in diagrams 1 and 2.

2. Fold the first point downwards so that the fold is about 1 cm/½ in above the half-way line as in diagram 3.

3. Continue folding the second and third points down, each one about 1 cm/½ in above the last as in diagrams 4 and 5.

4. When all three points are down, fold back the left and right hand points as in diagram 6.

5. Insert a flower (which has first had its stem thoroughly dried with paper towels) into the pocket which has formed in the centre.

Fan-Shaped Napkin

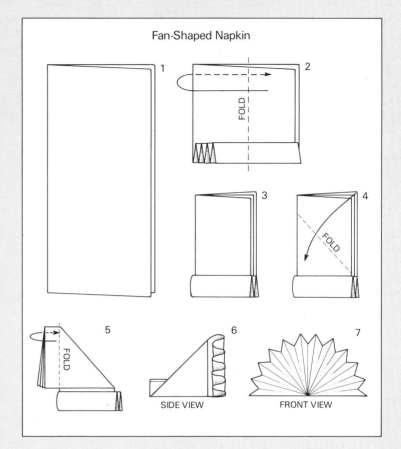

Flower-Holder Napkin

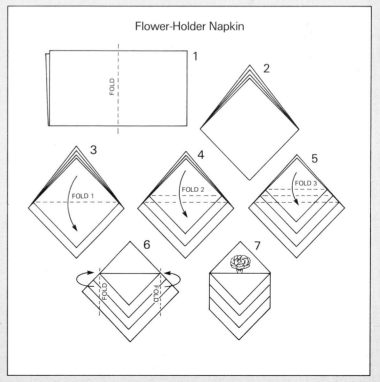

MENU PLANNING

This is one of the most important aspects of entertaining: a well-planned meal will always result in a successful and memorable evening. The list of dos and don'ts given below presents in a simplified form many of the major points of menu planning: using these principles, you will be able to avoid the usual pitfalls of host or hostess. Don't forget to use the **Meal Planners** in conjunction with overall menu planning: the two together provide a useful kit for helping you cope with all your entertaining requirements.

Do

1. Before you plan the meal, check that your guests have no special food or drink requirements.

2. When planning for the meal, always ensure that each course will contrast with both the preceding and following courses. Try to arrange contrasts in colour, texture and richness.

3. Use your freezer to the full: always check exactly what it contains before a dinner party, and use it in preparation.

4. Always plan exactly what you want to prepare well in advance, and check ingredients needed.

5. Check china, serving dishes and linen at least two days before the party to allow enough time to buy or replace any missing item.

6. Make separate lists for shopping for the meal and preparing for the meal. Remember to use them!

7. Prepare as much of the meal as you can in advance, particularly any complicated dishes.

8. Use all your kitchen equipment to the full during the preparation period. Some jobs are best done by hand, but many can be done using processors and liquidizers.

9. When preparing dishes or ingredients needing reduction (like stocks), keep the kitchen door shut and the window open, so that the smell does not permeate the house.

10. Keep a small entertaining book, listing date, menu and guest list, plus any comments that might be helpful for the future (that a guest dislikes carrots, say, or that a couple only drink white wine).

Don't

1. Don't leave invitations too late: the earlier you are able to invite people, the better.

2. Don't leave guests in any ambiguity about the nature of the occasion they are being invited to: if there will be a meal, let them know; if there will be only sherry and savouries, let them know this, too.

3. Don't omit to specify a time for your guests to arrive. If you wish to cook a dish in which timing is crucial, tell your guests (tactfully) that they should arrive on time.

4. Don't leave your planning until the last minute: for a number of dishes, this will be too late!

5. Don't ignore the seasons. Although most ingredients are available year-round nowadays, it is still true that seasonal ingredients taste best 'in season'.

6. When planning the menu, don't let 'hidden' ingredients (like cream) play a leading part in every course.

7. Don't plan for every course to be cold, nor for every course to be hot, either in summer or in winter.

8. Don't allow yourself to fall behind in your preparation, as you will then be too busy shortly before or just after your guests arrive.

9. Don't forget to prepare the house as well as the food. Top-to-bottom cleaning isn't necessary, but rooms to be used should be clean and tidy.

10. Don't forget to stock up with those things that you'll need in addition to the food: apéritifs, wine and perhaps an after-dinner spirit or liqueur; mineral water, candles, and of course your flowers.

GLASSES

Nothing enhances wine so much as serving it in an attractive glass, and six of the major types of wine glass are shown below, together with captions indicating their use. Always use clear, not cut, glass for serving wine (the thinner the better), and never overfill glasses: half-full is the maximum if the aroma of a wine is to be appreciated. Clean glasses with hot water but no detergent, then dry them quickly (while still warm) with a clean linen towel. Store upright, so that air can circulate freely in them.

Copita
A copita is a traditional sherry glass: smaller than other wine glasses, but based on the same tulip principle that funnels aroma up to the drinker. It can also be used for port, madeira or dessert wines.

Champagne flute
This glass is a perfect shape for champagne and sparkling wines. The first foam from a freshly opened champagne bottle has room to climb and die down in the tall glass, and the attractive bubbles are well-displayed.

Tulip glass
This is the classic white wine glass – indeed in many ways it is the classic wine glass, suitable for red, white and sparkling wines alike. Rosé wines are also most attractive served in this glass.

Anjou wine glass
This is the traditional wine glass of the Loire valley in France, and it makes a pleasing alternative to the tulip glass for light white and rosé wines. A green-stemmed Alsace wine glass is similar in shape.

Hock glass
This is the traditional Rhine wine (hock) glass, the thick brown stem reflecting colour in the wine. Like the Anjou glass, this is not a 'serious' taster's glass but an attractive occasional alternative.

The Paris goblet
This is the classic red wine glass, perfect for all red wines from simple country versions to fine burgundies or clarets. It is an easy glass to overfill, so try to find one of the large versions available.

Entertaining With Wine

It is difficult to imagine entertaining without wine: its colours, aromas and flavours seem to partner food so well, and promote such a civilized conviviality, that one's choice in most cases is not between wine and other drinks for serving with food, but rather among wines themselves. This is why some knowledge of wines is invaluable for anyone who entertains from time to time. When the right wine is matched with the right dish, a strange chemistry seems to take place: the wine makes the dish taste better, while the dish makes the wine taste finer; the combination of the two together, in fact, seems excitingly greater than the sum of its parts.

The information on these two pages will not tell you everything there is to know about wine, but it contains useful hints on buying, storing and serving it: the essential part, in short, of getting the most from wine.

Buying wine

The first step towards successful entertaining with wine is buying it. The sooner you can do this, the better, for all wines (even the cheapest) will benefit from a 'rest' of two or three months before they are served. Even if you buy your wine only a week before your dinner party, this will improve it, as wine never tastes at its best after a journey: just stand it in a cool quiet corner until it is needed.

Which wines should be bought for which foods? The only rule here is that there are no hard and fast rules: the wines which taste good to you with what you have cooked are the 'right' wines (for you at least) with those foods. That said, there are certain food/wine combinations that are known as always pleasing (like dry white wine with fish) and a number of foods that always present difficulties for wine (like

Food and Wine Matching Chart

Key — ♀ Good match ♀♀ Excellent match

WINE \ FOOD	Soups	Eggs	Pâtés and starters	Pasta	Seafood	Fish	Savoury flans	Poultry and white meat	Red meat	Game	Fruit desserts	Cheeses
Light red wine			♀	♀♀			♀	♀♀				♀
Medium-bodied red wine				♀				♀	♀♀			♀♀
Full-bodied red wine				♀					♀♀	♀♀		
Fine red wine								♀♀	♀♀	♀		♀
Light dry white wine		♀		♀	♀♀							
Full dry white wine			♀			♀♀	♀	♀♀				♀
Fine dry white wine					♀	♀♀	♀♀					
Medium sweet white wine	♀		♀				♀	♀		♀		
Sweet white or red wine			♀								♀♀	♀♀
Rosé wine		♀		♀				♀				
Champagne and sparkling wines					♀	♀	♀♀	♀			♀	
Sherry or Madeira	♀♀	♀										♀

EXAMPLES:

Examples of **light red wine**: Valpolicella, Bardolino, Alto Adige, Chinon, Beaujolais, German and New Zealand red wines.

Examples of **medium-bodied red wine**: Bordeaux red (claret), Bourgogne red (burgundy), most Vin de Pays, Rioja, Barbaresco, Chianti, Cabernet Sauvignon.

Examples of **full-bodied red wine**: Châteauneuf-du-Pape, Barolo, Dão, Syrah wines, many Australian and Californian red wines.

Examples of **fine red wine**: Bordeaux *crus classés*, Bourgogne domaine-bottled wines, Hermitage, Rioja Reserva, Brunello di Montalcino, top Californian and Australian Cabernet Sauvignon wines.

Examples of **light dry white wine**: Muscadet, Pouilly-Fumé, Sylvaner, Frascati, Vinho Verde.

Examples of **full dry white wine**: Bourgogne blanc (burgundy), Chablis, Graves, Riesling d'Alsace, Chardonnay, white Rioja, Soave.

Examples of **fine dry white wine**: Graves *crus classés*, Bourgogne domaine-bottled wines, Chablis *Premier* and *Grand Cru*, Hermitage blanc, top Australian and Californian Chardonnay wines.

Examples of **medium sweet white wine**: Anjou blanc, Vouvray, most German white wines, Orvieto abboccato, many English wines.

Examples of **sweet white or red wine**: Sauternes, German Auslese or Beerenauslese, Port, most Muscat wines, all 'Botrytis-affected' wines.

Examples of **rosé wine**: Rosé d'Anjou, Rosé de Provence, Tavel, Mateus Rosé.

Examples of **champagne and sparkling wines**: Vin Mousseux or Crémant, Clairette de Die, Blanquette de Limoux, Lambrusco, Asti Spumante, Cava.

Examples of **Sherry or Madeira**: Manzanilla, Fino, Amontillado, Oloroso; Sercial, Verdelho, Bual, Malmsey.

eggs, anything with vinegar in, very spicy food, or desserts based on chocolate). Some suggestions and guidelines in this field are summarised in the **Food and Wine Matching Chart** on page 149. Remember that as a general rule dry wines taste best before sweet wines, and white wines before reds.

The key to buying better wine lies in learning to read 'quality' from the label or bottle on the shop shelf. Many wine merchants now have 'wine selectors' to guide one towards the style of wine one is looking for (e.g. 'light dry red' or 'full sweet white'), and good wine merchants will always offer advice to customers who need it. Even so, there are times when one wishes to know what a certain word means on a label, and the **Wine Glossary** given on page 151 will be helpful here.

As to how much wine you should buy, the answer is always more than you need (for big parties, many wine merchants will let you have wine on a sale or return basis). If you cannot afford to have surplus supplies of wine to hand, though, a basic rule of thumb is one bottle for two people, plus an extra bottle for every subsequent multiple of two (three bottles for four people, four bottles for six people, and so on).

Storing wine
All wines have an optimum drinking age, and this varies between a matter of months for light, fresh, grapey white or rosé wines (like Muscadet or rosé d'Anjou) to twenty or even thirty years for vintage claret or port from an excellent year.

Most wines sold in this country will not benefit from long-term storage, and no inexpensive wine will do so. Short term storage of a month or so, for perhaps one or two dozen assorted bottles, is a good idea, as this short rest can often turn an apparently indifferent bottle into something good.

Ideally, the wine should be stored on its side in a dark, vibration-free place enjoying a constant, cool temperature. Few people though, are lucky enough to have a perfect cellar (where all these conditions are fulfilled) so improvisation is often necessary. An under-stairs cupboard, the bottom of a wardrobe, a corner of the garage, an old fireplace, even under a bed: all these places can be suitable, though in the short term a constant temperature and lack of vibration is probably more important than darkness.

Serving wine
Perhaps the most important factor affecting the serving of wine is temperature. Nearly all wines have a temperature band of (at most) four degrees centigrade at which they will taste at their best, and the difference between a wine served at its ideal temperature and one served several degrees too warm or cold can be startling. Use the box below to serve wine at its ideal temperature: a wineometer (a thermometer with an appropriate temperature band that can be inserted deep into the wine in the bottle) is a handy gadget to have here. Another, simpler, way of checking the wine is at the right temperature is to leave it in a room, larder or refrigerator which is already at the temperature required, for two to three hours.

Ideal serving temperature	
16°-19°C 61°-66°F	Old red wines, Rhône reds, Northern Italian reds, Californian and Australian reds.
14°-16°C 56°-61°F	Young red wines, Chianti, Rioja, Port, Madeira.
12°-14°C 53°-56°F	Light red wines (Beaujolais, Valpolicella), medium and sweet Sherry, white Port, best white Burgundy.
9°-12°C 48°-53°F	All other white and rosé wine. Dry Sherry. Champagne.
5°-9°C 40°-48°F	Other sparkling wines. All sweet white wines.

Opening bottles
There is a wide range of corkscrews available: four of the best designs are the Screwpull, the 'Waiter's Friend', the butterfly or lever action type, and the double action boxwood corkscrew. Any of these will give good results when opening ordinary bottles: which one you choose is largely a matter of personal preference.

Opening champagne bottles calls for special care. The best way to do it is as follows:
1 Have a glass ready.
2 Pointing the bottle well away from people or valuables, remove the foil and wire muzzle.

3 Grasp the cork firmly with the whole hand, and twist it slowly out of the tilted bottle, twisting the bottle slowly but firmly in the opposite direction as you do so.
4 Gently pour the first glass as soon as the cork is removed.

Decanting wine
Two types of wine seem to benefit most from decanting: fine old red wines that have thrown a sediment or deposit at the bottom of the bottle, and young, intensely concentrated red wines that need aerating in order to release their full flavours and aromas. The former should be decanted immediately before serving, and the latter anything between one hour (for young red Burgundy) and 6 or 8 hours (for young Italian Barolo or Australian Shiraz) before serving.
1 48 hours before decanting,

stand the bottle upright. (This is less important for young wines with little or no sediment than it is for older wines.)
2 Draw the cork. If the cork is very old and soft, make sure that you use a corkscrew with a worm thread rather than a gimlet thread: the Screwpull or double action boxwood are ideal for this job.
3 Wipe the lip of the bottle well.

4 Holding your decanter in one hand and the bottle in the other, slowly lift the bottle and pour its contents into the decanter over a bright light source (a candle is ideal). As soon as the sediment reaches the neck of the bottle (the candle light will show this clearly), stop pouring.

Wine baskets and decanting cradles are not normally necessary. They are primarily useful if you do not have the time to stand the bottle upright in advance (as the whole decanting process can then be carried out with the bottle horizontal) or if the wine has thrown a fine, light, easily disturbed sediment (as very old burgundy can).

Decanters for wine, like wine glasses themselves, are best made from clear glass rather than cut glass: the colour of a wine is an important part of the pleasure it offers the drinker, and clear glass shows this off to best effect. Cut glass decanters are ideal, though, for spirits.

All decanters should be sturdily weighted at the bottom and, like glasses, washed only in hot water.

Wine Glossary

Abbreviations: Fr = France   It = Italy   Sp = Spain   Gm = Germany   Pg = Portugal

Abboccato (It) or **Amabile** (It) slightly or semi-sweet

Amtliche Prüfungsnummer (A. P. Nr) (Gm) a control number supplied by the German government for each *QmP* wine, indicating that the wine has been tasted and analysed

Annata (It) vintage

Appellation Contrôlée (AOC or AC) (Fr) the highest French quality wine category. Every aspect of the wine is controlled, including grape varieties, quantity produced and alcohol level

Auslese (Gm) sweet, rich German wine, made from selected bunches of overripe grapes, sometimes affected by *botrytis*. The third wine up the *QmP* ladder

Beerenauslese (Gm) an intensely sweet, very rich German wine, made from selected individual grapes, generally affected by *botrytis*. The fourth wine up the *QmP* ladder

Bodega (Sp) literally 'a cellar', but is used to mean any wine firm or large producer

Botrytis cinerea, also known as 'noble rot': a mould that shrivels up grapes, concentrating their sugars and so being responsible for most of the world's great sweet wines

Brut (Fr) a term used to describe dry Champagne and other dry sparkling wines

Cabernet Sauvignon one of the world's finest red wine grapes, dominant in Bordeaux (for claret), and making excellent red wine in most other wine producing countries of the world

Cantina sociale (It) a cooperative

Casa vinicola (It) wine house, often buying in grapes from grape farmers to make wine with

Cépage (Fr) grape variety

Chardonnay one of the world's finest white wine grapes, dominant in Bourgogne for white Burgundy, and producing excellent wines elsewhere, especially in California and Australia

Classico (It) indicates wine from the most central or traditional part of a *DOC* area

Clos (Fr) a term used to describe many top quality single vineyard wines, especially in Burgundy and Alsace

Crémant (Fr) a term which means 'half-sparkling' in Champagne, but refers to top quality fully sparkling wines in Alsace, the

Loire and Burgundy

Cru (Fr) literally means a 'growth', i.e. a vineyard. The inclusion of the words *cru classé, grand cru* or *premier cru* in an *AC* should indicate a high quality wine

Cosecha (Sp) vintage

Côte, Côtes or **Coteaux** (Fr) literally means 'hill' or 'hillsides' and should therefore indicate wines of better-than-average quality as drainage and exposure to the sun are both superior on hillsides

Denominación de Origen (DO) (Sp) the Spanish quality wine category, roughly similar to France's *AC*, controlling grape varieties, wine-making methods and maximum yields

Denominazione di Origine Controllata (DOC) (It) the standard Italian quality wine category, roughly similar to France's *AC*, specifying grape types, zones, wine-making methods and maximum yields

Denominazione di Origine Controllata i Garantita (DOCG) (It) the top Italian quality wine category, roughly similar to Germany's *QmP*. Qualification procedures include a tasting panel

Deutscher Tafelwein (DTW) (Gm) table wine, equivalent to France's *vin de table*

Domaine (Fr) a single property, particularly in Burgundy, and there roughly equivalent to the 'château' used in Bordeaux

Erzeugerabfüllung (Gm) estate bottled

Frais (Fr) cool

Frizzante (It) lightly sparkling

Gamay a grape variety, best in France's Beaujolais, producing light red wines

Gewürztraminer a grape variety giving very spicy, perfumed white wines, both dry and sweet

Halbtrocken (Gm) literally 'half-dry': containing less sugar than most German wines excluding *trocken* wines

Kabinett (Gm) very light, delicate German wines made with no added sugar. The first wine up the *QmP* ladder

Landwein (Gm) a German wine category roughly equivalent to French *vin de pays*

Merlot a red grape variety widely used in Bordeaux and increasingly grown elsewhere for soft dry quality red wine

Millésime (Fr) year or vintage

Mise (en bouteilles) (Fr) bottled, generally followed by the place bottled, or the name of the merchant bottling the wine and his or her address. The best wines will be bottled at the château or estate where the wine was made

Moelleux (Fr) literally 'soft', used to describe semi-sweet or sweet Loire wines

Müller-Thurgau a white grape variety producing light, agreeable wines, mostly in Germany, though many English wines are now made from this grape variety

Muscat a grape variety found in nearly every wine-producing country of the world, and usually used to make sweet, often perfumed wines. These are sometimes very strong (as in Southern France), sometimes very light (as in Italy), and can occasionally be dry (as in Alsace)

Négociant (Fr) wine broker or merchant

Pétillant (Fr) very slightly sparkling

Pinot Noir (Fr) a red grape variety dominant in Bourgogne (for red Burgundy), and used with varying degrees of success elsewhere. Produces light or medium-bodied, richly flavoured dry red wine

Qualitätswein eines bestimmten Anbaugebietes (QbA) (Gm) German quality wine from a specified region, made from authorised grape varieties to a specific degree of ripeness. It is roughly equivalent to the French *appellation contrôlée*

Qualitätswein mit Prädikat (QmP) (Gm) literally 'quality wine with distinction', signifying wines made with no added sugar, according to specified methods and all officially tasted and tested. The ladder of richness begins with *Kabinett* and ends with *Trockenbeerenauslese*

Récolte (Fr) crop or vintage

Região Demarcada (Pg) the Portuguese version of France's *AC*

Reserva (Sp) applies to quality (*DO*) red wines, particularly riojas, that have been aged for at least 3 years. **Gran reserva** wines have been aged for longer, and should be better still

Riesling a white grape variety producing the finest wines of Germany and Alsace, and grown increasingly elsewhere. Finely balanced white wines of great breeding

Riserva (It) applies to *DOC* or *DOCG* wines that have undergone a specified (but variable) period of ageing

Sauvignon Blanc an aromatic white wine grape, chiefly used for the dry wines of the

Loire and Bordeaux, but also grown in California, where it is called Fumé Blanc

Sec (Fr), **Secco** (It) or **Seco** (Sp) dry

Spätlese (Gm) means 'late picked'. The second category on the *QmP* ladder, and usually a rich but still delicate wine

Spumante (It) sparkling

Supérieur (Fr) or **Superiore** (It) in general, means one degree or so more alcohol than the 'normal' version of the wine so described (though in Italy it can sometimes refer to a longer ageing period); it is not necessarily an indication of better quality

Tinto (Sp) full red wine

Trocken (Gm) dry

Trockenbeerenauslese (Gm) a very rich, very sweet German white wine, nearly always made from *botrytis*-affected grapes. The top of the *QmP* ladder

Uva (It) grape variety

Vigna, Vigneto (It) vineyard

Vins Délimités de Qualité Supérieure (VDQS) (Fr) the second rank of French wines, coming from traditional wine-making regions and subject to specific controls

Vin de Pays (Fr) the third rank of French wines, literally 'country wines'. Sometimes excellent; sometimes poor, too

Vin de Table (Fr) table wine. Not generally an impressive standard, though some brand names can be good

Vin Mousseux (Fr) sparkling wine

Vino da Tavola (It) table wine, but in Italy much used by renegade growers for first-class wines that do not fit the tradition-based specifications for *DOC* wines. Expensive examples can therefore be good

Vino de crianza (Sp) wine (particularly Rioja) aged for a minimum period, more than 'normal' but less than for a *reserva*

Vino de mesa (Sp) table wine

Vino de pasto (Sp) also table wine, but generally lighter than above

Vino novello (It) literally 'new wine', used for native Italian versions of French 'nouveau' wines (like that of Beaujolais)

VQPRD an EEC quality wine classification

VSQPRD an EEC quality sparkling wine classification

Weingut (Gm) wine estate

Entertaining With Flowers

The majority of people do not realise that the subjects of food and flowers have a great deal in common. In both cases it is the way in which they are displayed that is paramount: however beautiful blooms may be, or however carefully the frosting has been done on the sprigs of redcurrants, if they are not well displayed all can be lost. First impressions are all-important.

The same goes for the correct preparation of the raw materials. Without this, the finished article will not be up to standard. With flowers, it is particularly important, since the better prepared they are the greater their chance of lasting well – an argument which doesn't, admittedly, apply in quite the same way to food, since it doesn't have to last any length of time once it has reached the table.

But with flowers, it is well worth spending an hour or so on their preparation – an hour which can add a day or two to the life of the arrangement. People often ask about this, and many's the time that students have remarked on their amazement at how long the flowers have lasted once they have been treated properly.

QUALITY OF MATERIALS

To get a really first class arrangement, you must have top quality material, cut at just the right stage of its development. If flowers are to last, they should be picked and prepared when they are still in bud – but 'on the move', as too tight a bud may not develop in water. Fully open flowers may look good and give you the right effect, but they will last for only a very short time. And what a pity it would be to spend so much time and energy on something that doesn't give complete satisfaction.

Buying from a florist

If cutting from your own supply you can be very selective, but if you are buying from a florist, go

---

A Guide to Flower Arranging

• Find a suitable container for the flowers you have in mind. Picture where it is to stand, and pick or purchase with this in mind. In this way you will not over-cut or buy too much.

• Treat all your flowers before using them so that they last as long as possible (see Flower preparation, right).

• Secure the netting or other means of holding the stems in the vase. Whatever you use, make sure it gives the necessary support (see Materials, pages 154 and 155).

• Set the vase in its final position, or at least at the same height, before attempting to arrange it. Always work with a dust sheet next to you on which you can throw discarded material, rather than putting it down on the carpets or furniture coverings.

• Half fill the vase with warm water before starting to arrange it, and top up once all the stems are in place.

• Set the outline points – height, width and, if doing a facing arrangement, a good depth. There are no hard and fast rules or measurements for this – different flowers need different proportions. For instance, light grasses can be quite tall, whereas fruits and large flowers may need to be kept quite low down in the vase.

• Once a few of the outline stems are in position, stand well back and view the vase. Only you can decide if it looks the way you want it. Once your outline is fixed, you should keep all your materials within it. Make use of naturally curved materials to give shape to the arrangement.

• Gradually keep adding flowers and foliage, bringing different shapes and colours through the arrangement in sweeps rather than in blocks. No two flowers of the same height should be next to one another in your arrangements.

• Make use of flowers at every stage of development including buds, both half open and fully open, trying to keep the larger flowers lower down in the container.

• All stems should flow from the centre of the vase and not cross over in the vase.

• For a facing arrangement, the initial outline stems should be placed in the vase about three-quarters of the way back from the front of the vase.

• Place some large leaves over the rim of the vase to blend the arrangement and container.

---

to a reputable firm and see that you are given tiptop material. The barrowboy or florist with boxes of cut flowers standing on end and drying out in the wind outside the shop is not going to have top grade flowers.

You have got to establish a relationship with your florist and his assistants; once over this barrier, you will find it much easier. They will soon get to know the flowers and colours you like, and if you can tell them for precisely what purpose you need each lot of flowers, they should be able to provide you with the types and stem size you require.

Flower preparation

All flowers, whether from the garden, market or florist's shop, should spend a period of time in deep, clean water before being arranged. The time allowed depends on the flowers being used and their condition.

Above all, the water supply should be clean. For this reason, domestic tap water is best because it has been treated and is free from all bacteria. Pond water, or water from the rain butt, is teeming with 'life', and once this is brought into a warm room, activity increases and the water soon turns into a murky liquid which is far from pleasant. (You may have experienced something similar when using members of the cabbage (*brassica*) family, all of which tend to make the water smell. To avoid this, put these stems singly in a polythene bag with a spot of bleach in the water. They will not then contaminate the entire container.)

Containers

Use any type of container – a bucket is ideal – to give the flowers this initial drink, as long as it is thoroughly clean. The deeper the stems can go under water the better, and limp materials can even be laid horizontally under the water in a bath for two or three hours. Remove any unwanted foliage as this will also tend to make the water smell, but try to leave the stems looking as natural as possible. Do not pack stems too tightly but allow room for them to swell slightly as they absorb water, and leave in a cool damp place for four to six hours.

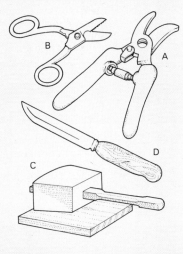

Equipment
You will need a good pair of secateurs (A) which should be kept oiled and sharp. Use these only for cutting plant material, and never force them. The best ones are those with one cutting blade, used with the blade kept uppermost. These, together with a pair of florist's scissors (B), a wooden mallet (C), a block on which to hammer and a sharp knife (D), make up all the equipment you need.

Chemicals
The use of chemicals in the water should not be necessary, as long as both water and vases are clean. The old idea of adding an aspirin to the flower vase water is not as silly as it sounds: it acts on the bacteria which tend to multiply and inhibit the stems' intake of water. Some people also suggest sugar in the water to encourage greater cell activity in the stem tissue. Proprietary chemical additives which you can buy to prolong the life of cut flowers should only be used with care, according to manufacturers' instructions, and never in good china or metal containers because they can all discolour the container sides.

Stem treatment
All stems should be cut at an angle to expose the widest possible surface for water absorption.

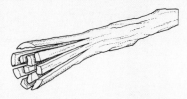

Hard woody stems
This group covers a very large range of plant material, including all foliage from trees and shrubs such as birch (*betula*), lime (*tilia*), *rhododendron* and mock orange (*philadelphus coronarius*); all blossom such as *prunus*; and many herbaceous plants such as golden rod (*solidago*), *phlox* and *chrysanthemum*. Cut the base of the stem and hammer 1-2.5 cm/ ½-1 inch of tissue to break it down. If the outside bark is thick, pare off with a knife down to the cambium layer (the white stem beneath).

Soft succulent stems
This is not such a large group but an important one, and includes hyacinth (*hyacinthus*), arum lily (*zantedeschia aethiopica*) and *crinum*. A clean slanting cut is all that is needed.

Hollow stems
Plants in this group are *delphinium*, hollyhock (*althaea rosa*) large *dahlia* and lupins (*lupinus polyphyllus*). To prevent the stem from drying out, cut it, invert and fill with water. Then plug with cotton wool and place it in deep water.

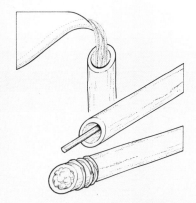

The amaryllis (*amaryllis hippeastrum*) needs a little extra treatment. Before filling the stem with water, thread a small piece of split bamboo cane up inside it to support the head of the flower, being careful not to puncture the stem tissue. Cut off the cane at base level, fill with water, plug and tie with an elastic band.

Stems which bleed
There are a number of plants with stems which, when freshly cut, exude a milky fluid, including *euphorbia* and poppy (*papaver*). The tips must be placed immediately after cutting into boiling water for 30 seconds or singed in a flame for a few seconds. The poinsettia (*euphorbia pulcherrima*), in addition, should have damaged leaves removed and the stem sealed with a flame.

FLOWER CATEGORIES
The stems described above cover most plants, but there are others that need special treatment.

Roses
Roses (*rosa*), for example, should have the base of the stem split up to 1 cm/½ inch, and the bottom leaves removed. Unless you are going to use a single stem in a specimen vase, the thorns should also be removed by rubbing the stem with the back of a closed pair of scissors. This helps with water absorption and facilitates the use of wire netting when arranging.

Limp roses
These should either be laid completely under water for a few hours, or have their stems recut, the tips put in boiling water for up to 30 seconds, and then be rolled in stiff paper and plunged into lukewarm water for a long drink;

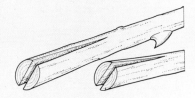

the paper holds the heads upright and enables the water to reach them. If the head hangs right over, it may crack the stem tissue, making it impossible to straighten the stem and revive the flower. Florists' roses are not always sufficiently advanced before picking and may not open properly. Some roses are longer lasting than others, and all you can do is try this treatment as soon as you see any sign of wilting.

Carnations
The flowers of the carnation (*dianthus caryophyllus*) family have woody, swollen stems at the leaf joints. Always make a cut through the thin part of the stem, not at a joint. Keep the carnation grass (leaves) for arranging.

Gerbera
It is essential with barberton daisies (*gerbera jamesonii*) to get the stems fully charged with water before arranging them. Cut and place the tip in boiling water or a flame for 30 seconds, and then put the stem in warm water for a few hours.

Lilac
This is of two types – the forced lilac (*syringa*) from Holland and garden lilac. With the Dutch forced lilac, hammer the stems, place the tips in boiling water and add the sachet of Chrysal generally supplied with the bunch; then top up with and stand in warm water for a few hours.

With garden lilac, remove all the leaves from the flower stems, thinning out weak twigs and odd-shaped branches but keeping side shoots of foliage to include in the arrangement. Hammer the stems and place in deep hot water.

Violets
Violets (*viola*) absorb water through their heads and should be arranged in small bunches deep down in the vase. Soak under water for a short time each day.

COLOUR

A colour scheme is a very personal thing and what may appeal to one person will not always appeal to another. All that one can say with flowers is that you should try to link them to the overall atmosphere of the room, and not create something so dominant that they stand out like a sore thumb.

Seasonal flowers

Please try to keep as far as possible to seasonal flowers. There is nothing worse than chrysanthemums in the spring or early summer, when one of life's great joys is to find the spring bulb flowers coming up in the garden.

The seasons seem to have lost some of their significance today, and with so many flowers coming from abroad it would be difficult to say what time of year it is just by looking in the modern flower shop window. There are, it is true, so many colours available that it is always easy to ring the changes, but it is still preferable to stick to the season wherever possible. So often the flowers themselves are better when growing in their true season.

Time of day

This will also have a bearing on what you use and the colours you choose. Remember, for instance, that blue is not a good colour under artificial light, and that green, or green against white, has a cooling effect on a hot evening.

Arrangements can be in one colour, subtly grouped using different shades or fully mixed as in a real garden.

Background

The background will make a big difference to the flowers and there is nothing more difficult to use for a table flower setting than an ordinary white tablecloth. It seems to kill the effect of the flowers straight away. Silver and glass vases in particular look so much better when they are able to reflect in a polished table surface.

Mixing colours

When using mixed colours, try to arrange these in sweeps and bring them from side to side. Dark flowers appear heavier than pale colours, and to start with you may well get better results from keeping these dark colours near the centre and low down in the vase (see the diagrams below). Later on you may like to move away from this rule, especially if you want to copy one of the arrangements painted by the seventeenth century Dutch Masters.

If only one stem of any particular colour is available, show this off to good advantage. And if you have two stems of any one colour, place these close together rather than putting them on opposite sides.

Colour changes

The colours of flowers change with age. The purple *cobaea*, for example, starts as a pure green trumpet but after two or three days in water it will become a deep beetroot colour.

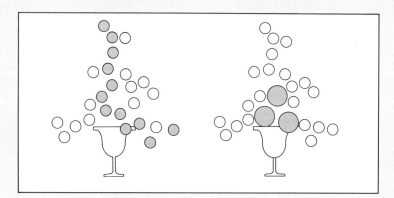

Left: sweeping a single colour through a mixed arrangement; Right: grouping dark colours and large blooms together low down in the vase.

MATERIALS

Netting

Once you have mastered the use of netting for arranging flowers, it will give the most pleasing results. Always use 5 cm/2 inch mesh and a gauge of between 19 and 22. The smaller mesh is no use, since once the netting has been rolled up and shaped to fit the container, the holes will be too small for most stems.

Plastic covered wire

This is recommended by some for use with delicate china and silver because it will not scratch the surface. A lot of people do not like it, however, and prefer to avoid scratching the vase by lining it with brown paper before putting in the netting.

What to do

You need four to five layers of wire with one layer flat on the bottom of the container and the top layer slightly domed. Try threading a pencil or small stick through the holes in the netting before you tie it to the vase.

Keep the wire for each vase separate and do not keep changing the shape. Each time you fold it up, the galvanising cracks and it will soon rust. After use, wash well and dry thoroughly.

Everyone has their own idea on netting and some find more is necessary than others. Whatever you do, do not use too much netting. Once you have a few stems firmly placed, other stems will stay in position easily.

Fixing

Secure the netting either by tying it to the vase or by folding the 'ears' over the edge of the vase. A rubber band will hold it firmly and does not show when the arrangement is complete.

Adding water

Add water after the netting has been secured. Provided that the stems have been properly prepared and are held below the water level, it does not matter at what angle they are lying – they will still take up water.

Netting is bought by the roll. Some florists will also sell a piece about 75 cm/30 inches square which should do for a large urn.

PINHOLDERS

These originated in Japan and consist of sharp brass or steel pinpoints set in a heavy metal base. The pins come in different sizes and the base size varies in size and shape. They are very useful for flowers with thick stems, but the water level must always be just above the pins if the flowers are to last.

It is a false economy to buy cheap pinholders, as they will not last. Plastic ones are totally useless and the rubber-based suction types tend not to anchor properly on the vase base. Some people like to use a little netting in addition to pinholders.

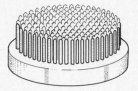

How to use them

A good heavy pinholder should stay in position without the addition of any adhesive. Keep pinholders dry when not in use, and make sure that any pins which have been displaced by hard woody stems are put back in the upright position. Special oasis pinholders, known in America as 'frogs', are also available. These are made up of about five to seven long pins round the perimeter of a heavy base, and hold the weightless dry plastic foam in position.

A range of different sized pinholders is useful to acquire as you build up your store of equipment. As with kitchen equipment, you will find some sizes more useful than others. To start, however, three sizes – 4 cm/1½ inches, 5 cm/2 inches and 7.5 cm/ 3 inches – should be enough to be going on with.

OASIS

This is a very popular medium in which to arrange flowers. It is a spongy cellular material which holds a lot of water. It must be soaked thoroughly before use and then always kept wet. Stems

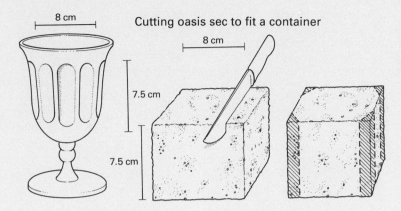

Measure the inside of your vase before cutting oasis sec to fit snugly.

should be prepared in the usual way and simply inserted into the wet block where they remain moist and steady. It is available in 'bricks' or 'rounds' and can be cut to the required size, always leaving plenty of room in the container for a water reservoir.

Oasis Springtime
This is a softer version which is useful for the less woody stems of spring flowers. Soak and use in the same way. If carefully handled, it can be used two or three times but it should always remain damp and be kept in a plastic bag between arrangements. Once it dries out completely, it will not absorb water again properly.

Oasis Sec
This is a hard version which is used without water for dried or wire stems. It should be cut to the shape of the vase because it needs to be firmly secured and needs no reservoir. First cut a square roughly the size of the vase and then carve it to the shape required by chipping away at the corners, trying it in the vase as you work. For cheapness and added weight, a smaller piece of Oasis Sec can be used in the centre of the vase with small bits of gravel around it.

FLORIST'S WIRE
Wire used by florists comes in two forms: stub and reel. The stub wires are used for mounting flower stems and foliage, the reel wires for making sprays and for binding materials together or on frames.

In flower arranging
Florist's wire is used to tie the wire netting, for hanging up vases, and for making leg mounts (see below). The flowers themselves should never be wired.

Black or blue annealed stub wires are sold in bundles, in gauges 20 to 24. Silver reel wire is sold on spools and in short lengths, and comes in gauges 24 to 36. The higher the gauge, the thinner the wire: use thinner wire for leg mounts, and thicker wire for tying and hanging.

Making single leg mounts

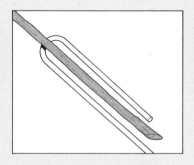

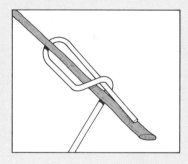

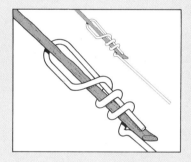

Place the stem on thin gauge florist's wire about three-quarters of the way along the wire.

Bend the two lengths of wire back along the stem. The short end of the wire should be no longer than the stem.

Bend the long end of the wire around the stem and short end two or three times. Finish at the end of the stem.

Straighten out the long wire: this forms the single leg mount. Insert into your supporting material.

Making double leg mounts

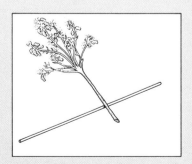

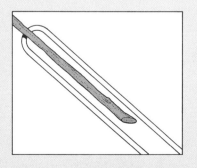

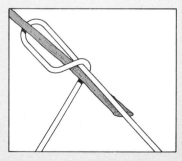

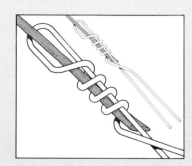

Place the stem on thin gauge florist's wire 2 cm/³⁄₄ in from the stem base, and 2.5 cm/1 in from the wire centre.

Bend the two wires down below the stem. The wire below the stem is 2.5 cm/1 in longer that the part above.

Holding the wires firmly, wind the longer wire around the shorter wire and stem two or three times.

Straighten out both wires to form the double leg mount. The two wires should now be of roughly equal length.

Directory Of Cooking Terms

al dente

Italian term used to describe food, and in particular pasta, which has been cooked until it is just firm to the bite. Before this stage is reached, the pasta will be hard and chewy; after this stage has passed, the pasta becomes overly soft.

bake blind

to bake a pastry case without a filling. This is done either when the filling ingredients require no further cooking, or when the filling ingredients are cooked at a lower temperature or for a shorter time than that needed to cook the pastry dough. Prick the pastry dough to prevent it from rising as you bake it, line it carefully with greaseproof paper or foil and fill with dried beans or rice. When the pastry is set, about two-thirds of the way through the blind baking period specified in the recipe, remove the beans and paper, and return the pastry to the oven to finish baking. (The pastry may need re-pricking at this point.)

The rice or beans used for blind baking should be replaced in a jar, when cool, for future use and kept specially for this purpose. Heavy ceramic beans, especially manufactured for blind baking, can be obtained from kitchenware shops, and these give excellent results.

beurre manié

this means, literally, kneaded butter, and refers to a liaison of butter and flour, in a proportion of 1½ parts butter to 1 part of flour. It is used to enrich and thicken a liquid in which food has been poached or simmered. Work both butter and flour together on a plate with a fork to a smooth paste. Add the beurre manié to a sauce, soup or stew in little pieces, off the heat, once the cooking is complete. After the beurre manié has been added, the pan should be gently shaken and turned (but not necessarily stirred) so that all is well blended. Where there are no pieces of meat, fish or vegetable that might be broken, a whisk may be used to incorporate the beurre manié. The contents of the pan are then brought gently to boiling point and simmered for a minute or two.

blanch

to treat food with boiling water in order to whiten it, preserve its original colour, loosen skin or remove too strong a flavour or tough a texture. Food can either be plunged into boiling water, as with sweetbreads, to make them firm before cooking and preserve their whiteness, or as with tomatoes prior to skinning them; or put into cold water and brought to the boil, as with bacon, salt pork and kippers to remove excess saltiness. Some vegetables are blanched to remove pungency (by dropping into fast boiling water in cases where it is important to preserve colour), and most are blanched before freezing to destroy harmful bacteria. Blanching is not a cooking process in itself, but a preliminary to cooking.

clarify

to remove all the impurities from liquids and fats. The most common form is the clarifying of butter, and this is done if the butter is going to be heated to a high temperature, to prevent the milk solids in the butter burning. Clarified butter will also keep for longer than ordinary butter, so it is used additionally for sealing potted shrimps, pâtés and duxelles.

Melt the butter in a small saucepan and heat it gently without allowing it to colour. Skim off any scum that rises to the top. Strain it through muslin or a nylon strainer into a bowl and leave it to set. When it is quite firm, turn out the 'cake' of clarified hardened butter, leaving the sediment behind. Wipe the base of the butter dry, and discard the sediment. Use as instructed in your recipe.

deglaze

to rinse out the sediment and concentrated juices left in a pan after roasting or sautéing, usually with hot stock or wine, to make a gravy or sauce. Pour the stock or wine into the pan, and scrape up the 'crust' left by the meat in the pan with a spatula, as the liquid bubbles and *reduces*. Deglazing a frying or cooking pan with a suitable liquid is one of the quickest and simplest ways to make a rapid sauce.

dry fry

to cook steaks with the minimum of fat. The pan must be heavy and preheated over a medium heat before the fat is put into it. Use 10 g/ ¼ oz of butter to 5-10 ml/1-2 tsp good olive oil. Put the steak in immediately after the fat, and fry on each side for the specified period.

flame

to ignite a spirit (usually brandy) or fortified wine and pour it, flaming, over food. This will give the food the flavour of the spirit or wine without giving it the (sometimes unpleasant) flavour of alcohol. The alcohol burns off, leaving the agreeable flavour of the spirit or wine behind. One can either flame a finished dish, as with Christmas pudding, or flame spirits or wine directly into the pan during cooking, as for certain ragoûts and game dishes. If the spirit is warmed beforehand it becomes volatile and the alcohol begins to evaporate, aiding combustion. Needless to say, great care must be taken when flaming food to minimise any risk of fire should the spirit accidentally spill.

julienne

thin matchstick slices or very fine shreds of vegetables about 4 cm/ 1½ inches long and 3 mm/⅛ inch wide, used as a garnish for clear soups or main course dishes. Strips of carrot, turnip, leek and celery can all be used as julienne vegetables. Heat them in a nut of butter until they just begin to change colour; then add a little liquid and simmer the vegetables gently until *al dente*. The term can also be used to describe the method of cutting vegetables into shreds of this size.

macerate

to soak and infuse food in the syrup or liquid in which it is to be served. This is done both to soften and flavour the food. Fresh fruit is commonly macerated in brandy, rum, kirsch or other liqueurs. The process is essentially the same as that of marinading meat or fish.

reduce

to boil a sauce or syrup quickly in an uncovered saucepan or frying pan in order to evaporate away the surplus liquid. This process both strengthens and intensifies the flavour (as what evaporates away is water) and produces a thicker consistency in the sauce. If you are doing a lot of reducing, try to keep the kitchen window open so that the moisture can escape.

refresh

to rinse freshly cooked or *blanched* vegetables or meats under cold water; they are then reheated before serving. The process of refreshing prevents the vegetable from cooking any further than the point to which you have already cooked it, and it simultaneously preserves the vegetable's colour (particularly important with green vegetables such as sprouts). Refreshed vegetables can be quickly reheated before they are served by tossing lightly in a small quantity of hot butter.

roux

a mixture of equal quantities of butter and plain flour which are cooked together to form the base, and thickening agent, for a sauce. Melt the butter slowly in a thick saucepan, remove from the heat, add the sifted flour and stir until the mixture is smooth. Return the pan to the heat for 1 or 2 minutes to heat the mixture through. Keep the heat moderate for this period, so that the roux does not brown. The liquid that is added to a roux should not be boiling but just warm, and added off the heat.

Roux may be made in advance and will keep for a few days provided no ingredients other than butter and flour are used. For a softer, richer roux and resulting sauce, use slightly more butter than plain flour. Wholemeal flour can be used to make a roux, but only for rich, darkly-coloured sauces, where the flecks of bran will not spoil the appearance and finish of the sauce.

sauté

to brown or cook vegetables or meat in hot fat over a high heat by tossing them in a sauté pan, which is a deep, straight-sided, heavy frying pan: an example is illustrated on page 144. After the initial sautéing, the meat or other food is generally removed from the pan, a sauce made, and the cooking of the food or meat finished in the sauce. While it may be convenient to use a frying pan for ordinary use, a sauté pan is ideal for proper sautéing as its deep sides will more readily hold the liquid often added to the cooking fat to make a sauce. *Clarified* butter, or a mixture of clarified butter and olive oil, is the best medium for sautéing.

Food Index

For Flower Index, see page 160.

Flower Index